AFTER MOTHER INDIA

AFTER MOTHER INDIA

HARRY H. FIELD

GYAN

Published by

GYAN

Gyan Publishing House
5, Ansari Road
Daryaganj, New Delhi-110002
Phone: 011-47034999, 9811692060
E-mail: books@gyanbooks.com

Distribution Network
gyanbooks.com
India, USA, Canada, UK, Australia

ISBN: 978-93-6780-526-8 (PB)

First Published, 1929

2nd Impression 2024

Printed at: Gyan Press, Delhi.

AFTER MOTHER INDIA
Author: HARRY H. FIELD

AFTER MOTHER INDIA

Being an examination of *Mother India*, of the first nine volumes written in reply thereto, and of other criticisms; together with certain new evidence mostly from Indian sources

BY

HARRY H. FIELD

JONATHAN CAPE
THIRTY BEDFORD SQUARE
LONDON

A STATEMENT from *India in 1927-28*—the official survey of India's progress prepared annually for presentation to the British Parliament in accordance with the Government of India Act:

> 'After the formation of the Statutory Commission the event which engrossed public attention more fully than anything else was the publication of Miss Katherine Mayo's book *Mother India* in the early summer of 1927. The main reason for the extraordinary effect produced by the book is its treatment of the subject of child marriage among Hindus, and certain other topics. Practically every newspaper in India denounced the book as a scurrilous libel on Hindus and Hinduism and it was freely alleged that Miss Mayo had been subsidised to produce it in order to degrade India in the eyes of the world, and to prejudice her case for self-government when the Statutory Enquiry ordered by Section 84-A of the Government of India Act came to be held. For months a violent agitation against the book was kept up in the Indian press and on public platforms in this country, and the controversy has extended to a great part of the civilised world.'—*India in 1927-28*, J. Coatman, Director of Public Information, Government of India, Government of India Central Publication Branch, Calcutta, 1928, pp. 3-4.

ACKNOWLEDGMENT

I WISH to express my indebtedness to certain individuals and organisations for help in securing material used in this volume ; and to certain friends for reading over the manuscript and making valuable suggestions.

I thank Miss Katherine Mayo for access to documents and for the use of her library. To Mrs. Annette Helen Doherty, Major-General A. Hooton, Mr. Albert Howard, C.I.E., M.A., The American Public Health Association, and the India Office in London, I am indebted for written statements and statistics. To Judge Daniel R. Williams, Edwin Muller, Jr., and Henry Kittredge Norton, I am under no slight obligation for reading and criticising either the whole or certain parts of my manuscript. I should also like to thank the staffs of the New York Public Library, the British Museum, the Missionary Research Library of the Foreign Missions Conference of North America, and the Office of the High Commissioner for India in London for the always courteous and untiring aid they have given me in their ordinary course of duty.

FOREWORD

LOOKING down the centuries, certain writings, here and there, stand out rather as material events than as mere records—rather as social forces than as records of thought. *The Origin of Species* and *Uncle Tom's Cabin* are instances.

If controversy be the measure, then *Mother India* bids fair to enter this class. The official review for India remarks, 'for months a violent agitation against the book was kept up in the Indian press and on public platforms.'[1] And already no fewer than nine books have been published denying the existence of many of the Hindu customs that *Mother India* brought within the searchlight beam of Western scrutiny. Quite naturally, those who believed themselves offended have done everything within their power to discredit the disturbing influence. Nevertheless, as the *Manchester Guardian*[2] stated on March 25th, 1929, 'No one who has followed Indian affairs can doubt that her [Miss Mayo's] book, in spite of glaring faults, has done more to help the cause of India's women than all that has been written by Indian social reformers in this century.'

Whatever help *Mother India* may have given, or may yet be able to give, to the least fortunate creatures of Hindu India, can be attributed to one fact and one alone: namely, that it brought to the knowledge of the Western world, and to the realisation of some Indians, a certain set of conditions that had hitherto been either

[1] *India in 1927-28*, quoted in the Epigraph of this book.
[2] Book review entitled "Miss Mayo Again."

unknown to them, or unsurveyed in their orderly and logical sequence. The reviews of the book that appeared in the Western press started the movement; but it was not until a large mass of people, on several continents, began to discuss its merits, both pro and con, that its real driving power was revealed for the improvement of the conditions exposed.

Here is a definite case of the influence and power of mass public opinion. And some Indians, besides Westerners, believe that *Mother India*, through this new influence, is opening a new era in Hindu social history.

But the effect of the mass of material published to controvert *Mother India* has been to build up a thick fog bank, so thick that clear vision of the central issues has become increasingly difficult.

Therefore it seems desirable that some of the charges levelled against the book should be examined in the light of such fresh evidence, mainly from Indian sources, as has been brought forth by the publication of the book.

No attempt will be found in these pages to examine all the criticisms of *Mother India* and its author; nor is the scope of this compilation as broad as was that volume's. *Mother India* itself disclaimed the pretension of being a whole or rounded picture of the great Hindu world in these words, 'That there are other facts, other columns of statistics, other angles left untouched by this research I do not contest.'[1]

[1] *Mother India*, Jonathan Cape, London, 1927, p. 363. References to *Mother India* throughout these pages are to the British edition.

FOREWORD

My motive in writing is the outgrowth of having assisted in the editing of *Mother India* and of having closely followed its history, from its inception. This experience has developed a deep conviction, already expressed, that Western public opinion, by holding the facts in true focus, has power to effect great reforms in Hindu India.

CONTENTS

		PAGE
ACKNOWLEDGMENT		7
FOREWORD		9
CHAP.		
I.	THE IMPACT	15
II.	'THE DRAIN INSPECTOR'S' REPORT'	25
III.	THE MESSENGER	38
IV.	'IN COMMON PRACTICE'	49
V.	WHEN DO THEY MATURE?	66
VI.	IS IT A CURSE?	74
VII.	A LIFE OF AUSTERITY	94
VIII.	FIVE ATTEMPTED REFORMS	105
IX.	DR. CLARK AND OTHERS	121
X.	THE NATIONAL CHRISTIAN COUNCIL	138
XI.	DEVADASIS AND PROSTITUTES	151
XII.	THEIR VOICE IS HEARD	163
XIII.	LEGENDS	180
XIV.	A CALF IS KILLED	197
XV.	ONE SUCCESSFUL METHOD	205
XVI.	SOME RESULTS	214
XVII.	MOTIVES	224
XVIII.	CONCLUSION	230
APPENDIX		
I.	LEGISLATORS AND 'MOTHER INDIA'	233
II.	'THE TIMES' EDITORIAL	250
III.	A SHORT BIOGRAPHY OF KATHERINE MAYO	253

CONTENTS

APPENDIX PAGE

IV. LORD NORTHCLIFFE'S STATEMENT 263

V. MEETINGS FAVOURABLE TO THE SARDA CHILD MARRIAGE BILL 267

VI. MEETINGS PROTESTING AGAINST THE SARDA CHILD MARRIAGE BILL 270

BIBLIOGRAPHY 273

INDEX 279

AFTER MOTHER INDIA

CHAPTER I

THE IMPACT

Mother India was first published in America on May 20th, 1927. Two months later, on July 14th, the British edition appeared in London.

As to India, it happened in the ordinary course that some of the British reviews of the book arrived there weeks ahead of the book itself. Outstanding amongst these was one appearing in a well-known Liberal London weekly, the *New Statesman*,[1] signed 'C. S.,' the editor's own initials. This completely favourable review was even more outspoken than *Mother India*, of which it declared in part:

> It is certainly the most fascinating, the most depressing and at the same time the most important and truthful book that has been written about India for a good deal more than a generation. To say that is no doubt to say a great deal, but it is not to say too much. Miss Mayo can observe accurately, can understand without prejudice, and can write—a combination of faculties that is unfortunately very rare. Her book is very heavily documented, almost every statement is a quotation from authority, yet it remains continuously readable. One is tempted to skip hardly a sentence throughout its four hundred pages. . . .

[1] Edited by Clifford Sharp.

In a sense it contains nothing that is really new. All who know anything of India are aware, of course, of the prime evils of Hinduism, of the horrors of the child marriage system, of the universality of sexual vice in its most extravagant forms, of the monstrously absurd brutalities of the caste system, of the filthy personal habits of even the most highly educated classes—which, like the degradation of Hindu women, are unequalled even amongst the most primitive African or Australian savages—of the universal cruelty to animals, and of the equally universal prevalence of laziness, untruthfulness, cowardice and personal corruption which in the code of *Mother India* are not recognised as faults at all. But these evils have never before, within living memory at any rate, been described for English readers as faithfully and as ruthlessly as Miss Mayo describes them. And the reason for this is not far to seek. English officials and even English missionaries have never cared to write quite frankly about India, because of the possibly disastrous repercussions of such frankness upon their own work out there. They have not sought to paint the Hindu as he is, simply because it was with the Hindu that they were seeking to establish friendly relations—and also perhaps because one or two efforts in this direction, made by early missionaries, produced some extremely embarrassing results. . . .

She tells without reticence what she has seen. And the picture she draws is so appalling that

> no civilised reader could fail to hope that its horrors are exaggerated. But they are not. The documented narrative is completely convincing; . . . Chiefly she espouses the cause of the baby girls, but the rest of her analysis of Indian social conditions is quite equally startling and convincing. She makes the claims for Swaraj[1] seem nonsense and the will to grant it almost a crime.[2]

As many Indian editors and political leaders had been accustomed to look to this journal for a sympathetic understanding of their aspirations, such a review as the above, coming from that source, seemed to them like treachery. Their immediate response was to attack both the book and the paper with equal violence. Said the leading editorial of an outstanding Swaraj newspaper published in Madras:

> We propose to deal briefly here with a Miss Katherine Mayo, who has perpetrated an atrocious piece of mendacious and malignant propaganda entitled *Mother India*. We have not yet seen a copy of this precious production. But we are enabled to gather a fairly clear idea of Miss Mayo's masterpiece from the deliriously enthusiastic full-dress reviews which have appeared in the press of Great Britain. . . . The virulence of the hack,

[1] Swaraj is an elastic term signifying home-rule, independence, or other varieties of increased political power, according to the views of the individual using it.

[2] The *New Statesman*, London, July 16th, 1927.

whose drivel besmirches the pages of the *New Statesman* and makes one wonder what has become of the sanity and good taste which once so distinguished that paper, simply passes all bounds of decency.[1]

Four days previously, the Indian-owned *Bombay Daily Mail*, in discussing the British reviews, had stated : 'One of the most bitter of them, that is to say, the most anti-Indian—appears over the initials C. S. (a very thin disguise for a well-known publicist) in the *New Statesman*.'[2] And it was on the strength of reviews alone that the Secretary of the Swaraj party tabled a resolution[3] in the Central Legislature of India demanding that the Government ban the book from the country. Ten days later, it was reported that Mr. Rangaswamy Iyengar, 'who has put down a proposal in the Assembly for prohibiting the book, has not yet read it, and is not likely to bring the question before the House until he has done so. He is prepared to withdraw his proposal if the book makes a different impression on him from the review in a London journal.'[4]

Mother India was never proscribed ; although requests that it be so were made in the Central Legislative Assembly and in at least one Provincial Legislature.[5]

[1] *The Hindu*, Madras, August 9th, 1927.
[2] *Bombay Daily Mail*, Bombay, August 5th, 1927.
[3] Reuter dispatch from Simla, India, August 13th, 1927.
[4] *Daily Express*, London, August 23rd, 1927, *Times of Malaya*, Ipoh, September 14th, 1927.
[5] Appendix I.

In England, less than a month after publication, ten prominent Indians, then visiting Europe, submitted to the London *Times*[1] a letter of protest and denunciation. Much has been made of the fact that *The Times* refused to print this letter.[2] Seven months later it explained its position in an editorial :

> To judge from a whole series of speeches, newspaper articles, and even published volumes, it seems by now to have become almost an accepted fact that *The Times* gave extraordinary publicity to *Mother India* when it first appeared, used it (with some mysterious object) as 'propaganda,' refused altogether to hear the other side of such questions as it raised, and violated the most elementary canons of controversy by 'suppressing' informed criticism.[3]

And, speaking directly of the ten Indians' communication, the editorial continues :

> This letter was declined with a courteous explanation that it was an established rule of *The Times* to decline all letters criticising publications other than those for which *The Times* itself was responsible. That is a rule for which there are very

[1] *The Times*, London, March 27th, 1928.

[2] Mrs. Besant's *New India* referred to this as a 'Suppression of Truth,' August 24th, 1927.

[3] *The Times*, London, March 27th, 1928. This editorial is reproduced, for those who desire to read it in its entirety, in Appendix II.

obvious practical reasons, for there would literally be no end to the correspondence demanding insertion if once it came to be recognised that anyone interested in, or aggrieved by, some volume or pamphlet or newspaper, in any part of the world, might look as a matter of right for space to challenge it in these columns. . . . No doubt every rule of the kind admits of variation, and it might be argued that the appearance of *Mother India* was an event of such overriding importance as to call for the immense advertisement of a protracted newspaper controversy in England. But is this really what the critics desired?

A point not mentioned in this editorial is the reasonable doubt whether all, or any, of the ten signatories of this letter had read the volume they denounced. The Allahabad *Leader*, an Indian-owned and -edited newspaper, gives the letter as including the phrase: 'It has never been our lot to read the book. . . .'[1] And the same paper adds three weeks later, in a despatch from its London correspondent:[2] 'One thing is to be borne in mind, . . . that the only authentic text of the letter circulated in India is the one appearing in your columns.'[3]

[1] *The Leader*, Allahabad, August 19th, 1927.
[2] *Ibid.*, September 5th, 1927.
[3] Other versions of the communication rejected by *The Times* use the phrase 'a book,' yet such an authoritative journal as the *Fortnightly Review* (February, 1928, p. 175) when discussing this matter says: 'Their letter states that "*it has never been our lot to read the book.*" . . .' Using the italics in so doing.

This fact that the book was being condemned without a reading, did not altogether escape public notice in India, where we find Mr. Himadri Bhusan Roy writing to the Calcutta *Statesman* on August 26th: 'The most amusing thing about the unfortunate controversy over Miss Mayo's *Mother India* is that not one in a thousand of her critics had any opportunity of reading her book and of knowing, at first-hand, what she had actually said.' Without regard to the facts, therefore, those wishing to attack bestowed upon their target any character which suited their purpose. Thus they advertised it as a 'Libel Against Indian Womanhood,'[1] or 'Gratuitous Insult, Indian Women Blasphemed.'[2] This characterisation was generally adopted by the Indian-owned press.

By September public meetings to denounce the book were being held up and down India. These meetings were assembled under such rallying captions as that heralding the one held in the Town Hall of Calcutta, on September 4th, under the chairmanship of the Mayor: 'To express indignation against and to repudiate the scurrilous attacks and malicious allegations made against the Indian womanhood by Miss Mayo. . . .'[3]

Meantime, the volume which occasioned all this high feeling remained practically unobtainable in India, owing to the difficulty, always widespread in the East, of distributing and selling foreign books.

[1] *Forward*, Calcutta, August 27th, 1927.
[2] *Amrita Bazar Patrika*, Calcutta, August 28th, 1927.
[3] *Forward*, Calcutta, September 4th, 1927.

In America, however, where the book was always procurable, it was not until late in 1927 or the beginning of 1928 that protest meetings, newspaper and magazine articles, pamphlets and volumes aimed to refute *Mother India*, began to appear.

The first book,[1] published 'in reply,' was placed on sale in London in November 1927, just four months after the English edition of *Mother India* appeared, but in America the first answer[2] was not issued until February, nine months after the original work was published in New York.

The American answer was written by a Bengali who left India when he was but eighteen years old, some twenty-one years ago.[3] After some wanderings he worked his way through an American college, married an American wife, and, it is understood, has but once revisited his native land in these two decades. His book was quickly followed by others from other hands, until, by the middle of 1928, no fewer than nine volumes,[4] all purporting to be replies to *Mother India*,

[1] *Father India*, C. S. Ranga Iyer ; Selwyn and Blount, London, 1927.

[2] *A Son of Mother India Answers*, D. G. Mukerji ; E. P. Dutton and Company, New York, 1928.

[3] *Daily Times*, Victoria, B.C., October 6th, 1928.

[4] *Sister India*, 'World Citizen' ; Sister India Office, Bombay, 1928.

Unhappy India, Lajpat Rai ; Banna Publishing Company, Calcutta, 1928.

India : Its Character, A Reply to 'Mother India,' J. A. Chapman ; Basil Blackwell, Oxford, England, 1928.

Miss Mayo's Mother India, A Rejoinder, K. Natarajan ; G. A. Natesan and Company, Madras, 1927.

had been published. Six of these contain much of the same material, each critic having collected and reprinted the material of his predecessors, until the latest arrival, *Unhappy India*, accumulates 513 pages, or something over 100 pages more than the original work that caused them all.

Thus, for instance, six of these 'replies' reprint, in whole, or in part, or both, Mr. Gandhi's review of *Mother India*; six quote Tagore and the National Christian Council, five use Dr. Margaret Balfour's theories, and all give reasons of their own as to why the offending book was ever written,[1] one author going so far as to offer his services as collaborator to rewrite the original work.[2]

But, of the many criticisms, that which first received any real attention in the West, and especially in America,[3] also attained the widest international circulation of them all: The twentieth-century Hindu saint, today an outstanding world-figure, Mohandas Karamchand Gandhi, expressed his views in his own paper

Mother India Ka Jawab, Mrs. C. Lakhanpal, B.A.; Gurukula Press, Dehradun, India, 1928. Translated from Hindi for the author.

Indian reviews report the eighth and ninth volumes as being chiefly restatements of other replies. They are: *Mother India Aur Uska Jawab*, Srimati Uma Nehru (Kashinath Bajpai, Allahabad, India, 1928) and *Miss Mayo's Grandhakhandanamu*, edited by Pandit Puranam Suryanarayana Thirthulu (G. L. Sastri and Company, Madras, India, 1928).

[1] A concise biographical sketch of Miss Mayo is given in Appendix III.

[2] *A Son of Mother India Answers*, p. 86.

[3] *The New York Times* devoted the best part of two news columns to this review on October 9th, 1927.

under the caption 'The Drain Inspector's Report.'[1] And because the world-wide following of the reviewer gave his words news value and importance, it appears wise, at the outset of this book, to examine his criticisms closely.

[1] *Young India*, edited by M. K. Gandhi, Ahmedabad, September 15th, 1927, pp. 308-11.

CHAPTER II

'THE DRAIN INSPECTOR'S REPORT'

Mother India's most serious arraignments of Hindu customs are substantiated in its text by quotations from Mr. Gandhi's own writings. This was possible since for years he has been battering his apathetic Hindu public with warnings against the 'curse' and the devitalising effects of child marriage;[1] the 'brutal crime' of enforced widowhood;[2] the monstrosity of Untouchability;[3] the appalling cruelty to animals;[4] the Hindus' filthy habits and 'total disregard of the elementary laws of health';[5] even the futility of 'mechanical contrivances.'[6]

Yet, when Mr. Gandhi's lead was followed by an alien stranger, his words quoted and sustained, he hastened to brand the work as 'doubly untruthful,'[7] the quotations as 'torn from their contexts,' the picture they made as 'wholly false,' and imputed the bought-and-paid-for motives of a hireling to the author whom he attacks through six and a half columns of his paper. Yet towards the end he writes:

> We may repudiate the charge as it has been framed by her, but we may not repudiate the substance underlying the many allegations she has made.[8]

[1] *Mother India*, p. 62. The words in quotation marks are from Gandhi's own writings. [2] *Ibid.*, p. 87.

[3] *Ibid.*, p. 154. [4] *Ibid.*, p. 221. [5] *Ibid.*, p. 322. [6] *Ibid.*, p. 36.

[7] These quotations appear in 'The Drain Inspector's Report.'

[8] *Young India*, September 15th, 1927.

But before making this statement Mr. Gandhi, forsaking his generalisations, specifically enumerates those parts of *Mother India* that are, he says, to his personal knowledge untrue. They are four in number ; briefly, as follows :

First : 'She has described the visit to me, and informed her readers that there are always with me two "secretaries" who write down every word I say.'[1]

Second : 'But the real crime committed against me is described by her at pages 387-88.'[2] (344-45 Cape edition.) This concerns *Mother India's* account of Mr. Gandhi's behaviour when stricken with appendicitis while serving a term in jail. The book records the report that he asked to be operated upon by the English surgeon in charge, instead of by his Indian physicians, and this in spite of his recent denunciations of all Western medical practice.

Third : 'Thus she describes an ovation said to have been given to the Prince of Wales, of which Indian India has no knowledge, but which could not possibly escape it if it had happened.'[3]

Fourth : 'I warn them [American and English readers] against believing this book. I do not remember having given the message Miss Mayo imputes to me. The only one present who took any notes at all has no recollection of the message imputed to me.'[4]

During the past eighteen months, these accusations have been reprinted in so many columns, pamphlets,

[1] *Young India*, September 15th, 1927.
[2] *Ibid.* [3] *Ibid.* [4] *Ibid.*

and press articles as material of first-class importance, that no excuse need be offered for examining them at length, despite their minor significance, whether true or false. So, taking the four in reverse order :

The fourth point. The 'message' which Mr. Gandhi does not remember is found on page 201 of the disputed book :

> 'What is my message to America ?' he repeated, in his light, dispassionate, even voice. 'My message to America is the hum of this spinning-wheel.'
>
> Then he speaks at length slowly, with pauses. And as he speaks the two young men, his secretaries, lying over their slant-topped desk, write down every word he says.

In attacking this passage Mr. Gandhi's memory betrayed him. For he not only forgot his 'message to America' but he also forgot that not his secretaries only, but his American visitor, from the beginning to the end, was herself taking verbatim notes.

At Mr. Gandhi's request, delivered by one of his attendants at the close of the interview, those notes, having been typed out in full, were sent back to Mr. Gandhi for revision and amplification. In due course Miss Mayo received back an approved transcript which Mr. Gandhi had caused to be retyped, together with his covering letter. The accompanying fascimile of both these documents[1] will enable the reader to judge for himself and will suffice to close this incident.

[1] See p. 29.

The third point presented in 'The Drain Inspector's Report' reads :

> Thus she describes an ovation said to have been given to the Prince of Wales, of which Indian India has no knowledge, but which could not possibly escape it if it had happened. A crowd is reported to have fought its way to the Prince's car somewhere in Bombay. 'The police,' Miss Mayo says, 'tried vainly to form a hedge around the car moving at a crawl unprotected now through a solid mass of shouting humanity which won through to the railway station at last.' Then at the railway station while there were three minutes for the train to steam out, the Prince is reported by Miss Mayo to have ordered the barriers to be dropped and the 'mobs' to be let in. The authoress then proceeds, 'Like the sweep of a river in flood(s), the interminable multitude[s] rolled in, and shouted and laughed and wept, and when the train started, ran alongside the Royal carriage till they could run no more.' All this is supposed to have happened in 1921 on the evening of November 22nd, whilst the dying embers of the riots were still hot. There is much of this kind of stuff in this romantic chapter, which is headed 'Behold a Light.'

All the world knows that Mr. Gandhi attempted to organise a boycott during the Prince of Wales' visit to India in 1921. One of the first instances of his failure was this same overpowering street demonstration in Bombay, spontaneously given to the Prince by the common crowds, a demonstration seriously out of

Interview with Mr. Gandhi, March 17th, 1926.

My message to America is simply the hum of this wheel Letters and newspaper cuttings I get from America show that one set of people overratesthe results of Non-violent Non-co-operation and the other not only underrateeit but impute a all kinds of motives to those whowere concerned with the movement. Don't exaggerate one way or the other. If therefore some earnest Americans will study the movement impartially and patiently then it is likely that the United States may know something of the movement which I do consider to be unique although I am the author of it. What I mean is that our movement is summed up in the spinning wheel with all its implications. It is to me a substitute for gun-powder. For, it brings the message of self-reliance and hope to the millions

ASHRAM

Sabarmati, 9-4-26.

Dear Friend,

I hope you received my previous letter in reply to your enquiry about the sources of my information on poverty of India.

I have now your 2nd letter enclosing copy of your notes. I have tried to fill in the gaps left by you. I have been obliged to do the same somewhat hurriedly but I hope it will answer the purpose.

Yours sincerely,

Miss. Katherine Mayo,
Bedford Hills,
New York,
U.S.A.

PART OF THE INTERVIEW MR. GANDHI GAVE TO MISS MAYO, TOGETHER WITH HIS COVERING LETTER.

Note that both the document and letter were typed on the same machine. Later Mr. Gandhi wrote: 'I do not remember the message Miss Mayo imputes to me.'

tune with the spirit of repudiation declared by Mr. Gandhi. Here is a contemporaneous newspaper report, dated November 24th, 1921 :

> At the Apollo Bandar and at Victoria Terminus there were demonstrations of enthusiasm such as must have surprised all who know the characteristics of the undemonstrative Indian. The police were almost helpless. They could not keep back the crowds which surged forward to get a closer glimpse of the Prince as he stood in his motor car and waved his hat, infected a little by the excitement of those enthusiastic thousands and by the warmth of a send-off which perhaps he had not expected. Traffic regulations went to the winds. The crowds surrounded his car and cheered. Such cheering has never been heard in Bombay before. Everybody did his best to make a cheerful noise. Even the wearers of the Gandhi caps—and there were many of them—took them off and waved them wildly in the air. Men and women of all classes and all communities helped in this wonderful send-off. The rich man in his motor-car, the poor man in his rags ; Hindus, Mahommedans, Parsis, Europeans,—all joined in this final demonstration of loyalty and affection. So large were the crowds that it took the Prince's motor-car ten minutes to cover the last hundred yards to the station entrance.[1]

To-day Mr. Gandhi would have us believe no such demonstration ever occurred.

[1] The *Times of India*, Bombay.

The second point: 'But the real crime committed against me is described by her at pages 387-88.' (344-45 Cape edition.) These pages in *Mother India* read:

> But once upon a time it chanced that Mr. Gandhi, having widely and publicly announced that 'hospitals are institutions for propagating sin';[1] that 'European doctors are the worst of all,' and that 'quacks whom we know are better than the doctors who put on an air of humaneness,'[2] himself fell suddenly ill of a pain in the side.
>
> As he happened to be in prison at the time, a British surgeon of the Indian Medical Service came straightway to see him.
>
> 'Mr. Gandhi,' said the surgeon, as the incident was reported, 'I am sorry to have to tell you that you have appendicitis. If you were my patient, I should operate at once. But you will probably prefer to call in your Aruvedic[3] physician.'
>
> Mr. Gandhi proved otherwise minded.
>
> 'I should prefer not to operate,' pursued the surgeon, 'because in case the outcome should be unfortunate, all your friends will lay it as a charge of malicious intent against us whose duty it is to care for you.'

[1] *Indian Home Rule*, Ganesh and Company, Madras, 1924, p. 61.

[2] *Ibid.*, p. 62.

[3] The spelling of Indian words in English is largely phonetic. This accounts for the various spellings of the same word met in several quotations in these pages. The author has throughout followed the exact text of the originals in all quotations, even to their sometimes inaccurate spelling and grammar.

'If you will only consent to operate,' pleaded Mr. Gandhi, 'I will call in my friends, now, and explain to them that you do so at my request.'

So, Mr. Gandhi wilfully went to an 'institution for propagating sin'; was operated upon by one of the 'worst of all,' an officer of the Indian Medical Service, and was attentively nursed through convalescence by an English Sister whom he is understood to have thought after all rather a useful sort of person.[1]

Mr. Gandhi disputes the above passage with these words:

This is a travesty of truth. I shall confine myself to correcting only what is libellous and not the other inaccuracies. There was no question here of calling in any Ayurvedic physician. Col. Maddock who performed the operation had the right if he had so chosen, to perform the operation without a reference to me, and even in spite of me. But he and Surgeon-General Hooton showed a delicate consideration to me, and asked me whether I would wait for my own doctors who were known to them and who were also trained in Western medical and surgical science. I would not be behindhand in returning their courtesy and consideration, and I immediately told them that they could perform the operation without waiting for my doctors to whom they had telegraphed, and

[1] For some reason of his own, Mr. Gandhi, in reproducing this passage from *Mother India*, quotes 'useful sort of person,' which is not done in the original text.

> that I would gladly give them a note for their protection in the event of the operation miscarrying. I endeavoured to show that I had no distrust either in their ability or their good faith. It was to me a happy opportunity of demonstrating my personal goodwill.
>
> So far as my opinion about hospitals and the like is concerned, it stands, in spite of my having subjected myself and my wards to treatment more than once by physicians and surgeons, Indians and Europeans, trained in the Western school of medicine.

It will thus be seen that Mr. Gandhi's objection to *Mother India's* account is not that it shows his general condemnation of Western medical science, but that it misinterprets his motive in accepting in his hour of need, the services of British doctors. He adhered, as he still implies, to his declared opinion of the skill of Western medical men; but as the two then present had the authority to operate upon him whether he desired it or not—yet refrained from exercising that authority—he would not be outdone in courtesy. Therefore, as a demonstration of goodwill and gallantry, he asked Colonel Maddock and Major-General Hooton to operate upon him.

Thus it appears the whole of Mr. Gandhi's case rests upon what he thought to the 'right' possessed by medical officers in charge of a prison to operate upon him, by main force and in spite of himself. No official ruling on this 'right' exists. But Major-General Hooton the senior medical officer, present on this specific occasion, states :

> With regard to the quotation from Mr. Gandhi's review of Miss Mayo's book to which you refer, I am unable to say what exactly is the legal position in India of a prisoner who wishes to refuse an operation which is considered desirable. All that I can say is that I, myself, never did and never should have forced an operation upon an unwilling prisoner, provided he was in his right mind and not a minor. In the case in point Mr. Gandhi was given entire freedom of choice and eventually requested Colonel Maddock to operate.
>
> (*Signed*) A. HOOTON.[1]

The India Office in London, being consulted for further information, states :

> There is apparently nothing in the gaol regulations (these are provincial) on the medical treatment of prisoners. The practice is, I understand, as in this country, to get permission from the prisoner (or his representatives if a minor) before operating. The Gandhi case is in point.[2]

It would therefore appear that the idea of operating by force upon a conscious and sane prisoner is as remote from British medical ethics in India as it would be to Western medical science the world over.

A further word from Surgeon-General Hooton carries interest :

[1] Letter to the author, dated March 28th, 1929.
[2] Letter to the author, dated May 8th, 1928.

During his convalescence I had a conversation with Mr. Gandhi, in the course of which I suggested that his action in resorting to European Surgery was not very consistent with his general attitude to Western medical science, and remarked that he had given us some very hard knocks in the past, even going so far as to call it 'Satanic.' He said yes, it was true he had been inconsistent, but that he knew his last hope of recovery lay in scientific surgery, and that he had thought that if he could live a little longer he might be able to serve his country further.

(*Signed*) A. HOOTON.[1]

And so, to the point first cited. Here it may be well to present Mr. Gandhi's statement together with Miss Mayo's reply to allow the reader to form his own opinion.

Mr. Gandhi[2]	*Miss Mayo*[3]
She has described the visit to me, and informed her readers that there are always with me 'two secretaries' who write down every word I say. I know this is not a wilful perversion of facts. Nevertheless	If Mr. Gandhi were to look on page 222[4] [p. 201, Cape edition] of my book he would discover that he has inserted the word 'always' into my text. I spoke only of the occasion when I sat with him and

[1] Letter to the author, dated May 9th, 1928.

[2] 'Drain Inspector's Report.'

[3] 'India,' Katherine Mayo, *Liberty Magazine*, New York, January 14th, 1928, p. 38.

[4] This passage has been quoted. See *ante*, p. 27.

the statement is not true. I beg to inform her, that I have no one near me who has been appointed or is expected to write down every word that I say. I have by me a co-worker called Mahadev Desai who is striving to out-Boswell Boswell and does, whenever he is near me, take down whatever he considers to be wisdom dropping from my lips.

his two young Indians, one or the other of whom, like myself, took down our conversation.

It will thus be seen that Mr. Gandhi's accusation, in this instance, is rendered possible only by his own interpolation into the text of the word 'always.'

It should be noted that not one of the four definite accusations is of any public moment; that not one proves a 'torn' context; that not one will stand close examination; and that in each the offence complained of affects Mr. Gandhi personally or his own claim to leadership. What is of even greater significance, however, is the fact that a man of Mr. Gandhi's reputation and one who, in all sincerity, has his country's interests at heart, should produce four such trifling matters to justify his attack on a volume to whose major contentions he himself is largely committed and which, if correct, presents the most urgent problems facing any people in the world to-day.

'The Drain Inspector's Report' is worthy of consideration on one other score : It openly displays an old anxiety that has beset this famous Hindu—an anxiety lest certain kinds of information calculated to hurt his political activities in Western eyes should come to be known or to be believed in white men's countries, there to embarrass both him and his cause. One other instance of this, hitherto, it is believed, unrealised, will help to illustrate the point.

CHAPTER III

THE MESSENGER

SHORTLY after writing 'The Drain Inspector's Report' Mr. Gandhi advocated that his associate, Mrs. Sarojini Naidu, the outstanding Hindu woman in politics, should go to America on a lecture tour ; these were his reasons as he gave them :

> No serious American can possibly be taken in by Miss Mayo's scurrilous writings. The seriously minded American does not need any refutation. And the general public that has been already affected by *Mother India* will never read the refutations however brilliant attempted in India. The idea therefore has been happily conceived in America of bringing out Sarojini Devi [Mrs. Naidu] on a lecturing tour by way of reply to *Mother India*. If Sarojini Devi would respond to the invitation, her visit is likely to undo some at least of the mischief wrought by Miss Mayo's novel.[1]

Nine months later—on October 26th, 1928, to be exact—Mrs. Naidu set foot on Manhattan Island, and in an early interview with an American reporter[2] gave as her reason for her first visit to America, 'Mahatma Gandhi ordered me to come.'

This was not the first occasion on which Mrs. Naidu had acted as an intermediary between Mr. Gandhi

[1] *Young India*, January 5th, 1928, p. 8.

[2] Esther Norton, *The Sun*, New York, October 30th, 1928.

and the American public. In a previous instance, it was not directly to America that she was sent, but to a stricken and helpless American girl, far away from home. The story does not leave a savoury taste in the mouth, and it belongs in these pages only in as far as it shows the consistent eagerness, as well as the continuity of method, with which Gandhi has nursed American public opinion, dating from years before *Mother India* appeared.

This incident occurred in 1921, during the visit of the Prince of Wales to Bombay, and when, as Mr. Gandhi has acknowledged,[1] riots and much bloodshed disturbed the peace, wholly because of his own preaching.

Professor Claude Van Tyne, head of the Department of History in the University of Michigan, visited India during 1921-22, and gives the following contemporaneous account of the Bombay happenings :

> 'Do not co-operate with the British in doing honour to 'the Prince,' Gandhi ordered. Then came the riot at Bombay, the deaths of fifty-four and the wounding of many, due to a clash between those who obeyed Gandhi, who gave the hour of the Prince's triumphal procession to burning foreign-made cloth, and those who could not resist the lure of a thrilling pageant. As is characteristic in India, the mob returning from a political meeting did the mischief. In general it was a fight between Hindus and Mussulmans on one side and

[1] *Gandhi's Letters on Indian Affairs*, V. Narayanan and Company, Madras, 1923, pp. 104-05.

> Parsis on the other, the police trying to quell the riot with as little bloodshed as possible. . . . In vain Gandhi had run wildly about the streets urging the rioters to go home. He was powerless when the mob's blood was up. When all was over he fasted in agony of spirit.[1]

As Dr. Van Tyne tells us, it was chiefly Indians who were killed, but the life of one American engineer was taken; and it was the news and circumstances of this murder that Mr. Gandhi was particularly anxious to keep from the people of the United States.[2]

William Francis Doherty, a young American citizen, went to India on the recommendation of the General Electric Company to enter the employ of the Indian-owned Tata Company of Bombay. Later he formed an engineering partnership with Mr. Richard Brenchley.

On the morning of November 19th, 1921, at about eleven-thirty o'clock, Mr. Doherty was quietly proceeding down Tankpakada Street, on his way to the Bombay Improvement Trust workshops, to expedite work on a machine needed in dredging. Suddenly arose an outcry, 'Sahib! Sahib! Maro! Maro!'—'A white man! A white man! Strike! Strike!' Immediately he was surrounded by a howling, murderous mob, which emerged simultaneously from hallways, yards, and houses along the street. An instant before, there had been nothing at all to show the presence of

[1] *India in Ferment*, Claude H. Van Tyne; D. Appleton and Company, New York, 1923, pp. 126-27.

[2] *Ibid.*, p. 126.

rioters, only the usual traffic occupying that thoroughfare.[1]

A terrible fight ensued. The young American, an athlete in splendid physical health, was, on account of the overwhelming odds, soon driven against a wall. Somehow, he wrenched a club from one of his attackers and, somehow, held his own for fifteen long minutes before the torrent of blows on his head, legs, and body did their inevitable work. Then he was left on the footpath for dead.

Witnesses to the incident, however, swear that a little later he recovered consciousness, and, seeing a water tap near by, dragged himself to it, and managed to turn the water on to his head. A few of the rioters, from their hiding-place, observed this move, and immediately reassembled the mob to beat him afresh, till they grew tired of beating. Then they robbed him of his valuables and stripped him bare. Finally, having gouged out his eyes, they dragged him naked through the streets, the length of two city blocks, while one of their company danced at their head, playing a suitable tune on the flute.

Not until one-thirty in the afternoon did the police pick up the still bleeding body to rush it to a hospital. There, ten minutes after he was admitted, Mr. Doherty breathed his last. For some ninety minutes, then, that young American citizen had lain naked, blinded and dying, under the broiling Indian sun.

When Mrs. Doherty discovered her husband's body, twenty-six hours later, it was so badly mutilated that

[1] This whole account is taken from a statement by Mrs. Doherty, in the possession of the author.

it could only be identified by certain scars on the legs —electrical burns received when the murdered man was a student at Stanford University in California.[1]

When Mr. Gandhi learned that one of the murders perpetrated in his name had been committed upon an innocent American citizen, his first anxiety was lest the news reach American shores, there, as he believed, to harm his cause amongst his many American sympathisers.

To the newly-made American widow, therefore, Mr. Gandhi hastened to send an emissary. This emissary, as attested by the widow herself, was the poetess, Mrs. Sarojini Naidu. Here is Mrs. Doherty's own statement on this matter—a statement attested before a notary public, and, in part, reproduced in fascimile in these pages :

State of California
County of Los Angeles }

ANNETTE H. DOHERTY, being first duly sworn on oath, deposes and says :

My deceased husband, William Francis Doherty, an American citizen, was a mechanical and electrical engineer and, at the time of his death, was managing engineer and business associate of Mr.

[1] These statements can be verified by the records of the court in Bombay which heard Mrs. Doherty's claim for compensation and the account of her husband's death. Lord Northcliffe's written statement concerning this murder appeared in a despatch dated Bombay, January 21st, 1922, in *The Daily Mail* of London, January 25th, 1922, and in the *Over-Seas Daily Mail* of January 28th, 1922, and is to be found in Appendix IV.

Richard J. Brenchley, engaged in sand extraction at Mumbra, adjacent to Bombay, India.

On November 19th, 1921, as he was quietly proceeding to the Bombay Improvement Trust workshops, he was set upon, his eyes were gouged out and eventually he was beaten to death by a group of rioters in a public street of Byculla, a suburb of Bombay.

This was during the visit of the Prince of Wales to India, when Gandhi was at the height of his popularity as saint and political leader, and had, through his violent speeches against the British, worked his followers into a frenzy of race hatred. My husband was probably mistaken for a Britisher when he was murdered by Gandhi's followers.

Within three days following this killing of my husband, word was brought me from Gandhi that he greatly desired an interview with me, begging me to set a time when I would receive him. I was then stopping with an American family in Bombay. Gandhi's emissary was Mrs. Sarojini Naidu, the Indian poetess and politician.

Mrs. Naidu was greatly agitated, and made many statements to me that I feel she would now like to unsay. Her chief concern, however, was that the American public should never be allowed to hear of this outrage committed upon my husband; and she very frankly asked me my price for refraining from ever discussing or advertising the affair in America and from myself returning to America. Under no condition, said Mrs. Naidu, would they be willing that the American public

State of California)
County of Los Angeles)

ANNETTE H. DOHERTY, being first duly sworn on oath, deposes and says:

My deceased husband, William Francis Doherty, an American citizen, was a mechanical and electrical engineer and, at time of his death, was maneging engineer and business associate of Mr. Richard J. Brenchley, engaged in sand extraction at Mumbra, adjacent to Bombay, India.

On November 19, 1921, as he was quietly proceeding to the Bombay Improvement Trust workshops, he was set upon, his eyes were gouged out and eventually he was beaten to death by a group of rioters in a public street of Byculla, a suburb of Bombay.

This was during the visit of the Prince of Wales to

* * * * * * *

At that time he was going about so unclothed that Mrs. Naidu suggested I call upon him rather than that he come to the American home where I was stopping - inasmuch as this latter might prove embarassing. It was therefore determined

* * * * * * *

and prejudice our people against him.

Subscribed and sworn to before me this 4th day of January, 1929.

Notary Public in and for the County of Los Angeles, State of California.
My commission expires

PART OF MRS. DOHERTY'S SWORN STATEMENT

Concerning the murder of her husband and Mrs. Sarojini Naidu's attempt to buy her silence.

should learn that they were killing people so promiscuously that even a white face cost a man's life.

As to Gandhi's request for an interview with me:

At that time he was going about so unclothed that Mrs. Naidu suggested I call upon him rather than that he come to the American home where I was stopping—inasmuch as this latter might prove embarrassing. It was therefore determined that I should see him at his own headquarters in Bombay, which I did, a motor car having been sent by him to fetch me.

Upon this occasion of my visit with Gandhi he repeated to me in substance what Mrs. Naidu had said, but even more emphatically stressed the point that Americans, because they were so much in sympathy with him in his political views, must on no account learn the details of the murder of my husband lest it hurt the success of his movement in America and prejudice our people against him.

ANNETTE HELEN DOHERTY.

Subscribed and sworn to before me this 4th day of January, 1929.

W. J. SCHISEL
Notary Public in and for the County of Los Angeles, State of California. My commission expires Jan. 18, 1931.

America must be kept from learning the actual

effects, upon Indian mobs, of Gandhi's fiery tongue. The Mahatma, not realising, we must believe, the insult involved, sends his skilful diplomatist to the bereaved American girl, to bargain for silence, almost over the dead husband's bier.

Six years later, history repeats itself. Again, so Gandhi thinks, an American woman endangers his prestige in the West. Though this time too late to bargain for silence, it is, perhaps, not too late to discredit her report. Again he turns to his old emissary. Mrs. Sarojini Naidu shall go to America.

'Mahatma Gandhi has been asking to use her great gifts in the American Continent to dispel the miasma of misunderstanding created by Miss Mayo and her writings,' says the *Indian National Herald*, of Bombay, on August 24th, 1928, in an article whose headlines read: 'TO UNDO MAYO'S MISCHIEF—Mrs. Sarojini Naidu sails for America on September 12th—INDIA'S GREATEST ORATOR—Tumultuous Reception Awaits our Unofficial Ambassador in the Land of Dollars.'

Mrs. Naidu lands in New York.

Questioned as to the purpose of her visit, 'Mahatma Gandhi ordered me to come,' she tells the reporter of the New York *Sun*.

But not all of the little body of India's educated women who knew of this mission, clearly grasped its intent. Among the imperfectly informed was *Stri-Dharma*, the official organ of the Indian Women's Association, which said editorially in the October issue, 1928:

> I do not believe Mrs. Naidu is one of those patriotic souls who would lie for the sake of their

TO UNDO MAYO'S MISCHIEF

Mrs. Sarojini Naidu sails for America on September 12

INDIA'S GREATEST ORATOR

Tumultuous Reception Awaits our Unofficial Ambassador in the Land of Dollars

It is with great pleasure that we are able to announce to-day that after all it has been possible for India's golden-voiced orator to find time

have done incalculable harm to the cause of India all over the world and especially in America. It was for this reason that Mahatma Gandhi

AN INDIAN-OWNED NEWSPAPER'S ANNOUNCEMENT (*Indian National Herald*, AUGUST 24TH, 1928.)

country. Doubtless, she will deny the gross libels and misrepresentations in Miss Mayo's book. But she will not deny the existence of the hundred and one vultures of tradition and convention that are eating away the heart of Mother India as time flies over head and the wind wearies the palm trees by the shores. The plague of Purdah system, the curse of child marriage, the meaningless 'untouchability,' the widow non-remarriage—those who deny these may as well deny the spots on the moon.

But alas for the confidence of *Stri-Dharma*. Less than six months later, another Indian paper[1] reports Mrs. Naidu, already launched on her American tour, as telling her audiences : 'Child marriage to us is what a betrothal is here. . . . As to widows remarrying—well, no law can order them to remarry and many of them have remarried.' 'Referring to Purdah,' continues this report, she said that 'it is a protective measure and not necessarily bad in its effect.' And again her words : 'We have early betrothals in India but as to child marriage in its real sense I doubt if there is any more in India than elsewhere.'[2]

Thus, a second time, we see Mrs. Naidu fulfilling her mission. 'The Land of Dollars' must be kept from discovering the facts.

[1] *Behar Herald*, Patna, December 15th, 1928.
[2] *San Francisco Chronicle*, January 23rd, 1929.

CHAPTER IV

'IN COMMON PRACTICE'

The Indian (Hindu)[1] girl, in common practice, looks for motherhood nine months after reaching puberty – or anywhere between the ages of fourteen and eight. The latter age is extreme, although in some sections not exceptional; the former is well above the average. – *Mother India*, p. 29-30.

THIS is perhaps the most frequently quoted paragraph in the whole of *Mother India*. Reviewer after reviewer has picked it out to gasp at, to commend, or to expostulate against. Debaters, newspaper and magazine articles, and books written in 'reply' have singled out this quotation as a target for their heaviest artillery.

Practically every one of the attacking forces have quoted Dr. Margaret I. Balfour's hospital statistics, which state that of 304 recorded mothers delivered of their first babies in Bombay hospitals, the average age was 18.7 years. Only three of these were fourteen and these three were the youngest. Again, Dr. Balfour says that in the Madras Maternity Hospital, for the years 1922-24, of 2,312 mothers delivered of their first babies the average was 19.4. Of these mothers seven, the youngest, were thirteen years old and twenty-two were aged fourteen. Dr. Balfour also cites reports of 3,964

[1] 'Hindu' replaced the word 'Indian' in an early edition of *Mother India*. And it is clear that the author spoke exclusively of Hindus in the first eight chapters of the book. Chapter IX of *Mother India* begins: 'The chapters preceding have chiefly dealt with the Hindu, who forms, roughly, three-quarters of the population of India.'

cases in other parts of India, unnamed, but including the North, of which only ten cases were below fifteen years, and thirteen was the youngest.

On first sight this evidence alone, given by a British lady doctor resident in India, working there, and, as she herself says, investigating these conditions, seems conclusive—sufficient to throw grave doubt on *Mother India's* statement, if not to put it actually out of court.

Yet, examine it more closely. Everyone knows that Bombay, India's second city, is much affected by its constant contact with the Western world, and that it is the home of the great body of the Parsis, a people who are advanced both in education and in social customs and who greatly influence the life of that city. Parsis do not practise child marriage ; 73 per cent. of their women are literate, as compared with 2 per cent. literacy in the total female population of India. As to Madras, Dr. Balfour's second field of observation, it is the oldest British settlement in India ; Elihu Yale, the benefactor of the Connecticut university, was its Governor in 1687. Both Western secular culture and Western Christian missionary effort have been active in Madras longer than in any other part of India ; wherefore the influence of both should be more apparent there than in other regions.

Briefly, Madras and Bombay alike are cities thoroughly saturated with Western civilisation, from many and differing sources.

Less, however, than 3 per cent. of the population of India live in cities of over 100,000 population. This latter fact, significant as it is, cannot be related to

Dr. Balfour's last figures, since she does not tell us where she secured them, other than that some came from the North. If, however, by 'North' she indicates the Punjab and the North-West Frontier Province, then be it borne in mind that these parts of India are principally inhabited by Muhammadans, with whom *Mother India* was not concerned.

The whole of British India, with its total population of 247 million people, has only 5,581 institutions for medical relief, containing under 75,000 beds.[1] And remembering that only 2 per cent. of the female population is literate, in a country admittedly full of ancient superstition and prejudice, it may be asked what kind of Hindus go to these hospitals, when a Hindu as enlightened as is Mr. Gandhi can term them all 'institutions for the propagation of sin.'[2] Little doubt that those women, of the great Hindu majority, who dare to transgress the customs and practice of their religion are the most adventurous, the most advanced, the most exceptional of their race.

And, since *Mother India* speaks of Hindu women only, it is necessary to know, before we place too much value on Dr. Balfour's statistics, exactly what percentage of the maternity cases quoted were Hindu and what percentage Christian, Muhammadans, or Parsis.

[1] Public, Local Fund and Private-aided Civil Hospitals and Dispensaries, 3,956 ; beds 41,086. Special and Railway Dispensaries, 908 ; beds 7,675. Mental Institutions, 23 ; beds 9,608. Non-aided Civil Hospitals and Dispensaries 601 ; beds 5,053. Leper Asylums 75 ; beds 9,734. Tuberculosis Sanatoria, 18 ; beds 921. (*Health Organisation in British India*, League of Nations Publication, 1928, p. 9.)

[2] *Indian Home Rule*, M. K. Gandhi, Ganesh and Company, Madras, 1924, p. 61.

A Baptist missionary with many years of work in India to his credit writes of Dr. Balfour's statistics :

> Figures which have been gathered at various hospitals are given to show that the average age is over eighteen. Such statistical figures seem at first reading quite convincing, but there are several considerations which will show that they are not as reliable as they seem. In the first place these statistics do not touch those classes of people among whom early marriages and early motherhood takes place, for girls of such homes are not brought to the hospitals nor are doctors called in, but the services (?) of the orthodox village midwife are procured. Statistics of such cases and conditions are hard to obtain, but there are those who know what they are. Again when young girls are brought to the hospital their ages are falsified, the parents not wishing it to be known how young they are. The common custom of India of counting a child one year old up to its first birthday and then two years old would make at least one year's difference in most of the cases.[1]

Whenever Oriental and Occidental ages are under comparison the common practice in the East of calling any infant two years old when it reaches the first anniversary of its birthday, which additional year it retains through life, should always be borne in mind.

Following Dr. Margaret Balfour's further writings,

[1] *The Baptist Missionary Review*, editorial. May 1928, pp 213-14.

we find this statement appearing in the *Times of India* over her name :

> One of the great handicaps which India meets in her competition with other countries and one of the great obstacles to her internal development is the poor health and feeble physique of her population. This leads to frequent disablement through illness and to a shortened expectation of life, little more than half that of people in England.[1]

And although Dr. Balfour at no time goes all the way with *Mother India* as to when the Hindu girl looks for motherhood, other authorities, equally experienced, are otherwise minded.

Compare, for instance, Dr. Balfour's average age of 19.4 for first deliveries with the evidence, given before the Age of Consent Committee, of Dr. G. E. Campbell, principal of the Lady Hardinge Medical College, Delhi : 'Witness said she must have attended more than one thousand Hindu girls for child-birth at the ages of from 12¾ to 16½ years.'[2]

Or, compare an Indian's statement, that of Dr. (Mrs.) Muthulakshmi Reddi, well-known medical practitioner and widely respected social worker :

> During the sixteen years of medical practice among the higher class Hindus, I have attended on many a child mother ranging from 12 to 15 not

[1] From a reprint sent the author by Dr. Balfour, who was unable to give its exact date. The article appeared, however, either late 1927 or early 1928.

[2] *Bombay Daily Mail*, Bombay, October 11th, 1928. See also *The Pioneer*, Allahabad, October 12th, 1928, and *Indian Social Reformer*, November 10th, 1928.

without many fears and misgivings as to the ultimate results of those unnatural labours.[1]

This is from a speech delivered by Dr. Reddi before the Madras Legislative Council, of which she is a member. Dr. Reddi was the first Indian lady to sit in any legislature, and so highly have her colleagues appreciated her public services that they have elected her to the responsible post of Deputy-President of the Council. This particular speech elicited from her fellow legislators such comments as: 'I do not think any one could champion the cause of women in India so well as Dr. Muthulakshmi [Reddi]';[2] 'I have greatest admiration for the lady Deputy-President,'[3] and '[she] has spoken with knowledge and experience.'[4] Continuing, Dr. Reddi proceeded to quote other medical women substantiating her case.

> This is a letter from Dr. Kugler, a lady who has spent 45 years of her precious life on this subject. She writes: 'It was in 1883 that I first arrived in India and my work as a physician among the women and children has afforded me very many opportunities of seeing the evils resulting from child marriage. I have often operated upon child mothers . . . so injured that they could not again function as wives. . . .'
>
> There is another lady doctor of Vellore, Dr. Ida Scudder who writes to me as follows: '. . . . I

[1] *Proceedings of the Legislative Council of Madras*, Official Report, March 27th, 1928, p. 32.

[2] *Proceedings of the Legislative Council of Madras*, March 27th, 1928, p. 40. [3] *Ibid.*, p. 37. [4] *Ibid.*

would probably have never studied medicine and would not have come back to India had it not been for three child wives ; none of them over 14 who died during one night in the station I was at the time. I was powerless to help. That was 30 years ago, but only a few months ago a girl of 13 or 14 came to me to be repaired for vesico vaginal fistula (a laceration of the private parts). She was like an innocent child and found it hard to understand what had happened to her.'

Dr. Macphail, for whom we all entertain a high regard, a lady who has spent 50 years in the service of Indian womanhood, tells the same tale. She writes : '. . . I have attended six young girls who were about twelve years old, certainly not yet thirteen and have attended many who were in their fourteenth or fifteenth year. Almost invariably these labours were abnormally long and difficult and the inevitable suffering was greatly increased by terror. In one case the young mother went insane during labour from terror and pain, and it was many months before she recovered from the nervous shock and strain and was able to take her place in the family. When they do survive this ordeal, the salvation of these young mothers lies in the fact that the babies are usually very small. . . .'

'It is cruelty to young girls from every point of view to have even the betrothal marriage at so early an age, but it is infinitely worse to allow the consummation to take place while she is still a child, especially if the husband is not a boy a few years older than his bride, but an elderly man who possibly has grandchildren older than his wife. Things are bad enough in Madras [city] but we all know that they are infinitely worse in the mufussal [country districts], where when a suitable bridegroom cannot be found for a young girl, her parents give her to any elderly man who is willing to take her, since religion demands that she must be married before attaining puberty.'[1]

Dr. Muthulakshmi Reddi, the Indian lady doctor, social reformer and legislator, then herself pleads for the child-mothers :

> How could you expect a girl child of 10 or 12 or even 13 to know the full significance of a married life, to understand its responsibilities and to perform the sacred function of a mother—the function of training her children to become patriotic, good and useful citizens ? How could you expect a girl of 12 or 13 or even 14 to maintain order and discipline in the home. . . .[2]

Finally she concludes with the words :

> Sir, on behalf of the innocent, helpless, suffering girl children of this land, on behalf of millions of child wives, child mothers and child widows, I appeal to all sections of the House. . . .[3]

This sounds very much like *Mother India*; many of its witnesses use the same kind of language. But the

[1] *Proceedings of the Legislative Council of Madras*, March 27th, 1928, pp. 32-33. [2] *Ibid.*, p. 35. [3] *Ibid.*, p. 37.

statements just quoted are of date more recent than the book.

Mr. Dhan Gopal Mukerji, who left India at the age of eighteen, offers us the information that these conditions were then unknown to him ; therefore, they do not exist. It might be questioned : What should a lad not out of his teens and not especially addressed to such a study, know of social conditions of this sort ?

Undaunted by this handicap, Mr. Mukerji, attacking the subject, quotes the passage from *Mother India* which heads this chapter and follows it with this statement :

> In defence of her allegations that a Hindu girl attains motherhood at an age much nearer eight than fourteen Miss Mayo refers us to the Indian census report of 1921, which I have looked up.[1]

By comparing Mr. Mukerji's statement with the original[2] the reader will discover that *Mother India* says nothing about the age at which the Hindu girl 'attains' motherhood ; it says that 'in common practice' the Hindu girl looks for motherhood anywhere between fourteen and eight.

Furthermore, Mr. Mukerji then proceeds to state that the Census of India for 1921 shows 601 girls out of every 1,000 as still unmarried between the ages of ten and fifteen years. Yet the Census, in fact, shows only 543 Hindu girls per mille as unmarried between these ages.[3] Mr. Mukerji used the figure inclusive

[1] *A Son of Mother India Answers*, p. 19.

[2] See *ante*, p. 49.

[3] *Census of India*, 1921, Vol. I, Part I, p. 164.

of all religions in India, while *Mother India* was speaking only of the great majority of girls, *i.e.*, of Hindu girls ; and Mr. Mukerji knew this, or he would not have specified 'Hindu girl' in the paragraph above quoted. On this showing, therefore, it would seem that over 45 per cent. of the Hindu girls between ten and fifteen were married, or were already widows, in 1921.

But the Census has something still further to say on this subject :

> Owing to the obloquy incurred by Hindu parents who have failed to marry their girls before puberty there is a strong inclination to understate the age of unmarried girls who have reached this age, which affects the age period of 10 to 15. On the other hand marriage and motherhood appear to convey an impression of age, and the age of young married women is more usually overstated than understated.[1]

Therefore, if a Hindu girl of fifteen is yet unmarried, her age is probably returned at a figure lower than it really is, thereby swelling the unmarried total. But, on the other hand, if she is married before she is fifteen years old, her age is probably returned, for census purposes, as greater than it really is, thereby lowering the married totals under fifteen. Seemingly—and by its own admission—it is impossible to get from the Census report any really accurate percentage of married girls.

But other statements in the Census point to the fact

[1] *Census of India*, 1921, Vol. I, Part I, p. 127.

that the number of Hindu girls married at fifteen or under is really greater than the figures recorded. For example, Mr. W. H. Thompson, the Census superintendent for Bengal, a man who has spent years working on the actual figures in Mr. Mukerji's own province, 'calculates on the basis of the age tables that the average age of marriage in Bengal is about twelve and a half for girls and rather under twenty for men.'[1] And again, the statement for the whole of India, given in Appendix VII of the Census, reads[2] : 'It can be assumed for all practical purposes that every woman is in the married state at or immediately after puberty and that cohabitation, therefore, begins in every case with puberty.'[3]

The actual Census figures for Hindu girls, however, read as follows :

Of 1,000 Hindu females in India[4]

Age	0-5	Unmarried	985,	Married	14,	Widowed	1
,,	5-10	,,	883,	,,	111,	,,	6
,,	10-15	,,	543,	,,	437,	,,	20
,,	15-20	,,	138,	,,	814,	,,	48

'The explanation of the discrepancy,' writes Miss Eleanor F. Rathbone, 'given to me by a leading statistical authority on India is that the generalisation in the Appendix, being based on common knowledge as to Indian customs, is probably nearer the truth than the figures.'[5]

[1] *Census of India*, 1921, Vol. I, Part I, p. 154.

[2] *Ibid.*, p. xix.

[3] See *post*, pp. 131-2.

[4] *Census of India*, 1921, Vol. I, Part I, p. 164.

[5] 'Has Katherine Mayo Slandered *Mother India*,' *Hibbert Journal*, London, January, 1929, p. 201.

Miss Rathbone, M.A., M.P., educated at Somerville College, Oxford J. P. President National Union of Societies for Equal

The 1921 Census shows 11,327,411 Hindu girls between the ages of ten and fifteen, of whom 4,947,266 were married and 232,147 were already widows, making a total of married and widowed of over 45 per cent.[1] Add to these admittedly inaccurate totals the general Census statements which increase them, and it appears difficult to quarrel with *Mother India* in regard to when the Hindu girl, ***in common practice***, looks for motherhood.[2]

Living India[3] and *A Son of Mother India Answers*[4] both quote the Census to prove that *Mother India* mixed betrothal and marriage; the passage quoted reads:

> It must be borne in mind, however, that the statistics of the married in India cannot be used without

Citizenship. Member of Parliament for the combined English Universities. Member, Liverpool City Council. Published various reports on women's work and on industrial problems. Author, *The Disinherited Family, a Plea for Family Endowment*, 1924. See *Who's Who*, London, 1928.

[1] *Census of India*, 1921, Vol. I, Part II, p. 46.

[2] Savel Zimand, in his *Living India* (Longmans, Green and Company, New York, 1928, p. 118), says: 'By comparing this situation with that of thirty years ago, we can gauge the progress that has been made. According to the Census, in 1891 the number of married girls per thousand in the age category of five to ten years was 126, and in 1921 it had dropped to 3 . . .' I refer my readers to Mr. Zimand's source. Here, in the Census for 1921, Vol. I, Part I, p. 164, they will find that the figure above cited by Mr. Zimand for 1891 as 126 is, in fact, 123, while his 3 for 1921 actually reads 88. These figures include all religions, but *Mother India* was concerned only with the Hindu figures, which, in Mr. Zimand's construction, would read from 146 to 111. Not all of Mr. Zimand's statistics are so easily checked, as for many of them he omits definite source references.

[3] Page 111.

[4] Pages 19, 20.

> close analysis. Owing to the custom of infant and child marriage among Hindus and Jains, the figures contain a large number of unions which are little more than irrevocable betrothals. A Hindu girl-wife, as a rule, returns after the wedding ceremony to her parents' house and lives there until she reaches puberty, when another ceremony is performed and she goes to her husband and enters upon the real duties of wifehood. At the younger ages, therefore, the wives are not wives at all for practical purposes, though their future lives are committed ;

At this point both end their Census quotation, substituting a period for the original's semicolon. The remainder of the sentence, which they omitted, reads :

> and from the eugenic point of view what is objectionable is not infant marriage itself but the extremely early age at which effective union takes place, girls becoming mothers before they are fit for the condition of motherhood, with serious consequences both to themselves and to the children whom they produce.[1]

Thus if Mr. Savel Zimand and Mr. Dhan Gopal Mukerji instead of printing only a part of the sentence had printed the whole of it, they would have left upon their reader's mind an impression entirely different from the one they actually effected.

Few Indians admit grounds for objection to child marriage, if it can be contended that the 'marriage' implies only betrothal, the practice being both con-

[1] *Census of India*, 1921, Vol. I, p. 152.

ceded and defended by most of those who have written to confound *Mother India*. *Unhappy India*, one of the seven volumes so written, in dealing with this subject says:

> Child marriage is beyond doubt having pernicious effects on the physique of Indians. . . . The fact is that a devastating factor like child marriage is seldom allowed by Society to go altogether without counterbalancing safeguards. In India this safeguard is provided in many of the child-marrying castes by postponing the *consummation* of marriage till a considerable period after the marriage ceremony. Marriage thus becomes a sort of betrothal and child marriage means only child betrothal.[1]

But apart from the question as to whether or not it is cruel to marry a girl before she has any idea what the ceremony entails, a real difficulty, according to some authorities, lies in keeping a man away from the girl he has married, whatever her youth and unreadiness, until she has reached puberty.

Dr. N. S. Phadke, an Indian who has studied eugenics in his own country, and who is now Professor of Mental and Moral Philosophy at Rajaram College, Kolhapur, presents this difficulty in his book, published in 1927: 'It is well-nigh impossible to marry a girl and then to keep her severely out of touch with her husband.'[2] Again, he says:

[1] *Unhappy India*, Lajpat Rai, pp. 188-189.

[2] *Sex Problem in India*, N. S. Phadke, M.A., with a foreword by Margaret Sanger; Taraporevala, Sons and Company, Bombay, 1927, p. 110.

> There is hardly any need to prove anew that early marriage leads to early cohabitation. It is mere idiocy to argue that when boys and girls are married at an early age a kind of steady love for each other arises in their hearts. If at all there are any inevitable consequences of early marriage they are that a depraved premature passion pollutes the hearts of the young couple. . . . the passion is encouraged and the girl experiences sexual relations with the husband long before attaining puberty, and that all chances are wiped away of the husband and the wife remaining aloof from each other for a certain period after the wife's maturity. In short premature cohabitation follows early marriage with an inevitable sequence. And with equally inevitable and cruel sequence cohabitation is followed by conception. It is no wonder if the fruits of such conceptions are putrid and short lived.[1]

Professor Phadke also expresses an opinion upon the age at which Hindu girls marry, in his chapter 'The Mother of the Race': 'Barring a few exceptional communities and speaking generally of the majority, girls in India are married at 14 at the latest,'[2] adding, two pages further on:

> It is a vain hope to look forward to a strong and fit race when those to whom the function of procreation is assigned by nature are hopeless and helpless going through life as through a mill that grinds young people old. . . .

[1] *Sex Problem in India*, pp. 100-101.
[2] *Ibid.*, p. 52.

Mrs. Brijlal Nehru, one of the two women members of the Age of Consent Committee, which toured India during 1928, was thus quoted, when addressing the All-India National Social Conference in December 1928:

> In India more than 80 per cent. of the people practised child marriage, and in some places the babies in arms were married. She based her experience as a member of the Age of Consent Committee and on the result of her tour in various parts of the country. The figures of child mortality in India were higher than any other country of the world. This was due principally to the early marriage.[1]

Another witness worthy of quoting on this subject is Surenda Nath Mallik, one of the Indian members of the Council of India—that august body which advises the Secretary of State for India in London—and, incidentally, one of those Indians who signed the *Mother India* protest letter to the London *Times*.[2] The official organ of the Royal Institute of Public Health, *The Journal of State Medicine*, carried in its May, 1928, number an article by Mr. Mallik, which reads in part:

> Amongst Hindus as a whole, child marriage is still prevalent though the influence of western education and ideas, as also for economic reasons, the marriageable age of girls is going up a bit. Amongst the agricultural classes, girls are married while they are only about eight years old or even

[1] *Indian Social Reformer*, January 5th, 1929, p. 296. See also *Times of India*, December 27th, 1928.

[2] See *ante*, pp. 19-20.

less, while in the higher castes in the rural areas the age for marriage of girls is slightly higher. In the town areas the age has gone up a little higher, and 12 may be taken as the general age. It is usual for these girls to be married to husbands who are mostly yet within their 'teens,' and as a general rule, they become mothers ordinarily at 14 or 15 years of age.[1]

In conclusion, it is obviously impossible to arrive at absolute figures of the age at which Hindu girls are married. The Census figures indicate that over 45 per cent. of them enter the married state by their fifteenth year. Other authorities would indicate that a much higher percentage of the Hindu girls are given in early marriage. The text of the Census, again, declares that among the great majority of the Hindu peoples, marriage is consummated at or immediately after puberty, and other authorities offer additional substantiating testimony. Finally, the laws of human nature, together with the absolute property right given by the Hindu code to a husband over his wife, point to consummation and therefore to a wife's looking for motherhood at the earliest possible moment.

But, because a girl cannot even look for motherhood until she reaches maturity, it is important to discover at what age the average Hindu girl attains that period.

[1] London, p. 285.

CHAPTER V

WHEN DO THEY MATURE?

Once the girl attains puberty the husband is made to know that she is at his service. . . . To serve the husband is the girl's *Dharma*[1] and the sooner she joins his service the better for her soul! In many parts [of India] for a girl to have her nuptials consummated within 16 days of puberty is again an unyielding mandate of the *Sastra!* – *Woman Awakened*, G. SUMATI BAI, B.A., L.T.; school teacher and medical practitioner; foreword by DR. ANNIE BESANT, Tagore and Company, Madras, 1928, p. 70.

Hindu religion lays down with sufficient definiteness the law of pre-puberty marriages and early post-puberty consummation. – D. P. KRISHNAMACHARYA, of the Vedantic school, *Madras Mail*, November 23rd, 1928.

THE main difficulties facing any attempt to decide the age at which the average Hindu girl matures are: first, the traditional reticence observed by Indians as to the subject of age; second, the lack of any effective official registration of births; and third, the fact that Hindus do not celebrate birthday anniversaries, and that although it is traditional for them to have a horoscope cast at the birth of a child, the practice is not all-inclusive, while in any case the document is seldom consulted in after years.[2]

'The ordinary educated Indian has very vague ideas about his own age. The uneducated Indian has practically no ideas at all,'[3] says Mr. Edye, the Census Com-

[1] *Dharma* means custom or duty.

[2] See *Census of India*, 1921, Vol. I, Part I, p. 26. [3] *Ibid.*

missioner for the United Provinces; and, when speaking of the guessing abilities of the Indian Census officials, this same authority remarks: 'During the period when the staff was being trained, I had my own age guessed by hundreds of supervisors and enumerators, and the estimates were seldom within five years of the truth, and varied between 16 and 60.'[1] With so large a range of error amongst supposed experts what would be the accuracy of the average Hindu's guess? Mr. Edye replies:

> The head of the house who answered the enumerator's questions not only for himself but also for his family, might have some idea of the age of his sons, especially if these attended school or had entered or hoped to enter Government service. He would have less idea of the age of his daughters; very little of that of his wife, which he had never accurately known; and practically none of that of the mothers-in-law and paternal aunts who happened to be quartered upon him.[2]

This being the case, what happens when it is important that a girl's age should be known—as court evidence, for instance, in case of rape? The answer is more simple than might be supposed; the parents either guess it, or employ the services of an astrologer, who decides the matter for them.

Some authorities, however, have made definite statements regarding the age at which the average Indian girl attains maturity. The most worth-while of these, although they vary rather violently, are presented.

[1] *Census of India*, 1921, Vol. I, Part I, p. 126. [2] *Ibid.*

Yet, before examining them, it is advisable, so that the reader may have a background on which to base his own judgment, to recall the age of a girl's pubescence in our own Occident, always remembering the widely accepted theory that both male and female mature much sooner in tropical countries than in our more temperate climes.

Every reader will recall, more or less, when he or she entered the adolescent period. Many will have children of their own on whom to base an inference. Turning from our own experiences to common authorities, we find the *Encyclopædia Britannica* stating: 'In northern countries males enter upon sexual maturity between fourteen and sixteen . . . females between twelve and fourteen. In tropical countries puberty is much earlier.'[1]

By Roman civil law and common law, and in England to-day, the legal age for puberty is twelve in the case of girls.[2] And *Webster's Dictionary* gives this same age as being generally accepted in the West.

Girls, then, in the tropics, Hindu girls, should be pubescent before they reach their twelfth year. But what do Indian opinions say on this subject?

The Bombay Presidency Social Reform Association in August 1928, made the following statement:

> Fourteen is perhaps the usual age at which girls attain puberty in most parts of India. It is probably not a question of castes and communities. The most recent opinion as regards age and sex

[1] *Encyclopædia Britannica*, eleventh edition, Vol. XXII, p. 626.

[2] *New Oxford Dictionary*. *Standard Dictionary*, Funk and Wagnalls.

distribution inclines to assign them to territorial rather than caste and communal peculiarities. Our Council, however, are of opinion that puberty is perhaps as much a psychological as a physiological incident. Puberty is earlier in girls brought up the old way, namely, without education and with constant thought of marriage as their sole purpose in life than in educated surroundings and with intellectual and social interests and with a broader outlook on life.[1]

Another authority from Bombay, the Mitra Mandal, whose president is a medical man, says in the course of its report to the Age of Consent Committee :

> In our part of the country the girls attain puberty between the ages of 13 and 15, it differs according to the position in society, environments and habits ; community makes no difference but we believe food does ; vegetarians attain puberty little later than non-vegetarians.[2]

From the Malabar coast, even further south, Khan Sahib T. M. Moidoo Sahib, member of the Legislative Council and president of the District Board, is reported as stating before the same Committee : 'Girls in Malabar generally attained puberty between 13 and 14. . . .'[3]

In the North we find Mr. Moti Lal Kaestha, Vice-Chairman of the District Board of Kangra (Punjab), affirming in September 1928 : 'The age of puberty in

[1] *Indian Social Reformer*, August 25th, 1928, p. 828.
[2] *Bombay Daily Mail*, October 17th, 1928.
[3] *The Hindu*, Madras, November 17th, 1928.

Kangra was between 14 and 16 in all classes.'[1] And Dr. Tarabai, L.C.P.S., L.M., recently in charge of a maternity home in Karachi, in reply to a direct question from a member of the Age of Consent Committee, said: 'Local girls generally attain their age at 13 and some of the Punjabi girls attain their age at 15.'[2] A lady doctor of standing gave evidence in Lahore. 'In the Punjab,' she said, 'girls attained puberty between the ages of 13 and 14 generally and in a few cases between 12 and 13.'[3] Again, at Lahore, Sardar Mangal Singh, an Akali-Sikh leader, is thus reported: 'The age of puberty among Sikh Jats was about 15, it was lower in the case of city girls.'[4]

These opinions are difficult to reconcile with, for instance, that of the one-time Christian missionary, Mr. C. F. Andrews, who affirms in his reply to *Mother India*: 'Womanhood, in a tropical climate like India, begins at least three years earlier than in a cold climate such as England.'[5] Or even that of *A Son of Mother India Answers*: '. . . . fourteen in the tropics would make a person as mature as seventeen in New York.'[6]

Other Indians, both by organisations and as individuals, believe a lower age prevails. The Marwari Association in Calcutta, for example, claims: 'Indian girls generally attain puberty between 11 and 12

[1] *Indian Social Reformer*, October 13th, 1928, p. 102.
[2] *Ibid.*, November 3rd, 1928, p. 154.
[3] *Ibid.*, October 6th, 1928, p. 86, Mrs. M. C. Shave, L.M. and S.
[4] *Indian Social Reformer*, October 6th, 1928, p. 88.
[5] 'The Facts About India, A Reply to Miss Mayo,' C. F. Andrews, *Young India*, Ahmedabad, June 21st, 1928, p. 209.
[6] Page 27.

years.'[1] Mrs. Bhat, lady Superintendent of the Seva Sedan at Poona, is said to have stated that 'consummation of marriage did not usually take place before puberty, but soon after puberty, and a little before the age of 13.'[2] And the Honourable Justice Ramesam of Madras in an opinion given in 1927 writes :

> I know cases of puberty (followed by monthly periods) at 9½, at 10 *y.* 2 *m.* Cases of attaining puberty at 11 are very common in South India. Cases below 9 may be regarded as pathological and may be ignored but the other instances cannot be ignored.[3]

Another intelligent witness, speaking of the Hindu girl, says : 'According to medical evidence, she attains puberty in her twelfth year.'[4]

And lastly, Dr. (Mrs.) Muthulakshmi Reddi, the Deputy-President of the Madras Council, testifies from her own personal experience in the South :

> If puberty is delayed beyond 14, the husband's people get ever-anxious and begin to consult the doctors. Many such cases have been brought to me for consultation. Sometimes the girl is made to live with her husband before even the first menses appears. I can bring to memory many such cases.[5]

[1] *Opinions on the Hindu Child Marriage Bill*, Government of India, Paper No. 1, p. 12, February, 1928.

[2] *Times of India*, Bombay, November 5th, 1928.

[3] *Opinions on the Hindu Child Marriage Bill*, Paper No. 1, p. 9, February 1928.

[4] *Ibid.*, Taw Sein Ko, C.I.E., I.S.O., p. 41.

[5] *Proceedings of the Madras Legislative Council*, March 27th, 1928, p. 31

One point completely broken down by this controversy concerns *Mother India*. For, while on the one hand many critics have charged that the book entirely disregards the fact of the Hindu girl's early development, on the other hand they have as repeatedly urged that it errs beyond reason in the age it assigns to the earliest chance of conception, since, they affirm, the Hindu girl is not pubescent until her fourteenth year.

As for the ancient Hindu scriptures, these, according to some authorities, concur in the theory of early maturity, since their text mentions ten as the possible age of a girl's pubescence. Here is Professor Phadke's citation of Marichi :

> He who offers a Gouri [a girl of eight] in marriage attains heaven, the giver of a Rohini [a girl of nine] Vaikunttha [a higher heaven], the giver of a Kanyā [a girl who has reached the 10th year but not puberty] is given a place in Brahma Loka [the highest heaven], and the giver of a mature woman is condemned to hell.[1]

From the evidence presented no exact conclusion can be reached. If a mean age were to be struck it would be somewhere between twelve and thirteen.[2] Yet twelve is the acknowledged age for our Western girls to mature, and, just as we have accepted this as

[1] *Sex Problem in India*, p. 81.

[2] An Indian woman medical practitioner writes : 'It is but a common practice besides with some to give a girl medicine to hasten puberty. This is especially so in joint families where a younger brother's wife happens to attain puberty before the elder brother's wife. The latter then is oft drugged to menstruate soon.' – *Woman Awakened*, G. Sumati Bai, B.A., L.T., foreword by Dr. Annie Besant, Tagore and Company, Madras, 1928, p. 100.

an average, we have also accepted the belief that females in tropical countries develop much earlier than those in colder climates.

The Age of Consent Committee—whose appointment was reported in a despatch of the *New York Times*[1] as being due to the publication of *Mother India*—is attempting to ascertain Indian opinion on this point, but of the witnesses[2] it has called, a sufficient number have been quoted in this chapter to show that the Committee's report must lack finality. And the only conclusion that we can reach, besides that of the need for further scientific research, is that the average Hindu girl matures before her thirteenth year.

[1] News item headed 'Miss Mayo's Book on India Gets Action on Child Marriage,' February 10th, 1928.

[2] Nine of the fifteen opinions above quoted were given before or sent to the Age of Consent Committee.

CHAPTER VI

IS IT A CURSE?

The whole pyramid of India's [the Hindu's][1] woes, material and spiritual – poverty, sickness, ignorance, political minority, melancholy, ineffectiveness, not forgetting that subconscious conviction of inferiority which he forever bares and advertises by his gnawing and imaginative alertness for social affronts – rests upon a rock-bottom physical base. This base is, simply, his manner of getting into the world and his sex-life thenceforward. – *Mother India*, p. 29.

The critics have invariably assailed this statement by endeavouring to show that consummated child marriages are non-existent; are practised only by some one particular Hindu community or are an exceptional practice, now quickly approaching the vanishing-point. These opinions are the natural reflex of *Mother India's* exposures. None of us likes to have his own faults pointed out before the world, and we are all apt to explode not only with resentment, but with argument to confound the exposer. The Indian, and especially the Hindu, has, however, shown himself so sensitive to world-opinion that his efforts have often resulted in his destroying his own arguments. For instance, *A Son of Mother India Answers* quotes the above paragraph twice; first, on page 19, to demolish it with the weapon of Dr. Margaret Balfour's hospital figures; and the second time, on page 50, to add:

[1] 'The Hindu's' replaced the word 'India's' after the first several editions of *Mother India*.

But to my mind the untenable thesis of *Mother India* is hard to maintain with accurate scientific data, from the psychopathic wards of different hospitals, for the reason that India has not an adequate number of hospitals, nor more than a dozen psychopathic wards to supply sufficient evidence.[1]

Exactly what psychopathic wards have to do with a man's being born into the world the text fails to make clear. But, if the author was trying to say that India has insufficient hospitals to afford generally representative scientific data upon maternity cases—a fact *Mother India* makes no attempt to override—he must have forgotten that only thirty pages previous, he himself produced these very same hospital statistics to establish what he now states cannot be so proven in India for lack of sufficient evidence.

A careful reading of *Mother India* discloses that its general thesis is based not upon statistics but, rather, upon the written evidence of Indians themselves. This fact has often been brought forward, but it remained for the editor of the *Baptist Missionary Review* actually to analyse the quotations :

> Wishing to know something of the sources from which Miss Mayo drew her information, we kept a careful record of all quotations of more than one line, both from written and spoken sources. We have noted a total of 269 quotations, 197 of these are from written records and 72 were spoken. Of the quotations from written records, 141 were with the name of the writer or speaker and only 16

[1] *A Son of Mother India Answers*, Dhan Gopal Mukerji, p. 50.

> without. Forty were from reports of commissions, census reports, etc. Of the spoken quotations the names of 18 of the speakers were given while 54 were not given. That is 199 of her quotations named the sources while 70 did not, though in the latter case the title or position of the speaker were given, in almost every case showing his or her right to be heard on the subject. Again we find that 102 of the quotations from written sources were Indian and 56 otherwise. As to the 40 references to reports, etc., the nationality of the writer of the report or the body making the report, could not be determined in every case. Of the spoken quotations 52 were from Indians and 20 otherwise. A total of 154 Indian and 76 foreign. More than two to one. . . . The author lets India speak for herself. . . . .[1]

Miss Mayo has been accused by Indian critics of misquoting at least five of her witnesses, a charge which arouses our interest when levelled against an author whose preceding works have been recognised for their accuracy.[2] The five[3] cases are dealt with elsewhere in these pages ; but, as may be noted here, these five have been re-paraded so many times, Chinese army fashion, that nobody could be blamed for believing a large majority of *Mother India's* quotations to have been challenged.

[1] *Baptist Missionary Review*, January, 1928, Kurnool, India.

[2] See Appendix III.

[3] Gandhi, Tagore, Lord Sinha, Miss Mona Bose, and the group at Mr. K. C. Roy's luncheon.

Meantime, since the book's publication, so much additional corroborative evidence of its thesis has appeared in Indian sources and in Indian print that it is difficult to choose where to begin its presentation.

For example, on February 9th, 1928, when introducing 'The Children's Protection Bill' in the Legislative Assembly at Delhi, Sir Hari Singh Gour[1] said :

> We have been reading in the newspapers, accounts given of speeches made in the House of Commons, of Indian babies weighing 1½ lbs. and 2 lbs. Sir, whether they weigh 1½ lbs. or 2 lbs., one fact remains and he who runs may see that the debility, the weakness of the Indian people, is due to these early marriages and early motherhood. The life of the people, according to the insurance statistics,[2] is not even half of what it is in England and other European countries. The reasons cannot be all climatic. One reason is the pernicious habit of early marriages and early cohabitation which is sapping the manhood and the womanhood of this

[1] Sir Hari Singh Gour, M.A., LL.D., Hindu ; barrister-at-law. Educated at Downing College, Cambridge ; Inner Temple, London : also LL.D. Trinity College, Dublin ; Vice-Chancellor Delhi University. Elected member Indian Legislative Assembly. Author of various books on law.

[2] The Phœnix Assurance Company Ltd. of Calcutta rules out Indian female policies as being too great a risk to underwrite, in these words : 'A small Extra Annual Charge, not exceeding ½ per cent. on the sum Assured, is made for European Female Lives. This extra will be removed on attainment of age 50. Proposals on Parsee Female Lives will also be considered on special terms. With this exception the Company grants Assurances on Female Lives in the case of Europeans only.' *Life Prospectus for India*, 1927, p. 16, Dalhousie Square, Calcutta.

country. It is an evil from which not only the persons directly concerned suffer, but it is an evil which cannot be described as anything but a national calamity. What is the result ? You have a child aged 11 or 12, wedded to a man or a boy who is at school. Early cohabitation prevents him from prosecuting his studies in the schools or colleges. She herself becomes a mother when she is about 13 or 14.[1]

Or again, at that earlier period when the Hindu protest meetings against *Mother India* were at their height—September 1927—a debate was held in the Central Legislative Assembly on a bill 'to regulate marriages of children amongst the Hindus.' Rai Sahib Harbilas Sarda,[2] the assemblyman who sponsored the bill, referred to the author of *Mother India* in his original motion :

> Just as there are slimy creatures who burrow in dirt, eat dirt and throw out dirt, so are there persons like that notorious writer of *Mother India*, whose attempt to revile the 'mother' has earned for her the contempt of all sensible people.[3]

Yet this in no way deterred him from giving, in the self-same speech, much information supporting the book's general thesis :

[1] *Legislative Assembly Debates*, February 9th, 1928, p. 255.

[2] Rai Sahib Harbilas Sarda, Hindu ; educated at Ajmer Government College and Agra College. Has occupied several posts in judiciary. Elected member, from Ajmer-Merwara, of Legislative Assembly. Author of several historical and descriptive works on Indian subjects.

[3] *Legislative Assembly Debates*, September 15th, 1927, p. 4,410.

> The gravity of the question will, however, be realised when we remember that out of every 1,000 Hindu married women 14 are under 5 years of age, 111 below 10, and 437 under 15 years of age. This means that a little over 11 per cent. of the Hindu women are supposed to lead a married life when they are below 10 years of age, *i.e.*, they are mere children, and that nearly 44 per cent. of them lead married lives when they are less than fifteen years of age, *i.e.*, when they are not yet out of their teens and before they have attained true and full puberty and are physically utterly unfit to bear the strain of marital relations.[1]

It must be admitted Rai Sahib Harbilas Sarda, like Sir Hari Singh Gour, does not leave much room for his fellow countrymen in America to argue that he has mixed marriage and betrothal—to declare, as they so often declare, that the Hindu marriage is merely a ceremony unattended by any physical act.

He continues, and, like others, quotes a doctor to substantiate the case:

> Sir, the secondary aim of the Bill is to remove the principal impediment to the physical and mental growth of the youth of both sexes and the chief cause of their premature decay and death. The measure I propose will help to remove the causes which lead to heavy mortality amongst Hindu married girls. The very high percentage of deaths among them is due to the fact that they are quite immature and are utterly unfit to begin married

[1] *Legislative Assembly Debates*, September 15th, 1927, p. 4,406.

life when they actually do so. Speaking of the strain imposed on girls by married relations, Dr. Lancaster in his book *Tuberculosis in India*, page 47, says:

'People forget the fearful strain upon the constitution of a delicate girl of 14 years or even less, which results from the thoughtless incontinence of the newly married boy, or still more, the pitiless incontinence of the re-married man. Serious as these causes of strain are upon the health of the young married girl, they sink into significance in comparison with the stress of maternity which follows.'[1]

And later, as if to justify *Mother India's* excursions into politics, he adds:

For we must remember, Sir, that even political emancipation, freedom or Swaraj, by whatever name you call that one fact, droppeth not like sweet manna from heavens. It has to be won. It has to be wrested from unwilling hands, and so long as these evils exist in this country, we will neither have the strength of arm nor the strength of character to win freedom.[2]

The next speaker, Mr. Kumar Ganganand Sinha,[3] begins by congratulating his colleague on bringing

[1] *Legislative Assembly Debates*, September 15th, 1927, p. 4,406.

[2] *Ibid.*, p. 4,407.

[3] Kumar Ganganand Sinha, M.A., Hindu; honorary research scholar, Calcutta University. Educated at Government Sanskrit College, Calcutta, and Calcutta University. Elected member, from Bhagalpur, of Legislative Assembly; founder of National Party therein. President, Purnea Hindu Sabha. Author of several works on Indian philosophical subjects.

forward 'this Bill to eradicate a deep-rooted evil from the Hindu society, namely, early marriage,' and continues in this vein :

> It is sapping the vitals of our race, and to let this continue is to commit racial suicide. . . The practical effects of child marriage, as I have stated before, are twofold. First, it implies cohabitation at an immature age, sometimes even before puberty, and practically always on the first signs of puberty. . . .[1]

But why follow further into horrors when enough has already been quoted to indicate the convictions of that leading Hindu assemblyman, Mr. Sinha?

This particular debate lasted over four hours ; by far the majority of the speakers supported the idea of reform, and others besides those already quoted found strong words to express their sense of impending doom for their race. Thus Munshi Iswar Saran, member for the Lucknow Division, declared :

> Sir, I submit that the Hindu race is dying and one of the causes responsible for our slow decay is early marriage. . . . What are we to-day ? We are feeble and weak, not morally but certainly physically, because of this early marriage.[2]

Opinion differed, however, as to which parts of the Hindu community are the worst offenders in the in-

[1] *Legislative Assembly Debates*, September 15th, 1927, pp. 4,412-13. [2] *Ibid.*, pp. 4,446-47.

human practice. The late Lala Lajpat Rai,[1] ardent Hindu politician and social reformer, stated:

> . . . in India the early marriages are confined mostly to what are known in the Hindu community as the 'higher castes.'[2]

But Pandit Madan Mohan Malaviya,[3] a Hindu of great influence, was otherwise minded:

> I wish to inform the House that our humblest fellow-subjects or the so-called depressed classes [untouchables] are the largest victims to this evil of early marriages.[4]

And a third, Sir Purshotamdas Thakurdas,[5] presented a third view:

> . . . it does not go by caste but it goes by the extent to which education may have reached that section or not—a certain section of the Hindu

[1] Lala Lajpat Rai, Hindu lawyer and journalist; proprietor, *Bande Mataram* and *The People*. Elected member, from Jullundur, of Legislative Assembly; author, *The Political Future of India*; *The Problem of National Education in India*, *Unhappy India*. Died November 1928.

[2] *Legislative Assembly Debates*, September 15th, 1927, p. 4,419.

[3] Pandit Madan Mohan Malaviya, Hindu. Educated in India; teacher, editor, jurist; President Indian National Congress, 1909 and 1918; member Imperial Legislative Council, 1910-19; Vice-Chancellor, Benares Hindu University; President, Hindu Mahasabha, 1923-24; elected member, from Allahabad, of Legislative Assembly.

[4] *Legislative Assembly Debates*, September 15th, 1927, p. 4,445.

[5] Sir Purshotamdas Thakurdas, cotton merchant, Hindu. Educated in India; president, East India Cotton Association; governor, Imperial Bank, Central Board; represents Indian commerce in Legislative Assembly.

> community do unfortunately mix this up with their religion.[1]

Any one ot these three Hindu leaders should be in possession of the facts ; yet no two agree. The author of *Mother India*, investigating this question, arrives, as the book itself shows, at the same conclusion as the last-quoted witness. Yet the significant fact remains ; all three Hindus agree that the evil of child marriage prevails somewhere.

Meantime the orthodox legislators grew uneasy in their seats at hearing the Western-educated members talk as if the Hindu masses were prepared to follow them in regulating Hindu marriages ; and one of the orthodox leaders, Mr. D. U. Belvi, assemblyman from Southern Bombay, gave voice to the following stricture :

> I do not care for those Hindus who have gone to England, and who have eaten beef and meat . . . we have to realise that the large bulk of the people of this country are orthodox. We have to legislate for those people.
>
> . . . . We must be taken as we are. We have got a certain set of tenets, a certain set of beliefs and customs. These must be respected, and the laws which you frame here must be suited to those customs and beliefs. . . . You are always on the top note, talking in hyperbolic language, and you do not want to consider the feelings of the millions of people who are outside this House. . . . Do you

[1] *Legislative Assembly Debates*, September 15th, 1927, p. 4,415.

> know that there is a large magazine of gunpowder outside this Legislative Assembly, and do you mean to throw into it a lighted match ?[1]

Mr. Belvi in voicing the opinion of the orthodox Hindus may seem to have used strong language against a bill which, at that time, only aimed to prevent Hindu girls from marrying before the age of twelve.

But a strong and audible Hindu cross section fights any and all attempts to change the custom of child marriage. For example, Mr. J. Manjiah, of the Spiritual Regeneration Movement, writing on the Sarda Child Marriage Bill in the *Bombay Daily Mail* on July 16th, 1928, said :

> Marriage of girls before puberty and age of 12 is a religious custom obtaining in practice from time immemorial. Exceptions, if any, only prove the rule. Aliens' modes of thinking can never get to the purposes at the root of customs. Persons like Miss Mayo display their feats of colossal ignorance only to our laughter or pity.

And because the majority of orthodox Hindus are illiterate—the literate minority (8 per cent.) being mostly unorthodox—it is difficult to judge to what extent any such reform will receive public backing. Social reformers themselves are prone to say they should lead public opinion, through legislation ; but, in this matter of marriage, in a country for centuries an addict to child marriage, the question must be

[1] *Legislative Assembly Debates*, September 15th, 1927, p. 4,427.

faced: 'Who is to enforce a law, in five hundred thousand villages, fixing the age at which a girl or boy may marry?'

What police, in what country, can enforce laws strictly pertaining to personal conduct in the intimate privacy of domestic life?

In 1891 an act was passed making it a crime for a man or boy married to a girl of twelve or under to have sexual relations with his wife. In 1925 the age of twelve was raised by statute to thirteen. This is the law to which *A Son of Mother India Answers* frequently refers, as:

> And since 1892 the Indian Penal Code has made intercourse with a girl below twelve a criminal offence.[1]

Again:

> Miss Mayo gives the following incident which startles me. She says that she came across a girl mother, at nine and a half, by Cæsarean operation, of a boy weighing *one and three quarter pounds.*
>
> Granted that Miss Mayo did not know of the Indian Penal Code and did not inform the Police about that case, still one more thing remains to be proven: namely, that this one personal experience of hers is not a criminal exception.[2]

And again:

> If the police forces and the Indian Penal Code can be trusted, then the conditions prevailing in 1891 do not apply to the India of to-day.[3]

[1] Page 20. [2] *Ibid.*, pp. 22-23. [3] *Ibid.*, pp. 48-49.

These suggestions are demolished by Assemblyman Rai Sahib Harbilas Sarda, proponent of the before-mentioned[1] bill to regulate Hindu child marriages, and in no uncertain terms :

> The law of the age of consent, so far as marital relations are concerned, is a dead letter, and has done little practical good except the slight educative effect which it has had on certain classes of people. The law regarding the age of consent has been in existence a pretty long time, but the last Census Report says :
>
> 'There is little evidence in the Census figures to suggest that the practice of infant marriage is dying out.'[2]

One difficulty of enforcing the Age of Consent Act, especially when relating to married people, was explained in March, 1927, by Mr. A. Y. G. Campbell, in the Madras Legislature :

> We have recently received from the High Court statistics of the number of prosecutions and convictions under Section 376 of the Indian Penal Code, which relates to rape, when the accused was the husband of the woman. The number of cases during the five years preceding the Act of 1925 was nil and the number of cases since the Act has also been nil. It is hardly to be wondered at that there were no prosecutions at all, for who will be the prosecutors ? The wife or the parents or guar-

[1] See *ante*, p. 78.

[2] *Legislative Assembly Debates*, September 15th, 1927, p. 4,408.

dian of the wife should be the prosecutor, and it is improbable that a wife or her parents or guardian would launch a prosecution against the husband or the son-in-law as the case may be. Therefore I am not surprised that the result of this legislation is nil.[1]

To this testimony from the South might be added that of an experienced Northerner, R. B. Diwan Chand, Obharai, advocate of Peshawar :

> The evil of child marriages is recognised and the penal measure of raising the age of consent has not checked this pernicious practice.[2]

Or, again, M. R. Ry. T. A. Ramalingam Chattiar, Avl., B.A., of Coimbatore, a leading Madrassee, thus expresses himself :

> The provision in the Age of Consent enactment that the persons specified should take action in cases of girls married makes it a dead letter so far as married girls are concerned, as it is not to the interest of the girl herself that the husband should be punished however unreasonable he may be.[3]

Turning next to those witnesses who have recently given evidence before the Age of Consent Committee,

[1] *Proceedings of the Legislative Council*, Madras, March 27th, 1927, p. 42.
[2] *Opinions on Hindu Child Marriage Bill*, Paper No. 1, Government of India, Legislative Department, p. 65. [3] *Ibid.* p. 4.

we find Mr. S. K. Bole, of Bombay, answering the Indian chairman's direct questions:

Chairman: Are you connected with the working classes?

Witness: Yes. I have been connected with the working classes since 20 years.

Chairman: Do you think that the law of Age of Consent is not known among the working classes?

Witness: No.

Chairman: Have you any reason to think that consummation takes place before the girl reaches the age of 13?

Witness: Yes.

Chairman: So apparently you are of the opinion that the law, as it stands, is violated to-day?

Witness: Yes.[1]

Lieutenant Kunwar Jamshed Ali Khan, a Muhammadan member of the United Provinces Legislature, expressed the view that 'the amendment of the Act in 1925 had practically failed to make the law more effective.'[2] Dr. Margaret I. Balfour, whose hospital statistics have been so widely broadcast in contradiction of *Mother India*, when asked if medical practitioners would report cases that came to their notice of infringements of the Age of Consent Law within the marital relation, replied that 'it was doubtful, because doctors would not like to lose their popularity.'[3]

[1] *Bombay Daily Mail*, Bombay, October 20th, 1928.
[2] *The Pioneer*, Allahabad, October 11th, 1928.
[3] *Bombay Daily Mail*, October 24th, 1928.

Nor is it apparent why the mere passing of a law by a handful of men, most of whom are widely separated in thought and education from the great majority of the people, should effectively influence the majority opinion. Not eight per cent. of the people can be reached by any printed words. And more than once legislators have recently acknowledged that, in the past, they have made little or no personal effort to instruct and lead their constituencies. Thus, Pandit Madan Mohan Malaviya, one of the most distinguished Hindu Assemblymen and a member of the Central-Indian Legislature's Select Committee on the Child Marriage Bill, does not hesitate to affirm that the reforming element, for all their years of talk, have never made sufficient or sincere efforts toward creating a public opinion in favour of a more humane marriage age. He says in part :

> . . . . I know what we have done, Sir. It is no good telling me that I do not know what we have done. We have delivered speeches, we have published pamphlets ; we have passed resolutions, but we have not gone from house to house to bring the evils of early marriages home to the people at large. We have not carried on such an agitation. We have not carried on even such an agitation as the temperance people are carrying on in some places against drink. We have not carried on an agitation commensurate with the enormity of this evil, and we are not entitled to claim that we have done all that we could.[1]

[1] *Legislative Assembly Debates,* September 15th, 1927, p. 4,443.

Few Hindu professional men have as yet recognised it as a duty to acquaint their nation with its danger. An honourable exception is the Hindu scientist, Professor Phadke, who writes in his *Sex Problem in India* :

> The saddest consequence of this tyranny of religion has been the sanction which it has accorded to child marriage and the censure which it has heaped on late marriage. If we leave out of consideration a few small sects like the Rajputs in some parts of northern India, we have to take child marriage as the form of marriage most prevalent in India—from the Himalayas to Cape Comorin, and from Calcutta to Peshawar.[1]

In summing up this author says :

> Our people are suffering from a miserable degeneration ; our race is to-day void of all stamina, mental as well as physical ; disease is undermining the health of our men and women ; the average span of expected life in our country is as low as 24 years ; our country's death rate is shockingly huge compared with that of any other nation—all these facts are so patent that he who runs may read them.[2]

Unfortunately Professor Phadke's book was published in India only, thereby escaping Western attention. Consequently it received little notice from the Hindu world that it aimed to serve.

A second outspoken book whose potential usefulness has, for the same reason, been largely nullified is

[1] 1928, pp. 71-72.

[2] *Ibid.*, p. 329.

Woman Awakened. This recent work was written by a Hindu woman medical practitioner, but as it was published in India only it has aroused little Hindu comment. Yet it abounds in passages such as this :

> What vitality can there be in a nation where often a unit quantity of food meant for one has to suffice for three, the mother, the baby in the womb and the child at the breast ? Should we glorify child-marriage for this ? In this connection it may be said that child-marriage is all right provided early consummation of it is forbidden. But what should be said of the husbands that ravish their child-wives even before puberty ? Because it is the husband his offence is no rape to the people around him and even if law condemns the act who should complain about him—not surely the ignorant frightened child-wife of his ![1]

Turning now to the various Indian women's conferences held since *Mother India* first appeared, we find the same consciousness voiced by their leaders. Her Highness the Maharani Chimana Saheb Gaekwar of Baroda, in her presidential speech at the first All-India Women's Conference in January 1927, used these words :

> Before even the girl's body has reached maturity, almost before she is aware that she has a soul of her own, she is made the plaything, either of a youth as sinned against as herself, or of a man who can neither respect her nor arouse her re-

[1] *Woman Awakened*, G. Sumati Bai, B.A., L.T., Tagore and Company, Madras, 1928, p. 51.

spect. . . . . If we are to have strong vigorous sons and daughters, we must have strong and mature mothers.[1]

At the third session of the same conference Mrs. Jelal Shah, speaking on child marriage, said :

> It is a system ruinous to boys and girls alike, physically, mentally and morally, and, if allowed to continue, will most certainly do irreparable and still greater harm in course of time to generations still unborn. . . . They [child-wives] are the poor miserable wrecks who become the mothers of a physically weak and delicate nation.[2]

Later in 1927, at a Bombay meeting favouring the Sarda Child Marriage Bill, the chairman, Mrs. F. S. Talyarkhan, a well-known Parsee social reformer, asked :

> What respect can any country command which believes that the proper place for a girl of 12 is not the nursery but the marriage bed ? Speaking as a woman I have no hesitation to say that child marriage among Hindus is a reproach and a disgrace to our sex, no matter to what race we belong ; it is a curse to the country and a sin in the eyes of God.'[3]

Finally, the testimony of Mrs. Annie Besant's new Messiah, J. Krishnamurti, is important in view of its

[1] *All-India Women's Conference on Educational Reform*, Poona, January 1927, pp. 16-17. Report printed by Scottish Mission Industries Company, Poona. [2] *Ibid.*, p. 29.

[3] *Bombay Daily Mail*, October 21st, 1927.

total difference from the pictures he paints for American audiences and gives out in interviews to Western newspapers. Addressing his own countrymen in India, Mr. J. Krishnamurti stated, in March 1928:

> We have a splendid spiritual heritage; but it has grown stale and profitless through lack of the one thing which alone can keep any tradition fresh and profitable; and that is the spirit of real affection and consideration for others. The most potent survivals from our immemorial past are now—what? Crystallised cruelties and selfishness, infant marriage, the heartless restrictions which we place on widows, our treatment of women generally, the whole system of untouchability, what are these but matters in which the dead weight of custom has crushed out of us the ordinary decent feelings which should sweeten and harmonise the life of human beings? And what is caste itself but a system of organised selfishness—the desire of every man to feel himself different from others, and to be conscious of possessing something which others do not possess. These and many similar things, are our heritage to-day; and it is under the weight of this heritage that we are groaning.[1]

Notwithstanding such realisation of his country's needs, this man who claims spiritual leadership in both the East and West denounced *Mother India*, in the American press, as 'grossly exaggerated and most unfair.'[2]

[1] *New India*, Madras, March 22nd, 1928.
[2] *New York World*, April 10th, 1928.

CHAPTER VII

A LIFE OF AUSTERITY

THE number of Hindu girls who are already widows at ten years of age or under is still over 96,000, while no fewer than 329,076 Hindu widows are fifteen years old or less,[1] and so long as orthodox Hinduism maintains its present tenets, there seems little hope of this number being seriously diminished.[2]

The causes of this condition are in part explained in the last Census of India :

> The large number of Indian widows is due partly to the early age of marriage, partly to the disparity in the ages of husbands and wives but chiefly to the prejudice against the remarriage of widows. The higher castes of Hindus forbid it altogether and, as the custom is held to be a mark of social respectability, many of the more ambitious of the lower castes have adopted it by way of raising their social status. . . .[3]

The fact that since 1856[4] it has been legal for Hindu girls to remarry has scarcely affected the situation.

Mother India stated the case of the Hindu child

[1] *Census of India*, 1921, Vol. I, Part II, p. 46.

[2] The Vidhva Vivaha Sahayak Sabha, a reform organisation of twenty-three years' standing claiming 600 branches all over India, reports a grand total of 13,000 widows' remarriages. In 1927 it claims to have arranged 2,500 remarriages in the whole of India. (*Indian Social Reformer*, August 11th, 1928, p. 794.)

[3] *Census of India*, 1921, Vol. I, Part I, p. 155.

[4] The Hindu Widow Remarriage Reform Act of 1856.

widow, and its author has continued, in more recent writings, to appeal on their behalf, just as the Brahman widow, Pandita Ramabai, besieging America for hearing and help, found courage to do before her.[1]

Both in speeches and in writing the Indian social reformer to-day shows that he is aware of this evil and would gladly banish it from his civilisation if he but knew how to do so.

'I shall not take the time of the House,' said a legislator recently,[2] 'by narrating what Hindu widowhood means. There is no Hindu who does not know it from practical experience in his household. It is a life of agony, pains and suffering and austerity.' Or, as says Lalbhai D. Dholakiya of Patan, writing in the *Bombay Daily Mail* of October 16th, 1928, to advocate legislation for the removal of child widowhood :

> One need not go to Miss Katherine Mayo, who has given a graphic description of the poor lot of Hindu widows in her wretched book the *Mother India*, to study the 'horrors' of widowhood in India. The moment a young woman becomes a widow she is doomed for ever. . . .

It will not, however, be attempted here, to elaborate a picture of the misery the Hindu widow must endure. Rather, the purpose of this chapter is to show the attitude, in this matter, of educated Indians holding responsible positions. Their views are mainly determined by practical facts. Most of them recognise the evils of

[1] *Pandita Ramabai Sarasvati*, Clementina Butler ; F. H. Revell Company, New York, 1922.

[2] *Legislative Assembly Debates*, September 15th, 1927, p. 4,414.

enforced widowhood ; the question they face is, what steps should be taken to rid their country of this evil ?

One suggested remedy is the bill mentioned in the preceding chapter, introduced by Rai Sahib Harbilas Sarda into the Central Indian Legislature, and since commonly known as the Sarda Child Marriage Bill.

In October 1927, this bill was circulated throughout India for opinions. The views thus elicited were published by the Government in a Paper dated February 1928. This Paper, containing statements by Indian justices, by bar associations, by leading educators and examiners, by business and landowners' organisations, by district commissioners and deputy commissioners, and by governors in council, gives an enlightening cross section of educated opinion. In the statement of the principal of the Sanskrit College at Benares, the reader finds an outline of the generally accepted objectives of the bill, as it then stood, and also the individual opinion of this important educational authority :

> The main objects of the Bill are (i) to put a stop to the possibility of widowhood in case of girls below 12 years of age by declaring their marriages invalid and (ii) to prevent to a certain extent the physical and moral deterioration of boys and girls by laying down their minimum marriageable ages.
>
> The Bill involves certain important socio-religious changes. In my opinion reforms of the society, whenever they are necessary, must come from within the society itself and must not, as far as possible, be imposed from without, e.g. through

legislature. The Hindu Society—I am speaking of the orthodox section of it, which represents the major portion of Hindu population—is governed by the dictates of the Shastras [the Hindu books of holy laws] as interpreted by the Pandits. These Pandits are learned Brahmans and are recognised as the leaders of Hindu Society. Their verdict on all matters connected with socio-religious discipline of the Society is considered as final. . . . Whatever reforms may be introduced in the Society in defiance or disregard of the views of the Pandits is bound to create unrest in the country. . . .

As regards the details of the Bill in question the object of the Bill is certainly noble. But the only effective manner in which that object can be secured is, in my opinion, by educating the public opinion and not by legislation. When public opinion is sufficiently enlightened the reform will take place smoothly and as a matter of course.[1]

Justice Venkatasubba Rao, of Madras, was differently minded; he wrote: 'There can be no objection, in my opinion, to there being legislation on such matters as infant marriages. If the removal of social evils is left to public opinion, I am afraid it may take some centuries before such evils disappear from Hindu society.'[2]

Another legal opinion elucidates the Hindu marriage custom, gives three reasons for holding the proposed

[1] *Opinions on Hindu Child Marriage Bill*, Government of India, Legislative Department, 1928, p. 26. [2] *Ibid*, p. 8.

legislation improper, and points out two of its main weaknesses :

> Marriage among Hindus is not a contract between *sui juris*. It is a sacrament. It is completed on going through certain religious ceremonies and becomes irrevocable afterwards. In the present state of Hindu society, to invalidate it on the ground that the girl or boy or both are below 12 and 15 years of age, respectively, is improper because (*a*) it offends against religious sentiments, (*b*) it will render the girl unhappy for life, as no one will marry her again and (*c*) it is vicarious in that it punishes the innocent and not those who bring about such marriages.
>
> It is impracticable because (1) the age can easily be evaded by giving out higher age and (2) those who bring it about will pass it off as valid and no one is interested in exposing it.[1]

Mr. Justice Ramesam, another Madrassee, made this suggestion, equally informing :

> Instead of this legislation, I would suggest a slightly different one—less ambitious as to age but more effective in diminishing the number of widows. All marriages of girls below the age of 8½ should be made criminal offences and those who bring about such marriages should be punished. . . . .
>
> As the Bill stands, it is mixed up with anomalies and hardships. It will be a dead letter and I object

[1] *Opinions on Hindu Child Marriage Bill*, Rai Bahadur, T. M. Narasimhacharlu, p. 1.

to it. Instead of unremarried child widows, we will have unmarried maidens living secretly immoral lives. Is this desirable ?[1]

In Bengal, the Marwari Association of Calcutta, a powerful and important organisation of business men, again emphasised the Hindu religion's demands on its adherents :

> In plain language, the Bill proposes to prohibit the marriage of Hindu girls before they reach the thirteenth year of age, that is to say, before they attain puberty, for Indian girls generally attain puberty between 11 and 12 years. . . . If any one had deliberately intended to hurt the religious feelings of the orthodox Hindu community, to change the face of the Hindu society and to insult the Hindu religion, he could not have hit upon or devised a more effective means. But in the opinion of my Committee, no Hindu having any faith in his religion, can agree to such a provision.[2]

And the Honorary Secretary of the Bar Library Club of the High Court of Calcutta reported, shortly after the Calcutta meetings organised under the chairmanship of the mayor to protest against *Mother India* :

> While fully conscious of the evils which the proposed Bill aims at and appreciating the object with which it has been introduced, the Bar is of opinion that legislation should not be undertaken, as it is sure to raise a storm of protest throughout the land as interference with the religious

[1] *Opinions on Hindu Child Marriage Bill*, p. 10.
[2] *Ibid.*, pp. 12-13.

> tenets and deep-rooted sentiments of the vast majority of the orthodox Hindu population. The Bar is of the opinion that social reform in the direction of advancing the marriageable age of girls should be effected from within, and not imposed upon the community by the legislature, unless there is very great demand for it.[1]

Or again, the Incorporated Law Society of Calcutta made a very similar statement on December 17th, two months after the first public meeting in Calcutta protesting against *Mother India*.[2]

Just as some of the evils exposed by *Mother India* were unknown to men who had spent their whole lives among the Indian people, so, it appears, the existence of baby widows was unknown to the Advocate-General of Madras ; yet he showed courage in stating :

> I dislike legislation of the kind. But I confess to a shocked feeling on reading the note by the author that the census reports show widows under five years and even under one year of age. . . . I am personally inclined to allow the legislation which will have the effect of preventing marriages during the years of life most subject to mortality.[3]

In the United Provinces, an outstanding Hindu advocate of Cawnpore, Rai Bahadur B. Vikramjit Singh, B.A., LL.B., M.L.C., also considered the bill an infringement on religious and personal rights :

> As a President of the Sanatan Dharm Maha-

[1] *Opinions on Hindu Child Marriage Bill*, p. 21.
[2] *Ibid.*, p. 22. [3] *Ibid.*, p. 10.

mandal I can voice the opinion of the Sanatan Dharmist Hindus. The Bill is an encroachment on religious sentiments of the people and is an interference with religion. No Government or Legislature has a right to interfere by legislation with what the Shastras enjoin. I therefore desire that this piece of legislation should be opposed.[1]

And Vice-Chancellor M. M. Dr. Ganganatha Jha, M.A., D.Litt., of Allahabad University, said: 'In my humble opinion it is dangerous to society to deal with social matters by penal legislation. . . . I call the proposal positively "dangerous," specially in view of the possibility of criminal proceedings being launched for the offence contemplated.'[2]

But in the Muhammadan North, the Punjab, opinions almost unanimously favoured legislation to end Hindu child marriages, although some thought the Bill, as it then stood, unfortunate in its method, and did not hesitate to say so. The district and sessions judge at Ambala, knowing his Hindu neighbours, thus expressed himself:

This Bill, if passed, will prove a godsend to the legal practitioners of India. Every marriage of a boy under 15 or of a girl under 11 will be null and void once and for ever and even if the marriage is not consummated until several years later, whatever children may eventually be born, will be born bastards. The Bill should have been entitled 'A Bill for the promotion of bastardy in India. . . .'

Another aspect of the matter concerns the traffic

[1] *Opinions on Hindu Child Marriage Bill*, p. 27. [2] *Ibid.*, p. 27.

> in women, a traffic that is rife in Northern India.[1] This business thrives or declines very much in proportion to the supply of women who are accessible to easy abduction. The Bill will create a large class of concubines whom any man will be permitted to abduct with impunity as soon as they reach the age of 16 years. The husband being no husband at all will have no redress at law. A more direct stimulation to the traffic in women it would be difficult to devise. No doubt in the long run, bitter experience of such cases should teach the community to eschew child marriages and would thus further the purpose of the Bill, but the more immediate evil of the nearer future is too high a price to pay for the ultimate result.[2]

Again, in the Rawalpindi Division of the Punjab, the Gurukal section of the Arya Samaj[3] registered discontent with the ages of twelve and fourteen provided in the Bill, proposing sixteen for girls and twenty-five for men, as the proper ages at which marriage should be permitted.[4] Four other organisations

[1] *The Times of India* in an editorial on August 8th, 1928, said: 'Reports of the kidnapping of minor girls are numerous. No one knows the fullest extent of this fearful trade; but the Sind police, according to a report which appeared in our columns yesterday, have obtained unmistakable evidence of nefarious organisations in Sind, Marway, Gujerat and the Punjab. The public are fully aware of the evil, and the Maha Sabha authorities in Delhi and elsewhere are doing their best to expose the traffic. . . . Publicity will reveal something of the magnitude of the trade; and to be forewarned is to be forearmed. Publicity will also discourage many from committing an unpardonable crime."

[2] *Opinions on Hindu Child Marriage Bill*, p. 32.

[3] See *post*, pp. 176-77.

[4] *Opinions on Hindu Child Marriage Bill*, p. 37.

joined in endorsing the spirit underlying the Bill. But from this same district comes the report :

> The remaining bodies and Associations, however, consider the Bill as an outrageous encroachment on the fundamental principles of Hindu Law. In their opinion, the Hindu marriage being a sacrament, its validity should not be called into question by any Act of legislature.[1]

In far away Burma, where two-thirds of the population are not Hindus but Buddhists, and are, therefore, not addicts to child marriage, the majority of the opinions expressed were favourable to the Bill, many of them going so far as to criticise the age of twelve for girls as being too low. Mr. Taw Sein Ko, C.I.E., I.S.O., the examiner in Chinese, Burma, Maymyo, made the following comment in his preliminary remarks :

> The Bill is, no doubt, one of the tangible results of Miss Mayo's work on Indian Sociology entitled *Mother India*, which exposes the seamy side of Hindu domestic life, and which paints, in lurid colours, its sadness, suffering, and misery, due primarily to child marriage and early marriage, thereby straining to a breaking point the economic resources of the people, and retarding their material, intellectual, moral, and political development on their path toward Progress and Home Rule.
>
> In enacting this salutary law, it may, perhaps, be essential to elicit public opinion and to postpone the above legislation for about two years. These

[1] *Opinions on Hindu Child Marriage Bill*, p. 37.

pernicious and inhuman customs and practices relating to Hindu marriage have prevailed for more than two thousand years, and a period of two years is a mere drop in the ocean, when compared with the life-history of a nation, which numbers over two hundred million souls, and whose history stretches to over 5,000 years in the past. . . .

The time-limit of marriageable age for a Hindu girl is fixed too low. According to medical evidence, she attains puberty in her twelfth year. It would, indeed, be a crime as well as a physiological disaster, if she was given away in marriage as soon as she had completed her twelfth year.[1]

Sufficient has now been quoted to show that so far as educated and informed Indian opinion is concerned, the present custom of child marriages, with its consequent production of baby widows, is, amongst the small educated class, more generally deplored than not ; yet divergent opinions are held as to the proper means and hope of amelioration. Most social reformers and reform organisations have expressed themselves as strongly favouring the Sarda Bill to regulate marriages ; but the practical men in the field point out grave dangers lying in wait for this piece of legislation. In view of their warnings that it will become a 'dead letter,' that it is 'positively dangerous,' and that it will further immorality, has India stored up any previous experience that might serve as a guide in this urgent matter ? Has legislation ever been aimed to rid the country of other harmful Hindu religious customs ? If so, what guidance does it give ?

[1] *Opinions on Hindu Child Marriage Bill*, pp. 39-41.

CHAPTER VIII

FIVE ATTEMPTED REFORMS

By their very nature Governments are but interpreters and executors of the expressed will of the people whom they govern, and even the most autocratic Government will find itself unable to impose a reform which its people cannot assimilate. – M. K. GANDHI in *Young India*, October 20th, 1927, p. 354.

MR. GANDHI notwithstanding, an examination of the British record shows that on five major occasions, the Government of India has attempted to impose social reforms upon British India. In each case, such advance as has been achieved, has been won, not only against the religious beliefs of the Hindu majority, but against the open hostilities of many Hindu leaders. The evils attacked were: suttee, thuggee, infanticide, enforced widowhood, and consummated child marriage. Only two of these five attempted reforms—those of suttee and thuggee—have, however, been enforced to any degree approaching success, while in the three remaining instances the effort has proved almost totally ineffective. In briefly reviewing the Government's five attempts to lift the Hindu social status by law enactments, it is important to remember that a small educated Hindu minority, in every case, has materially helped.

In 1829, Lord William Bentinck, the then Governor-General, promulgated Regulation XVII, declaring the Hindu religious custom of burning widows alive to be culpable homicide.[1] This act met with opposition from

[1] *Encyclopædia Britannica*, eleventh edition, Vol. XIV, p. 441.

the learned babus of Calcutta, who fiercely objected to the loss of an ancient religious privilege. By these militant obstructionists a committee was formed and over 800 signatures obtained to an appeal to the Privy Council to permit suttee.[1] Although the mission failed, it showed the seriousness of the opposition.

One Hindu's name will always be honourably associated with the effort of Governor-General Lord William Bentinck ; honour is due to Raja Rammohan Roy for strongly attacking this vicious rite, although he did not advocate its summary abolition by law. Says Professor Edward Thompson in his recent historical research : 'Rammohan Roy was a valiant fighter against suttee, but he thought the prohibition an inexpedient measure,'[2] and, if praise must be given, this authority awards it to a single individual, the Governor-General : 'The credit is almost entirely personal, and it is Bentinck's.'[3]

Obviously, prevention of suttee is largely within the range of police enforcement, and to this one fact is due, in wide measure, the success of Regulation XVII. For it is difficult to burn a widow, with due ceremony, on her husband's funeral pyre, without the events coming to the knowledge of some Government authority. Hence, while cases still occur in various parts of the country, these are as nothing when compared to the 839 cases of widow-burning—probably a small fraction

[1] *Suttee*, Edward Thompson ; Allen and Unwin, London, 1928, p. 79. See also *Life and Letters of Raja Rammohun Roy*, by Sophia Dobson Collet, edited by Hem Chandra Sarkar, published by A. C. Sarkar, Calcutta, 1913, pp. 150-152. [2] *Suttee*, p. 78.

[3] *Ibid.*, pp. 77-78. See also *Life and Letters of Raja Rammohun Roy*, pp. 146, 147.

of those which actually took place—officially reported in 1818, forty-nine of whose victims were under twenty years old.[1]

An Indian writer, in the July 1928 issue of the official organ of the Indian Women's Association, speaking of the tragedy of widowhood, said :

> In former times numbers of them were burnt with their husbands. An early Governor-General stopped this practice. Sir John Woodroffe objects to references to this obsolete custom in judging present-day Hindu society. He would be right if Indians themselves had stopped this practice as westerners stopped the burning of witches. But it was not Hindu humanity but British legislation that ended *Sati* [suttee].[2]

During the same Governor-General's term, the ancient custom of thuggee was first vigorously and successfully attacked, the system being gradually unmasked and finally stamped out.[3]

The thugs were a peninsula-wide, well-organised confederacy of professional assassins. The members worked in gangs of from ten to two hundred who, under various guises, wormed themselves into the confidence of wealthy travellers, only to await a favourable opportunity to strangle, plunder, and bury their victims. Under both Hindu and Muhammadan rulers, thuggee was a recognised, tax-paying, religious profession, whose members staunchly worshipped Kali, the Hindu

[1] *Suttee*, Edward Thompson, pp. 69, 71.
[2] N. Yagnesvara Sastry, *Stri-Dharma*, July, 1928.
[3] *Encyclopædia Britannica*, eleventh edition, Vol. XXVI, p. 896.

goddess of destruction, and who invariably gave some share of the spoils to her. The initiated always regarded their victims as sacrifices to Kali, upon whose protection they relied with unquestioning faith.[1]

Through the unremitting vigilance of Lord William Bentinck's officers, and especially that of Sir William Sleeman, K.C.B., otherwise known as 'Thuggee Sleeman,' the confederacy was practically annihilated by 1835.[2]

Now we come to the less successful attempts of the Government to wipe out ancient evil customs embedded in the religious concepts of the Hindu peoples. The first of these is infanticide. In the crusade against this practice, such names as those of Jonathan Duncan and Major Walker[3] stood out at the end of the eighteenth century. Always a stubborn crime to check because of the extreme difficulty of detection, the Government's efforts have been only partially fruitful, even up to the present day. The latest census presents a table showing the sex ratio of groups with and without a tradition of female infanticide. Thus we read, of the Punjab in 1921, that castes having the tradition averaged 794 females for every 1,000 males, while the rate of females to males among those castes not traditionally addicted to infanticide was as 869 to every 1,000. Similarly, in the United Provinces, the castes without the tradition average 924 females per 1,000 males, while those with the tradition of killing girl babies report only 809 girls

[1] *Encyclopædia Britannica*, eleventh edition, Vol. XXVI, p. 896. See also Vol. XV, p. 641.

[2] *The Oxford History of India*, Vincent A. Smith, C.I.E.; Clarendon Press, Oxford, 1923, pp. 666-668.

[3] *Encyclopædia Britannica*, eleventh edition, Vol. XIV, p. 517.

per 1,000 boys,—a discrepancy of over 13 per cent. On this comparison, the Census Commissioner comments :

> . . . in these particular communities it seems to be quite useless and quite unnecessary to insist upon reasons for the low sex-ratio other than that which these figures suggest, viz., the continued deliberate destruction of female infant life either by active or by passive means . . .[1]

The present law against infanticide provides that if female children, in any particular locality, fall below a certain percentage, that locality shall be placed under police supervision, the cost being charged to the local inhabitants.[2]

A second ineffective Government attempt to induce social reform by legislative enactment is found in the Hindu Widow Remarriage Act of 1856, which, during its seventy years of life, has proved a miserable failure. This piece of legislation was purely 'permissive,' in that it merely legalises the remarriage of Hindu widows within the jurisdiction of British India. Its aim was to diminish the number of widows in Hindustan. But one glance at present-day figures will prove its utter futility. The last Census, taken in 1921, shows that, between the ages of fifteen and twenty, out of every 1,000 Hindu girls no fewer than 48 were widows and that Hindu India reported 191 widows to every 1,000 population,[3] as against 73.2 per 1,000 recorded in England and Wales.[4] The total number of Hindu

[1] *Census of India*, 1921, Vol. I, Part I, App. VI, p. xviii.
[2] *Encyclopædia Britannica*, eleventh edition, Vol. XIV, p. 517.
[3] *Census of India*, 1921, Vol. I, Part I, p. 164.
[4] *Ibid.*, p. 155, 1911 figures.

widows, as given in the Legislative Assembly in 1927, reached over 20,200,000.[1]

The Select Committee which examined the Widow Remarriage Bill at the time of its origin reported having received twenty-three petitions signed by 5,191 Hindus in favour of the proposed measure, and twenty-eight petitions signed by 55,746 Hindus against the measure—a majority of over ten to one against the reform.[2] One of the majority petitions quotes no less than eight Hindu 'bibles' and holy law-givers, each to this effect:

> Him to whom her father has given her or her brother with the paternal assent, let her obsequiously honour, while he lives; and when he dies let her never neglect him.
>
> Let her emaciate her body, by living voluntarily on pure flowers, roots, and fruit; but let her not, when her lord is deceased, even pronounce the name of another man.
>
> Let her emaciate till death forgiving all injuries, performing harsh duties, avoiding every sensual pleasure, and cheerfully practising the incomparable rules of virtue, which have been followed by such women as were devoted to one only husband.[3]

But the Honourable Mr. J. P. Grant, introducing the bill, is reported as saying:

> Every candid Hindu would admit that, in the

[1] *Legislative Assembly Debates*, September 15th, 1927, p. 4,413.

[2] *The Indian Social Reformer*, Bombay, August 11th, 1928, p. 795.

[3] *Ibid.*, pp. 781-782.

majority of cases, young Hindu widows fall into vice; that in comparatively few cases are these severe rules for a life of mortification virtuously observed; that in many cases, a licentious and profligate life is entered upon in secret; and that, in many other cases the wretched widows are impelled to desert their homes and to live a life that brings open disgrace upon their families.[1]

Finally, we turn to the fifth major attempt of Government to impose a social reform upon Hindu India—the attempt to protect girl children from premature sexual use. As a preliminary step in 1860, the Indian Penal Code fixed the legal age of consent within the marriage bond at ten years. In 1891 the Government returned to the attack and, by main force, against fierce opposition, attempted to lift the Hindu people out of their social pit. This fight resulted in a paper victory, which raised the age for girls within the marriage bond from ten to twelve. And again, in 1925, a law was passed, making it a criminal offence for a husband to have intercourse with his wife before she reached her thirteenth year or for an unmarried girl to be subjected to sexual relations before she reached fourteen.[2]

What has been the result of thus raising the age of consent? As we have heard from the Indian witnesses quoted in earlier chapters and as has been shown from court records, this law, for all intents and purposes, is a dead letter.

[1] *The Indian Social Reformer*, Bombay, August 11th, 1928, p. 764.
[2] *Legislative Assembly Debates*, September 3rd, 1925.

Yet in total disregard of past experiences, and in spite of Mr. Gandhi's statement, most Indian social reformers and many Indian politicians still believe the passing of laws to be a sufficient panacea for all social evils. And if the Government, remembering the past, deems it wisdom to sound out public opinion on a bill regulating Hindu marriages before allowing it to come to a vote, such action is defeated and stamped as being 'strongly opposed' to Hindu reform.

This is precisely what happened in September 1927, when the Sarda Bill to regulate Hindu marriages lay before the Legislative Assembly.

The Home Member's[1] amendment, 'that the Bill be circulated for the purpose of eliciting opinions thereon,'[2] was defeated in a division by fifty-six votes to fifty-one.

The Government's action is referred to in *Unhappy India*:

> Another Bill fixing the minimum age for marriage, brought forward by R. B. Har Bilas Sarda, a Hindu Assemblyman, was very strongly opposed by the official members. . . .[3]

Another motion offered the same day by a prominent Hindu 'that the Bill be referred to a Select Committee,' was adopted without a division,[4] and, when *Unhappy India* was written, was still in that stage.[5]

The advantages of circulating a Bill for opinion are

[1] 'The Home Member' is the official spokesman for the Government of India in the Assembly. In this case a Briton.

[2] *Legislative Assembly Debates*, September 15th, 1927, p. 4,416.

[3] *Unhappy India*, p. 183.

[4] *Legislative Assembly Debates*, September 15th, 1927, p. 4,415.

[5] *Unhappy India*, p. 183.

twofold. First, it is brought before every representative body in the country, giving each a chance to express its views ; and, second, it receives, meantime, a large amount of publicity in the press, while public meetings are usually held and resolutions are passed, whether for or against the measure. So the mere act of circulation develops, of itself, a considerable educational value.

Yet Indians were not alone in criticising the Government's desire for circulation, various sinister interpretations being placed upon it ; and at least one American has misquoted the debate of September 15th.[1]

In March 1928 the Select Committee, which was dominated by Hindus,[2] made its report to the House. This reads in part :

> The object of the Bill as introduced in the Legislature was to impose restraint upon the solemnisation of child marriages, and the method adopted was, broadly speaking, that of declaring all marriages of boys or girls below a certain age to be invalid. The Bill has been circulated under the orders of Government and has elicited a strong expression of feeling that it is objectionable, both on religious and on legal grounds, to interfere with the validity of a marriage which has been performed. In our opinion, these objections are at present insuperable, and we have accordingly acted upon a suggestion . . . that the Bill should

[1] *Living India*, Savel Zimand, misdates the debate and, purporting to quote Mr. M. R. Jayakar, puts words into his mouth that are not in the official record.

[2] The Committee consisted of fifteen members of the Assembly, of whom at least nine were Hindus.

effect its purpose . . . by imposing punishments upon those who participate in them [child marriages].[1]

The Committee's recommendations and the Government's consequent policy throughout this matter were ably explained in March 1928 by Mr. Sarda, who originally proposed the measure, and who at this time moved that the changed Bill be recirculated for the purpose of eliciting further opinions :

When I introduced the Bill, I confined its operations to Hindus only, for two reasons. There is a fundamental difference of opinion with regard to the institution of marriage between the Hindus and Mussalmans. The former regard marriage as a sacrament, the latter only as a civil contract. Moreover, amongst the Hindus, there is such a thing as enforced widowhood. Among the Muslins no such thing obtains. . . . As, however, the Select Committee made this Bill a penal measure, it thought it would be advisable to apply it to all Indians, whether Hindus, Muslims, or Christians.

Two questions now arose for decision : the first was, up to what age was the marriage to be held a child marriage ? And secondly, what were the penalties to be imposed on those who performed such marriages ? The Committee unanimously decided that 18 was the minimum marriageable age for boys ; as for girls, the Muslim opinion, as the Bill now applies to Mussalmans also, in the Select Committee was dead against fixing the age below

[1] *The Gazette of India*, Part V, March 31, 1928, Delhi.

14; consequently, the age was fixed at 14 in the case of girls. . . . I have just a word to say as regards the attitude of Government before I conclude. When I introduced the Bill, Sir Alexander Muddiman, the then Home Member, declared that he would oppose it at every stage. These apprehensions have been found to be unfounded. The Honourable the Home Member, has given all possible assistance to the passage of the Bill. . . .[1]

This speech was immediately followed by one from the Home Member, who again pledged the Government's support, and in these words:

> . . . I should like to relieve any apprehensions that may have been entertained by the Honourable the Mover by saying at once that Government not only do not intend to oppose his motion but that it has their cordial support. The Honourable Member has been good enough to say that the Government have rendered every assistance in the transmutation of his original measure into the form in which it has been reported to the House. That is perfectly true; and I only wish to say, with regard to the statement made by the Honourable Member that my predecessor, Sir Alexander Muddiman, had declared that the Bill would be opposed at all stages, that the Bill against which Sir Alexander Muddiman entered a caveat was a very different measure from that which has now emerged. . . .
>
> It will, I hope, receive the general approval of

[1] *Legislative Assembly Debates*, March 26th, 1928, pp. 1,967-68.

> this House and I trust that though, as I have observed in my note appended to the Report of the Committee, Government must reserve a final judgment on some of the expedients proposed in the Bill, it will receive very general support after it has been circulated.[1]

But before the motion for recirculation was carried, the Bill received severe criticism from at least one member who had supported it in the debate of September 15th, 1927. Said Mr. M. K. Acharya :

> I have received from several people, from several bodies and several institutions, from several recognised heads of religious institutions, strong statements calling upon us in fact to object to this Bill. It is true that on the last occasion I also was one of those who supported the general principle of that Bill . . . but now I am sorry I am forced to raise a voice of protest against this present measure. As I said just now this is a penal legislation, and I am opposed on principle, I am very strongly opposed on principle to penal legislation coming in to the aid of social reform. . . . I would warn Government to take note of the fact that there is a great deal of strong orthodox Hindu opinion which is opposed to penal legislation of this kind. . . . Marriage among us does not necessarily denote the immediate living together as man and wife. In fact, among Hindus, especially young Brahmans and certain others, there are two ceremonies ; the first and more im-

[1] *Legislative Assembly Debates*, March 26th, 1928, p. 1,968.

portant and more sacred ceremony is really the ceremony of betrothal. . . .[1]

He then elaborated the argument used so frequently by the Indian critics of *Mother India*—that Hindu marriages are mere betrothals; but Mr. Acharya must have felt the force of the reply of a Hindu colleague, Munshi Iswar Saran :

> Mr. Acharya talks about betrothal, Sir, but if he had taken the trouble of studying this Bill, he would have seen that there is not a word in it against betrothal. You may betroth the child before even the child's father is born. There is no objection to it. Betroth the child whenever you like. But what we object to is that you have no business to marry a child. . . .[2]

Those who talk about betrothals are seldom serious. More often than not they do so to raise a screen before the real evils of child marriage. Additional light is thrown on this point by C. V. Visvanatha Sastri, advocating the Sarda Child Marriage Bill in a letter to the *Madras Mail* dated February 14th, 1928 :

> The Mahasabha [General Hindu Convention] must admit that marriage is an act which is made public as soon as it takes place ; and that consummation can take place without its being known to anyone besides the two parties to it. I personally know of three cases where such consummation

[1] *Legislative Assembly Debates*, March 26th, 1928, pp. 1,968, 1,970. M. K. Acharya, B.A., Hindu ; journalist ; educated at Madras Christian College ; headmaster 1902-17 ; independent political worker since 1917. Elected member from South Arcot *cum* Chinglepet. Prominent member *Swaraj* party and National Congress. [2] *Ibid.*, p. 1,976.

> took place in secret; and became known only when the young girls were in an advanced state of pregnancy; so cleverly did they conceal this for seven months. . . . The bride has to go to her husband's home on various occasions; and the chances of their husband[s] meeting them are frequent. . . . Such is the fear of our Law givers that it is enjoined that even a brother and sister must not be together alone.

Later, the motion for recirculation having been adopted without a division, the Government issued orders to Collectors and District Officers once more to sound the state of public opinion upon the Sarda Child Marriage Bill.[1] Again the officials in each district were instructed to gather and transmit the opinions of the leading members of their communities together with their own opinions.[2]

In addition, public meetings were held both in favour of and in protest against the Bill, while some of the newspapers carried columns of correspondence, as well as reports of the various meetings. Unfortunately, no collection of newspaper clippings on this subject can be complete, but I have before me reports of seventy-five organisations and meetings which have taken action in this matter, together with much correspondence and many notices of lectures which have appeared in

[1] *The Hindu*, Madras, May 17th, 1928.

[2] This document had not been secured up to the time of going to press. However, Rai Sahib Harbilas Sarda summarised it in his speech in the Legislative Assembly on January 29th, 1929. As a strong advocate for raising the age of consent he is apt to belittle the opinions against the reform, which appear to be heavily in the minority.

the Indian press. Of the seventy-five no fewer than thirty-eight record action favouring the proposed legislation, while thirty-seven meetings are reported as protesting and passing resolutions against it.[1]

A further analysis shows that, while the meetings in favour are principally held in the large cities, as Bombay, Calcutta, Madras, Simla, etc., the thirty-seven protest meetings have, in most cases, occurred in the villages and towns of the South. Similarly, while Indians of all religions seem to attend the gatherings favouring the Bill, its opponents appear to be predominantly orthodox Hindus. Women are active in the favourable conclaves, while men, apparently, form the majority of the opposition.

True to custom, resolutions are passed at all the meetings ; and these show a monotonous similarity. On the one hand it is resolved :

> That this meeting of the citizens of Madras heartily approves of the principles underlying Mr. Harbilas Sarda's Child Marriage Bill and appeals to the country to make honest and strenuous efforts to see that the said Bill is passed into law.[2]

And, on the other hand :

> This meeting of the citizens of Alwartirunagare records its emphatic protest against the Child Marriage Bill of Mr. Sarda . . . as it strikes at the very foundation of Shastraic principles guiding the Hindu society and regrets the unwarranted interference of legislatures in a matter of purely affecting the religious life of the Hindus. To

[1] A list of the dates and places of these meetings appears in Appendix V and VI.

[2] *The Hindu*, Madras, May 22nd, 1928.

regulate marriages by legislative enactments and to punish the orthodox section of the public for the breach of the provisions of such measures is against the spirit and letter of the Proclamation of Queen Victoria and hence requests the Government to veto it.[1]

These divergencies explain, perhaps, the Home Member's words: 'Government must reserve a final judgment on some of the expedients proposed in the Bill.'[2]

For better or for worse, the British have, with the main exceptions of suttee, thuggee, infanticide, widow remarriage, and the age of consent, refused even an attempt to interfere with the Hindu religion, and their present-day policy in general opposes the passage of any law that is incapable of enforcement. The people of the United States, with their 94 per cent. of literacy, will be the first to appreciate the danger of endeavouring to enforce laws affecting personal rights and religious customs among peoples full of superstition, only 8 per cent. literate in any language, and easily excited to violence by the emotional appeal.

[1] *The Hindu*, Madras, June 15th, 1928.

[2] The Hindu Child Marriage Bill was again brought before the Assembly by its sponsor, Rai Sahib Harbilas Sarda, on January 29th, 1929. Unofficial members opposing the bill brought up two 'points of order' to prevent the bill from being taken into consideration ; both were overruled by the President, one with the aid of the Governor General's spokesman. The following amendment was then offered again, by an unofficial member : 'That the consideration of the Bill be postponed till the report of the Age of Consent Committee becomes available to the Members of the House.' This was accepted by the majority of members, official members voting in its favour. Thus when next the bill comes under consideration the additional light thrown upon it by the Age of Consent Committee will help guide the Legislature on this difficult and much-debated subject. See *Legislative Assembly Debates*, January 29th, 1929.

CHAPTER IX

DR. CLARK AND OTHERS

IN December, 1927, the Indian press reported the publication of a booklet of protest, assured of a wide circulation in America, 'against the injustice of Miss Mayo,' which booklet carried this letter, signed by seven prominent American missionaries then in India :

> As Americans we wish to express our sense of deep regret that a country-woman of ours should, after a brief stay in India, write so unfairly and offensively of this country.
>
> It is clearly apparent that Miss Mayo saw only a part of India and did not see that part in the proper perspective. In many things her accuracy as an observer will not bear scrutiny and the many highly exaggerated conclusions give a false picture of India as a whole. . . .
>
> We wish to express our sense of humiliation that an American should write with such unfairness and apparent prejudice in presenting India.[1]

In no place does this letter give any instance of the 'many things' that will not bear scrutiny, and it seems absurd to imply that *Mother India* was ever intended as a whole or complete picture of India, in view of its author's statement : 'Leaving untouched the realms of religion, of politics, and of the arts, I would confine

[1] *The Hindu*, Madras, December 17th, 1927.

my inquiry to such workaday ground as public health and its contributing factors.'[1]

Nevertheless, one of the seven signatories was a bishop. Another, the Reverend E. Stanley Jones, is reported in the *Times of Malaya* of September 14th, 1927, to have said, in a speech at Masulipatam[2] :

> Miss Mayo's book, I must say, is a terrible book. . . . I am prepared to discount 70 per cent., say even 90 per cent., of all that she says of India and Indian peoples. She has never seen India and never studied India at close quarters. Most of what she writes is based upon what she has learnt through hearsay or reports by interested foreigners.
>
> I must concede that she is an expert investigator. She was asked by the Y.M.C.A. to review the work of the Y.M.C.A. in the Great War and write a book on it. She told the Y.M.C.A. authorities point blank, that the results might prove distasteful to them. The Y.M.C.A. entrusted her with the work and her promise came too true. It was a very bad compliment for the trust reposed in her by the authorities of the Y.M.C.A. when they asked her to write the book.[3]

[1] *Mother India*, p. 20-21.

[2] See *The Hindu*, Madras, August 23rd and 27th, 1927; also *Indian Daily Mail*, Bombay, September 5th, 1927.

[3] At the beginning of *That Damn Y* (Houghton Mifflin Company, Boston, 1920, p. 2) Miss Mayo states the circumstances under which she undertook this investigation. Without having actual knowledge of the Y.M.C.A., she had, she says, already acquired a considerable aversion to it, and disliked the idea of coming into contact with the machine. 'Said the other party to the argument,' she proceeds : ' "Every word that you say may be true – and more

To print this statement, 'She has never seen India and never studied India at close quarters,' so generally quoted in the Indian-owned press as coming from the lips of the author of *Christ of the Indian Road*, is to give it sufficient answer.

With regard to Dr. Jones's second paragraph about Miss Mayo's war book, *That Damn Y*, a glance at the official Y.M.C.A. organ for July 1920, when the book was first made public, shows us the feeling of the organisation toward her work:

> The best perspective and survey of the Association's part in the war work has been produced in a recent book by Katherine Mayo. . . . It is the most complete, the fairest, and most readable study of the war service yet produced. Miss Mayo is a trained correspondent and a keen analyst. . . . People who jumped at conclusions from partial and hasty reports will read her book with a new vision.[1]

also. But if it is true, then what an awful thing that the American people should be entrusting to its hands millions of dollars to spend for our boys in France! Not because of the waste of money, though that would be bad enough – but because an army of simple supporters think the job is being done. If they are deceived – why, can't you see that the best service you can possibly render is to get over there, go through the field with care, and then tell America exactly what you find?"

'Finally, unwillingly persuaded,' Miss Mayo adds, 'I stated my terms: I would go to France a free agent, paying my own expenses from the start, beholden to the organisation for nothing but the right to wear its uniform and for free access to all its records and all its work. . . . I specifically emphasised my intention to state the facts as I found them, to the best of my judgment, without regard to whose feelings they might hurt.'

[1] *Association Men*, New York, July, 1920.

Not all American missionaries, by long odds, followed the seven signatories alluded to at the beginning of this chapter, and some openly resented the attacks upon *Mother India*, spread both at home and abroad by these individuals. But to declare publicly for the book needed real courage : pressure was exerted upon most missionaries to join in the attack, and those who catered to the Hindus in this instance stood to gain in prestige and popularity among the most powerful section of their public. Any missionary who supported *Mother India* had, on the other hand, nothing whatever to gain, except unpopularity and the consciousness of having honestly stood behind a conviction. Indeed, the opinion has been offered that no missionary could have written *Mother India* and remained in the country, without grave danger to his life.[1] Therefore, it would seem that both missionaries and Indians who speak out in support of the book should be given more weight than is accorded those who attack it. An example of this courage is found in the editorial of the official organ for the Baptist Mission's work in the Indian Empire, issue of January 1928 :

> Dr. Stanley Jones chose to write one side of the story only. He says in his Preface to the Sixth Edition [*Christ of the Indian Road*], 'Some of my readers have observed the absence from this text-book of certain notes usual in missionary text-books. . . Have these dark lines hitherto so common in the picture, faded out ? Is it all sweetness and light ? No these things are still there. But I

[1] See *post*, p. 147.

have left them out of the picture for three reasons.' But is he criticised for leaving them out? No! He is telling the hopeful and pleasing side. He leaves unmentioned the fact that hundreds of thousands of uneducated and educated high caste Hindus are spurning Christ and His message with all the power of their inherited bigotry and all the fervour of their ancient antagonisms. He is quiet concerning the persecution and abuse heaped on converts throughout the length and breadth of the land. He tells nothing of the disabilities of the Indian Christians in the enjoyment of public rights and privileges. But is he condemned for telling only one side of the story? No! He tells the pleasing side. But woe to the man who tells the unpleasant and forgets to soften the telling with assurances that there is another side. Miss Mayo was keenly aware of the reception her book would be accorded, for she says in Chapter I, 'In shouldering this task myself, I am fully aware of the resentments I shall incur: of the accusations of muck-raking; of injustice; of material mindedness; of lack of sympathy; of falsehood perhaps; perhaps of prudence.' Strange that word 'of falsehood *perhaps*.' If she were to write that paragraph over again after reading a few of the reviews published she would leave out the word 'perhaps.'[1]

A third one of the seven missionaries who signed the letter of protest is Dr. Alden H. Clark, M.A., D.D.

[1] *The Baptist Missionary Review*, editor, Rev. W. J. Longley, Ramapatnam, Nellore District, published by Orissa Mission Press, Cuttack, January, 1928, pp. 20, 21.

He also wrote an article, published in *The Young Men of India* and in the *Atlantic Monthly*,[1] which he named 'Is India Dying ?' He might better have called it 'Miss Mayo Lying,' for such was its burden. 'I shall attempt in this article to prove, beyond any reasonable doubt, that her basic assertions are not true,' wrote Dr. Clark ; yet in the very next paragraph he stated : 'It seems to me that she had a fresh and very powerful message on the baleful effects of sex exaggeration and on other prominent abuses, if only she had been able to present it in a balanced and friendly way.'

Dr. Clark's attack was delivered against three main points—cattle-feeding, outdoor sports, and the physical status of the male Hindu. This is the first issue as he presented it [2] :

> It seems impossible that a traveller in India could avoid seeing mile on mile of fields full of waving millet. In the villages no one could fail to note the great stacks of this fodder. . . .
>
> It seems to me in keeping with the accuracy of the other parts of the book that, in speaking of the food of cattle, it wholly neglects to notice that Indian farmers devote about forty million acres to good fodder crops and that the chapter in question closes with the assertion, 'They will not raise food for their mother the cow.'[3]

Dr. Clark gives us no authority for his total of 40,000,000 acres of fodder crops ; therefore we may

[1] 'Is India Dying ?' *Atlantic Monthly*, Boston, February 1928. Also *Young Men of India, Burma and Ceylon*, Calcutta, March 1928. [2] 'Is India Dying ?' [3] *Mother India*, p. 211.

turn to the Royal Commission on Agriculture, to which were appointed five Indian and five British members, who for two years and with every resource at their disposal investigated these conditions. In their Report, dated June 1928, we read :

> Even when all possible use has been made of existing resources of supply, a shortage of fodder is likely to arise in many parts of the country. In these circumstances, the only remedy is the cultivation of fodder crops on the cultivator's holding. For this there would appear not only to be much need, but much room, since the total area under fodder crops is somewhat less than 9,000,000 acres, or 3.5 per cent of the total area sown, as compared with 16.6 per cent. in Egypt.[1]

Or, we might take the evidence of the Director of the Institute of Plant Industry at Indore, a man who spends his life working on crop improvement and who is the author of several books on this subject. He writes : 'Practically all the millet seed grown is used for human food and practically all the dry stalks are fed to the cattle and buffaloes.'[2]

These statements, however, still leave unanswered the question as to how much so-called fodder is actually fed to cows as distinct from draught cattle, which are

[1] *Report of the Royal Commission on Agriculture in India*, His Majesty's Stationery Office, printed in India, June 1928, p. 209.

[2] Albert Howard, C.I.E., M.A., A.R.C.S., F.L.S., author of *Crop Production in India* and *Development of Indian Agriculture*, in a letter addressed to the author, dated March 25th, 1928, Institute of Plant Industry, Indore, Central India.

always the Indian cultivator's first care. The Indian and British Commissioners again testify that the cow

> . . . gets little stall feeding and has to seek the greater part of her food where she can ; young cattle and the male offspring of her rival, the she-buffalo, share her fate and pick up their livelihood on common grazing grounds . . . In nearly every part of the country, the common grazing lands, and all grass lands close to villages, are hopelessly overstocked. This view was impressed upon us by many witnesses. Expressions such as 'every village overstocked with herds of wretched starving cattle,' 'deplorably poor cattle,' 'weedy cattle eating up food,' were repeated with variations almost everywhere ; and that these statements were true we had many opportunities of seeing for ourselves.[1]

Dr. Clark's next statement, chosen to justify his condemnation of *Mother India*, may be paralleled with a second made by the same Indian and British Commissioners, who investigated the actual conditions over the period 1926-28 :

Dr. Clark

In Western India, to my personal knowledge, the farmer and his family have an affection for their cattle, each one of which is

The Commission

But he [the Indian farmer] is by no means willing to make an unusual sacrifice on behalf of his cattle. It is in this

[1] *Report of the Royal Commission on Agriculture in India*, 1928, pp. 197-198.

named. In times of scarcity the family deprives itself in order that the cattle may be fed. The concluding chapter [of *Mother India*] avers that this book states living facts. . . . But it must be plain that the general assertion that 'They will not raise food for their mother the cow' has been very easily disproved. Nor do I recollect a single one of the twenty-nine descriptive chapters which does not create its sombre impression by a similar method.[1]

last respect that he differs from the peasant of many western countries. In western lands, the stock-owner is held responsible for finding food for his cattle. . . . In India, the position is entirely different ; the custom is that the animal, when not working, should find its own food on the village common, or on uncropped land, or in the jungle, when there is no fodder available on the holding.[2]

A further charge in Dr. Clark's article is directed against *Mother India's* failure to credit Hindu mass life with an element of outdoor sport and in its implication that lack of physical exercise is in part responsible for the Hindu's sex exaggeration and frequent bodily weakness. 'What traveller could fail,' asks Dr. Clark, 'to see the little children all over India with their tops and marbles, their kites and their various ball games ? Did no one give Miss Mayo an opportunity to witness the wild excitement aroused by a wrestling match in

[1] 'Is India Dying ?'

[2] *Report of the Royal Commission on Agriculture in India*, 1928, p. 199.

village or city ?'[1] Cricket and football are enjoyed after school, he says, and his friends among the princes and Brahmans often beat him at tennis.

Let another missionary confront him :

> In regard to the play-life of the boys of India Dr. Clark takes the following words from Miss Mayo, 'give him no outlet in sports,' and in answer he refers to the little children all over India with their marbles and kites and their various ball-games and the wrestling matches in village and city. He mentions the after-school hours when every boy and young man is engaged in football, cricket and other games. He then cites the Boy Scouts and the supervised municipal play-grounds as evidence that the Indian youth has a sufficient outlet in sport. . . . Those who have toured through the villages of India know for a certainty that there is absolutely no common or general body-building and character-developing sport for the millions of boys and girls. There are a number of indigenous games which are played by the older boys and young men especially on moonlight nights. There is also the circular dance with the hitting of sticks . . . but this is often far more harmful than helpful as it is often carried on past midnight until the dancers fall exhausted. . . . Where are these play-grounds ? Certainly not in the hundreds of thousands of the villages of India. Our attention is called to the Boy Scout Movement to show that the Indian boy had an outlet

[1] 'Is India Dying ?'

> in sport. But this also is of very recent origin. In 1924 there were about 6,000 Boy Scouts in all India. To-day there are in all India, Burma and Assam 27,336 Scouts and 4,739 Cubs. (The *Indian Year Book*, 1928, page 356). That is there are about 32,000 Scouts out of over 32,000,000 boys between the ages of ten and twenty. . . . We say after as many years of village experience as our friend Dr. Clark has had that the average Indian boy has absolutely no outlet in healthful, helpful, organised, directed, body-building and character developing play or sport.[1]

Yet, after presenting his evidence, Dr. Clark wrote in condemnation of *Mother India* : 'Its sentence about "no outlet in sport" is obviously untrue.'

A third argument offered to controvert *Mother India* concerns the age of motherhood. After repeating the stock statements already used at the Hindu 'protest meetings,' Dr. Clark quotes, in their support, the words of a census investigator in the Punjab, completely ignoring the facts that the Punjab is one of the few Provinces where the Muhammadans, with whom early marriage is not a religious custom, are in the majority ; and that *Mother India* on the point of early marriages explicitly limited itself to the Hindus. The Punjab investigator, Clark announces,

> discovered that 'in the majority of cases the first child is born in the third year of effective marriage.' Apparently he is the only census investigator who studied this question, but there is no reason

[1] *The Baptist Missionary Review*, May 1928, pp. 212-213.

to suppose that his finding would not be true of other parts of India. This would bring motherhood in most cases to the fifteenth year at the lowest.[1]

According to this analysis, then, even in the Punjab cohabitation begins at twelve. This is the ground upon which Dr. Clark challenged the statement that 'the Hindu girl, in common practice, looks for motherhood . . . between the ages of fourteen and eight.'[2]

The Baptist Missionary Review, above quoted, is edited and published in India. From that vantage point it tears to pieces Clark's words denying the evils of child marriage, and then proceeds to bring forward an incontrovertible native authority—Dr. (Mrs.) Muthulakshmi Reddi, M.L.C. This lady practitioner wrote in the *Madras Mail* of February 23rd, 1928, championing the cause of those millions of voiceless sufferers whose miseries Dr. Clark seeks to belittle:

> As in my experience of 16 years of medical practice among the higher class Hindus, I have come across many sad facts which if revealed would be shocking to the civilised world, I feel that fairness and justice demand that I should express what I feel on this important question. . . . First of all I am prompted to ask, what glory, what culture, what boast of civilisation, what mutual happiness between the husband and wife and what beauty of womanhood could there be in a system that makes tender children of twelve, thirteen and fourteen with . . . immature generative organs to undergo

[1] 'Is India Dying?' [2] *Mother India*, pp. 29-30.

the severe ordeal of wifehood and motherhood with the result that very often the organ of reproduction expels the products of conception ending in abortions and miscarriages which Brahmin girls seldom escape. . . . There is a Brahmin patient under my care just now who with all the facilities of treatment that modern science could afford has been repeatedly miscarrying in her eighth month of pregnancy and thus has been denied the supreme happiness of clasping the precious form of her own dear babe to her breast. There is another patient who has been sharing in a similar fate and suffering from repeated missed abortions, herself having been nuptialised in her twelfth year. I can quote hundreds of such cases. . . . . They deserve our fullest sympathy and deep consideration, but what to think of those B.A.'s, M.A.'s, and B.L.'s who cry that 'Religion is in danger.' . . .

Again it was only last year that I attended on a similar case, a girl of 13 and that too in a medico's house, the girl did not even understand why she was suffering, was crying day and night like a small helpless babe cursing her parents and when the baby was actually born she got so cross that she would not handle it nor nurse it for the first two days. . . .[1]

And, answering specifically all those who denounce *Mother India* as based on evidence that is ancient and out of date, this lady concludes :

[1] *The Baptist Missionary Review*, May 1928, pp. 214-215.

> So, if the orthodox should still persist . . . I will be put to the necessity of publishing a list of cases, many of such are even to-day to be found at Madras in the well-to-do and educated families, to support Miss Mayo on the evils of early marriage and the incontinence of the Brahmin youth in spite of his weak and undeveloped physique and poor diet.[1]

In addition to his *Atlantic Monthly* article Dr. Clark has written two letters addressed to the Indian press about *Mother India* and its author. The first reported the action he was taking :

> The very day on which I first had opportunity to read *Mother India*, I sent to America a brief review of it, which has just been published, in which I said, among other things, that I was ashamed that a fellow American should write a book whose picture of India was a 'slimy caricature.' . . . I myself had 400 copies of this statement [National Christian Council] struck off and am sending them to a wide constituency in America. . . . I have myself gathered what seems

[1] Dr. (Mrs.) S. Muthulakshmi actually adduced, as illustrative of her argument, the following two cases, similar to those in Appendix I of *Mother India*, in the Madras Legislative Council :

'I. The Triplicane case of a child wife having been burnt to death because she would not satisfy the animal passion of the husband is still fresh in our memory.

'II. I can never forget the case of a girl wife of 12 who looked in her development like a child of 10 having been forced to live with her husband who was an M.A., and who was well over 40, a huge figure, even before the girl attained her puberty.'

Proceedings of the Legislative Council of Madras, official report, March 27th, 1928, p. 31.

to me to be conclusive evidence against many of Miss Mayo's worst mis-statements and have sent it to Miss Mayo in the form of a letter with an appeal to her, in the name of truth and goodwill, to withdraw the book.[1]

(Signed) A. H. CLARK.[2]

Dr. Clark's second letter makes an interesting sequel to the above :

> We agree with Mahatma Gandhi, Mrs. Sarojini Naidu and many other candid readers that the book contains much terrible truth. We hope and believe that this truth, even as presented by Miss Mayo, may do good. But this is not the side of the case which we are emphasising to America. In America, by pen and by voice we are repudiating the fundamental attitude of *Mother India* and are doing our best to refute its repulsive errors.[3]

And so Dr. Stanley Jones, Bishop Fred B. Fisher, the Rev Dr. Alden H. Clark, and their four brother missionaries[4] proclaim *Mother India* unjust and untrue, and themselves humiliated that an American should have written it.

Another instance of reckless irresponsibility emanating from a Western member of holy orders, this time

[1] Miss Mayo informs me that she does not recall having received this or any other communication from Dr. Clark.

[2] *Indian Social Reformer*, Bombay, December 10th, 1927.

[3] Letter from the Rev. Alden H. Clark of the American Marathi Mission, Ahmednagar, in *The Hindu*, Madras, March 10th, 1928.

[4] The names of the other four who signed the letter of protest (see *ante* p. 121) are : Alice B. Van Doren, J. DeBoer, Mason Olcott, and D. F. McClelland. *The Hindu*, Madras, December 17th, 1927.

a British Y.M.C.A. official, is contained in a document addressed to a prominent New Yorker and written on the Association's official letterhead from its Calcutta headquarters. Referring to the author of *Mother India*, it reads :

> . . . she is nothing but a paid propagandist for a group of die-hards in England. . . . I have heard from very good authorities certain things which bear this out, and the book itself is the strongest evidence for it. . . Either Miss Mayo is one of the most ignorant investigators, who have ever set out on such a survey, or she is one of the most clever and malicious propagandists that the world has seen.

This same writer interviewed Miss Mona Bose, principal of the Victoria School for girls, Lahore, one of the Indian witnesses quoted in *Mother India*, and thus reported his inquiry : 'I have consulted this lady and find that a great many of the things printed in inverted commas were never spoken.'[1] Then after entering into details of the inaccuracies, he adds :

> I have felt it necessary to deal with this rather extensively because it is a case which I have been able to investigate, and here we find an entire lack of appreciation for strict accuracy. It is most likely that in the innumerable quotations given without names the same inaccuracy would be found.[2]

[1] The original signed article appeared in *The Indian Witness*, September 7th, 1927. It has been largely used in the replies ; for instance, see *Unhappy India*, p. li ; K. Natarajan's *Miss Mayo's Mother India, A Rejoinder*, p. 98. [2] *Ibid.*

In this case I have seen the notes Miss Mayo took at the time, which she did not return to Miss Bose for correction. I find, however, that two witnesses[1] were present throughout the interview, and both have confirmed the report set down in *Mother India* from the notes.

But what seems equally pertinent to the case is the comment of the American editor of *The Baptist Missionary Review*, himself a missionary in India. Referring to the Y.M.C.A. secretary's statement, just quoted, that 'a great many of the things printed in inverted commas were never spoken,' he says :

> If the reader will turn to page 138-9 of *Mother India* (American edition) [132-33 Cape edition] he will see that the 'many things' consist of three paragraphs. That Miss Bose would find it necessary to deny these statements we cannot understand, for they certainly are correct as to conditions existing in many schools. They are not startling statements but simply the fact that girls from the high caste homes will not sit or eat with low caste girls and that Indians are not over anxious to pay for the education of their girls. Both of these facts are undeniable.[2]

[1] These two witnesses, one American and one British, are both women of unquestionable responsibility. Their names are withheld at their own request.

[2] *The Baptist Missionary Review*, January 1928, p. 23.

CHAPTER X

THE NATIONAL CHRISTIAN COUNCIL

THE National Christian Council of India, Burma, and Ceylon issued a statement in October 1927 'to the people of India,' with the object of denouncing *Mother India*, of publicly washing their hands of it, and of repudiating any possible idea 'that the book was promoted in the interests of missionary propaganda.' It continued :

> . . . the picture of India which emerges from Miss Mayo's book is untrue to facts and unjust to the people of India. The sweeping generalisations that are deduced from the incidents that came to the notice of the author, or, that are suggested by the manner in which these incidents are presented, are entirely untrue as a description of India as a whole.[1]

This statement, signed by the Rev. Dr. Macnicol and Mr. P. C. Philip, secretaries, was broadcasted far and wide, so that it is not surprising if, in some quarters, it has come to be regarded as the repesentative view of the Christian missionaries in India.

That the majority of missionaries in the field were misrepresented by this action of the upper few, can scarcely be doubted ; nor should they be asked to

[1] This statement was sent around the world. I find it in the following Indian-owned papers : *Bombay Daily Mail*, October 18th, 1927 ; *Indian National Herald*, Bombay, October 18th, 1927 ; *Amrita Bazar Patrika*, Calcutta, October 20th, 1927 ; *Indian Social Reformer*, October 22nd, 1927, etc.

accept its responsibility. But their voices, in support of *Mother India*, were slow to reach America, and for two reasons: first, because, until quite recently, whether by order or by choice, many have kept their views private, excepting for personal letters to their friends; and second, because magazines supported by missionary funds, while welcoming critical views, have in several known instances refused statements supporting *Mother India*.

The following letter, appearing in *The Times of India*, from the pen of the Rev. James Smith, is of the kind that missionary magazines have refused:

> There appeared in your issue of the 19th instant a statement purporting to be from the National Christian Council of India, Burmah and Ceylon. I note that Bishop J. W. Robinson dissented from it and I wonder how many more members of the Committee would have dissented, if they had been consulted.[1] I am quite certain that the vast body of missionaries would have done so. Had Dr. Macnicol stopped at repudiating missionary connection with the book, no-one would have cared, but even that was not necessary in my opinion, as no responsible person has charged us with having any connection with Miss Mayo or her book. The book was written for one purpose only, to depict certain social evils, the existence of which had been denied in America and the author has

[1] In a letter appearing in the same paper on November 8th, 1927, Dr. Macnicol states: 'All members of the Committee were consulted with the exception of the Metropolitan and Dr. S. K. Datta, both of whom are out of India.'

confined herself closely to her subject. There was no occasion whatever in such a book to dilate upon 'culture, kindliness, charm, religion and piety' as Dr. Macnicol and his friends desire. These virtues had never been denied by anybody. She has supported her charges of the ill-treatment of women and children by many incidents that have not been and cannot be denied. I can from my own personal recollection tell many incidents of equal atrocity with any Miss Mayo has told in her book, and it is because of my knowledge of such abominations that my sympathies go out to the countless millions who undergo such cruelties. I have seen thousands of wedding processions and cannot recall ever having seen one 'marriageable' bride, while several of them were babies under a year old. I knew at least three men of 40 to 45 that married children of 7 to 10 years. These three were all Brahmins too, and one of them a graduate of very high culture and charm of manner.[1]

Another missionary opinion, which has remained unbroadcast since it differs from that of the National Christian Council, notes that body's widely published repudiation of *Mother India* as 'missionary propaganda,' and then asks :

> Are not sin, superstition, idolatry, bigotry, lack of compassion as shown in the evils of the caste system, are not these challenges to the Gospel of Christ ? We do not want the book used as 'Missionary Propaganda,'—we hate that word. Let

[1] *The Times of India*, Bombay, November 1st, 1927.

> us stop using it! But we honestly believe that every missionary, every Indian pastor and Christian worker and every reformer and social service worker, should have this book and read and study it carefully and then consecrate himself anew to the freeing of 'Mother India' from these terrible conditions. The Apostle Paul did not mince matters. . . . Read the Epistle to the Romans from the 18th verse of first chapter, through the second chapter and you will find things much worse than anything shown in Miss Mayo's book.[1]

And *The Indian Witness*, the Methodist official mouthpiece in Southern Asia, after editorially denouncing the book as 'not a true picture of India,' proceeds in a totally different vein :

> The writer was publicly questioned last year after an address to an audience composed mainly of non-Christians [Indians] as to why missionaries and other Christians in India were now saying so little against child marriage, enforced widowhood and the *purdah* system and the questioners declared themselves unsatisfied by the reply that Hindus and Moslems are now dealing so vigorously with these evils that there does not seem to be the same need as there was in former years for Christians to deal with them. They declared their fear that familiarity had made Christians condone what they once condemned. There is no doubt that acquaintance with bad custom, if unaccom-

[1] Editorial in *The Baptist Missionary Review*, editor, Rev. W. J. Longley, January 1928, pp. 21-22.

panied by persistent effort to destroy it, tends to make one indifferent to it or even unconscious of its evil aspects.[1]

Whether or not this last sentence is an admission that certain missionaries have ceased making efforts to rid India of evil customs, the reader must judge for himself. The editorial continues :

> Missionaries are criticised by Miss Mayo for not writing and talking more about these conditions in Indian life. She suggests that they have betrayed the weak, the mistreated, the suffering by keeping quiet. The same charge is made by a Hindu friend who in a personal letter to the Editor praises Miss Mayo's book, refers to her as 'the noble lady who by her book has done more for India than any living person,' and says 'you missionaries have sought the favour of oppressors whom you meet and have forgotten the oppressed who are hidden from your sight.''[2]

And this pronouncement of the official organ of the Methodist Episcopal Church frankly adds : 'There may be some truth in what Miss Mayo and our Hindu correspondent suggest.'

Eight weeks later, the same paper prints a letter from Bhagat Ram, whom it describes as 'a Hindu gentleman of the Punjab who carries on an active propaganda for better treatment of women, children and dumb animals.' The letter runs :

[1] *The Indian Witness*, J. Waskom Pickett, editor, Lucknow, November 2nd, 1927. [2] *Ibid.*

> It is said that the great Saviour came here to seek and save the sick and sorrowful. Being led by mere paper arguments of some of the Indian politicians, or perhaps being influenced by some of their friends among the mighty Indian millionaires, it appears that a few Christians have begun speaking against that sympathiser of Indian womanhood, Miss Katherine Mayo. It may be easy to leave suffering humanity in the lurch, and it is not so easy to help the helpless women here. To take the side of the mighty to the detriment of the oppressed, I fear, will never be acceptable to the Merciful Lord.
>
> So it would be quite in keeping with the ministry of the Lord of Sorrows, if His servants should choose to do everything that can be done to help on the cause of the poor helpless women and children of India.[1]

Such reproofs, coming, as they do, from Hindus themselves, should make members of the National Christian Council pause to reflect. Alarmed at the acknowledged inroads that Christianity is making among their traditional slaves, the Untouchables, have the Brahmans determined to distract the missionary's effort by courting his friendship and by affecting to 'accept Christ,' the better to drown Him in their bottomless sea of thirty-three million gods? By cunning, not by open force, throughout the centuries the Brahman has ruled his people—has overcome Buddhism and driven it into the mountains and beyond the

[1] *The Indian Witness*, December 28th, 1927.

seas. That cunning seems more than a match for the uncertain Western missionary.

That the idea of Christ is influencing a greater number of persons in India than the less than 2 per cent.[1] who actually profess Christianity is probably true. Yet when the Protestant missions face the facts regarding their fully fledged members they have very real cause for consternation. At a representative conference, where over a score of different churches and missionary societies were represented, the report of the enquiry into the quality of Christian leadership in business and public service bears the following note:

> There are in India to-day about 49,000 paid Indian Christian workers and the number of communicants or church members in full standing is about 740,000. This means that about one in fifteen of the adult church membership of the Protestant Churches in India are the employees of missions. It is safe to assume that one earning member supports on the average at least two adults. If that is so the economic dependence of the Indian Christian community on foreign missions is seen in its true proportions.[2]

By accepting the assumption that each worker supports two other communicants, we find that not one

[1] The total number of Indian Christians is 4,332,578, excluding Burma and Ceylon. *Biennial Survey of Occupation and Directory of Christian Missions in India, Burma, and Ceylon*, Scottish Mission Industries Company, Ajmer, 1926-27, p. xxiv.

[2] The Kodaikanal Missionary Union's Annual Conference, May 1928, as reported in *The Baptist Missionary Review*, August 1928, p. 352.

in fifteen but almost one in five of the total Indian Protestant communicants are dependent for their livelihood on the funds of foreign missions!

At the 1928 meeting of the Fellowship Council—a conference largely attended by Christian missionaries as well as by Hindus and Moslems—the question was raised as to[1] 'how far the Fellowship could remain true to its ideal, if those who belonged to it wished to convert others to their own Faith?' Mr. Gandhi personally took part in this debate; and his stand is thus reported by his friend, C. F. Andrews, also present:

> At the back of the question, there was a definite challenge to the whole Christian missionary position in India. Missionaries of a liberal type of mind had been finding great joy in the Fellowship. . . . Then came Mahatma Gandhi's declaration. He stated that if in doing so, or in joining the Fellowship, there was the slightest wish, or even the slightest thought at the back of the mind, to influence, or convert, any other member of the Fellowship, then the spirit of the movement could be destroyed. Anyone who had such a wish ought to leave the Fellowship.[2]

Did these apostles of Christianity reaffirm their vows to spread the Gospel? We read on: 'This,' says Mr. Andrews, 'puts the Christian missionaries into a very difficult position.'[3]

[1] 'The Basis of Inter-religious Fellowship,' by C. F. Andrews, M.A., in *The Young Men of India, Burma and Ceylon*, June 1928, Vol. XL, No 6, pp. 322-323. [2] *Ibid.* [3] *Ibid.*

Yet they did muster spirit to challenge the Indian 'saint'; they did ask him 'whether, if they possessed the greatest treasure in all the world, they would be wrong in wishing to share it.'

But Gandhi was quick to rebuff their presumption. 'He was adamant,'[1] Mr. Andrews tells us. 'Even the idea of such a desire was wrong, he said emphatically; and he would not move from that position at all.'

And so our Christian soldiers, American or British, took their orders, while the Y.M.C.A.'s official organ obligingly continues:

> On the whole, the International Fellowship Council was wise in not passing any resolution on the subject. The matter was left open. . . .[2]

Some Christians in India, however, are not quite so docile. Says the official Baptist mouthpiece, speaking editorially of Mr. Andrews's article:

> It seems to us unbelievable that any true Christian can hesitate a moment on such a proposition. Not only does Mr. Gandhi interdict open and verbal propaganda, but he places his ban on the secret thoughts of the heart. . . . We believe it would have been far better if the Council had taken a definite action either upholding Mr. Gandhi's position or emphatically repudiating it.[3]

Meanwhile, the attack of the National Christian Council drove more and more conscience-smitten mis-

[1] *Young Men of India, Burma and Ceylon*, June 1928, p. 323.
[2] *Ibid.*
[3] *The Baptist Missionary Review*, August 1928, pp. 363-364.

sionaries to voice indignant protests. Many of these have crossed the seas in the form of personal letters. But it would be unfair, by quoting these, to expose generous-minded men and women hard at work in their field to such disciplinary measures as their seniors on the Council might see fit to visit upon them. Little harm, however, can come from publishing the expressions of those who have definitely retired from missionary labours. Such a one is this :

> I went to India, a single lady missionary, in 1878 ; and returned finally from there in 1924. I have just completed reading your book *Mother India* and feel like telling you how thankful I am that you have had an opportunity of seeing at first hand, and that you have been able to put it into print as you have. . . . I think every phase of Indian affairs that you discuss, religious, political, economic, social and moral has been handled very impartially, and so many of your statements are amply supported by satisfactory proofs. It is an awful book, but warranted by prevailing conditions there ; and I am glad you have so clearly let the light in.
>
> It confirms all that some missionaries have stated, but no missionary could have written it and remained in the country ; his life would not have been worth much. I know the soul suffering that I often endured while at work there ; but, were I young, I would return to-morrow.[1]

[1] The author has copied the original document which is in Miss Mayo's possession.

In this communication the writer, Mrs. C. H. Archibald, requested that her name be left unknown. But less than a month later came another note from her, saying: 'I have been reading some things about your book that have stirred me considerably. And I now give you permission to use the statements in my first letter, my name, too.'

In a third letter, this same lady writes: 'I have this last week the opinions of three of our missionaries, all commending the book and calling upon others that it be read.'[1]

Another missionary, of over thirty-three years' medical service, the founder and principal of the famous Women's Christian Medical College at Ludhiana—in the Punjab—is reported in *The Christian* of May 31st, 1928, to have recently made a six weeks' tour inspecting the field work of forty-seven women medical graduates from her college. This lady, Dr. Edith Brown, was accompanied by her London secretary. Their home organisation reports:

> During their 5,000 mile tour these friends asked many of the lady doctors they met, 'Is *Mother India* true?' All sadly confirmed the medical statements therein.

And finally, because of the value of the witness and because of his original criticism of *Mother India*, the following letter, addressed to Miss Mayo by the Right Reverend Henry Whitehead, for twenty-three years Bishop of Madras, must be cited:

[1] Taken from the originals in the possession of the addressed.

May I state the impression that the book [*Mother India*] has left on my own mind? It did not tell me anything new. During the time of my service in India, close on 40 years, I came to know of all the moral and social evils that you describe; most of them have been discussed publicly in India during the last sixty or seventy years, and efforts have been made by a series of earnest and able social reformers, both Indian and European, to find a remedy for them, though with singularly little success.

But *Mother India* did disquiet my conscience. It compelled me to ask whether I ought not to have made far more effort to awaken the Hindus, to whom I was sent, to the cruelty and inhumanity which those evils involve.

The view I took was that the evils you describe are deeply rooted in the Hindu religion, and that my business as a Christian Missionary was to lay the axe to the root of the tree rather than to deal with the fruits. But I am not sure that I was right. St. John Baptist's call to repentance came before the preaching of the Kingdom of God.

If I may venture to make one small criticism of your book, it is that, though the connection of the evils you describe with Hindu religious ideas is mentioned, it might be more strongly emphasised.

It is this religious sanction that has made the efforts, often the splendid and courageous efforts, of Indian social reformers so ineffective.

Take the case of sexual immorality. I do not think that the people of the West are by nature purer than the peoples of India. But we in the West have the inestimable advantage of a religion that stands for purity and righteousness.

Try to imagine what London would be like if in St. Paul's Cathedral, Westminster Abbey and other leading churches large establishments of prostitutes had been kept for centuries past for the use of the clergy and worshippers. What chance would reformers have of raising or even maintaining the standard of sexual morality?

Yet that would be parallel to the state of affairs actually existing in South India where the *Devadasis*, women and little children married to the god and maintained as prostitutes, have for many centuries been kept in the large temples. You have described the system in one of the chapters of your book and your description is painfully true. It is the consecration of immorality by the sanction of religion. . . .[1]

Sulham House, HENRY WHITEHEAD
Pangbourne, June 2nd, 1928. Bishop

[1] *Slaves of the Gods*, Katherine Mayo; Jonathan Cape, London, 1929, pp. 12-15.

CHAPTER XI

DEVADASIS AND PROSTITUTES

DURING a meeting that I attended in London, at which *Mother India* was the subject of discussion, the lately retired Bishop of Madras made a criticism identical with that which he expresses in the letter just transcribed. On that occasion, shortly after the Bishop resumed his seat, he withdrew from the meeting; whereupon a young Madrassee Hindu rose to his feet to deny categorically the very existence of devadasis in India. 'It is not true that Hindu temples have girls who act as prostitutes to the priests and worshippers,' he said in effect.

This pronouncement was received with a gasp, which seemed to fill the room; for not only the Bishop but the majority of people in the audience had spent the best part of their lives in India.

When the meeting was over two ladies of long Indian experience asked the Hindu spokesman why he denied the Bishop's statement, which they themselves, from their own personal experience, knew to be the bare truth. The Hindu's eyes dilated; his expression grew excited; at last he exclaimed, vehemently, 'It's true to you, but not true to me!'

And it was useless to point out to this young man that a fellow-countrywoman of his—herself a Madrassee—less than six months previous had proposed a resolution in the Madras Legislature which read:

This Council recommends to the Government to

> undertake legislation or if that is for any reason impracticable, to recommend to the Government of India to undertake legislation at a very early date to put a stop to the practice of dedication of young girls and young women to Hindu temples for immoral purposes under the pretext of caste, custom or religion.[1]

To that young man in London, with his Hindu training and his Hindu mind, the life of a devadasi appeared not as one of shame but of sacred consecration to the Hindu gods. Here we face sharply what appears to the Western mind an untenable position, but what is in reality a perfectly normal working of a Hindu-trained brain. Facts which are for any reason whatsoever inconvenient or shameful can be banished in the twinkling of an eye—for, the whole material world being rated as an illusion, it follows that any material phenomenon, especially if its appearance is embarrassing, may be declared not to exist. Yet, in her speech introducing the above resolution, Dr. (Mrs.) Muthulakshmi Reddi pointed out that thousands of young innocent children are condemned to a life of 'immorality and vice,' of suffering and disease, and finally of death, resulting from infections and venereal diseases contracted in the pursuit of their profession as Hindu religious prostitutes.[2]

Another Hindu, this time a member of the Central Legislature and author of *Father India*, gives us a further example of the Hindu mind at work. First he

[1] *Proceedings of the Legislative Council of Madras*, official report, November 4th, 1927, p. 415.

[2] *Ibid*, p. 415. See her entire speech.

freely acknowledges that devadasis exist 'in the parts of India which Miss Mayo mentions.'[1] But to him their life is not abhorrent, and for what is, to his way of thinking, a perfectly good reason :

> In India, the prostitutes form a class by themselves. It is untrue to say that they belong to respectable families of rank and position. The mother of a prostitute was a prostitute once. The daughter becomes a prostitute. . . . The idea of allowing the young girls of the prostitute class to grow in the atmosphere of the temples is to instil into them some religion, some fear of God, so that when they come of age they may not indulge in promiscuity, but be the mistress of one man. The prostitutes of India are, therefore, one of the most god-fearing and loyal class of mistresses known to that unfortunate profession.[2]

Accepting Mr. Ranga Iyer's standard as faithful to his religion, accepting his explanation, therefore, as sincere, we find nevertheless that in his major statement he is misleading us. Only daughters of prostitutes, he would have us believe, are recruited to the devadasi ranks. But turning to our former and unchallengeable authority, we find her addressing her fellow Hindus in the Madras Legislature in these words :

> It is a well-known fact that the devadasis are recruited from various castes among the Hindus having different names in different districts and

[1] *Father India*, C. S. Ranga Iyer, p. 51.
[2] *Ibid.*, pp. 51-52.

> that their strength is kept up by adoption from other Hindu communities because when the old devadasis become sterile, which they very often are by the nature of their profession, they buy girls from other caste-Hindus and so, every Hindu community at one time or other shares in the degradation and misery of such a life.[1]

Or again :

> I may point out for the benefit of the non-Hindu Members of this Council that these women do not belong to the brothel class and that they are only the victims of tradition, custom or mistaken religious fervour. . . .[2]

Regarding the kind of religion that, as *Father India* pleads, the temples instil into these children, this lady doctor says :[3]

> First of all, these innocent children are made victims and are prepared for an immoral life by a course of training from their early days. Secondly, the temple and the illiterate Hindu public are responsible for developing a kind of mentality in those children which makes them, when they grow to be women, view a criminal, unholy and anti-social act . . . as a hereditary right and a caste *dharma*.[4]

[1] Dr. (Mrs.) S. Muthulakshmi Reddi in the *Legislative Council of Madras*, official report, November 4th, 1927, p. 416.

[2] *Ibid.*, November 5th, 1927, p. 514.

[3] Dr. (Mrs.) S. Muthulakshmi Reddi in the *Legislative Council of Madras*, November 5th, 1927, p. 514.

[4] *Dharma* means custom or duty.

In following the legislative debate upon Dr. Reddi's resolution, we are struck with the frequency with which the author of *Mother India* is mentioned: 'Why should we sanctify vice by giving it the cloak of a religious custom and allow persons like Miss Mayo to hold us up to ridicule for tolerating such a sinful practice in the temples?'[1] asks one member while supporting the motion. But the Diwan Bahadur M. Krishnan Nayar is even more explicit in his brief and pointed speech:

> I wish to say just a word on this resolution. My party has resolved to support this motion. The resolution is on very sound lines; and it is the existence of customs like the one referred to in this resolution that gives a handle to enemies of India like Miss Mayo to write books like *Mother India.* The abolition of this custom will prevent the existence of at least one source of adverse comment from persons like Miss Mayo. I have no desire to say more than this; and indeed, no further words in support of the resolution seem necessary.[2]

Here, again, is evidence, all the stronger for its grudging nature, of a new hope for some of the victims of the Hindu social system—hope directly attributed to a frank American exposé often bitterly resented by those whose ancient advantages it threatens.

The resolution to do away with the condemnation of children to temple prostitution called forth a manifesto,

[1] Mr. A. B. Shetty in the *Legislative Council Debates of Madras,* November 5th, 1927, p. 519. [2] *Ibid.*, p. 522.

addressed to Government, from the members of the Devadasi Association of Madras. This body—claiming to represent 200,000 members[1]—humbly submits to the Government for consideration :

> . . . that we have to our credit the support of the entire Devadasi class, with very few honourable exceptions who are our enemies ; the support of Sastras such as, Pancharatra, Vaikhanasa, Puranas, Upanishads,[2] Customs and Traditions, the support of the Pandits and the Hindu society in general drawn from all classes and castes ; the support of the public as may be known from the several protest meetings held all over the presidency and the volume of opinion gathering every day from the press.[3]

Finally, the manifesto makes 'An Appeal to the Public' :

> The Devadasis are to-day proposed to be destroyed ; Hindu girls may follow next, widows may take their chance later ; temples may be demolished, worship desecrated and we shall be torn asunder from all traditions. Our Hindu brethren who love Hindu Gods and who worship in the Hindu Temples come to our rescue and save us from peril.[4]

[1] *The Dedication Bill, Manifesto to the Madras Government by the Members of the Devadasi Association*, Aurora Press, Madras, December 1927, p. 9.

[2] This is a list of leading Hindu sacred writings.

[3] *Manifesto to the Madras Government by the Members of the Devadasi Association*, December 1927, p. 16.

[4] *Ibid.*, last page.

Just one sample of the distorted appeals made in the name of the Hindu religion to the orthodox millions who worship in Hindu temples, and this one represented as emanating from the victims themselves !

Sections 372 and 373 of the Indian Penal Code prohibit the disposal and possession of girls under eighteen with the intent that they be employed, or used, for the purpose of prostitution. And, it is claimed, Hindu religious tenets prohibit the practice above sixteen ; therefore, those who defend the infamous institution hold that, between the law and their church, there is no need for further legislation.[1]

But, says an article in the *Madras Law College Magazine* : 'The legislative efforts . . . have not resulted in placing on the Statute Book an Act to effectively prevent the dedication of minor girls to temples and consigning them to lives of open prostitution in the name of religious ritual or social custom.'[2]

And Dr. Reddi unveils one way of getting around the Penal Code :

> . . . to my personal knowledge the law has been rendered ineffective by the guardians or the parents of the girls waiting till the completion of the

[1] 'Above the age of 16, the religious tenets prohibit their [Devadasis'] enrolment. A girl to be dedicated according to the rules, which have been observed from time immemorial, must be a virgin, and therefore they took care when this practice was instituted to dedicate girls under the age of 14. No temple authority would ever think of dedicating a girl to the temple who is above the age of 14.' Rao Bahadur T. Rangachariar, member for Madras City. *Legislative Assembly Debates*, February 27th, 1922, p. 2,604.

[2] Reprinted in *The Indian Social Reformer*, September 22nd, 1928.

> eighteenth year and then dedicating them to the temples. Many a girl has been brought to me for a certificate to say the girl has attained 18. . . . I will repeat once more that any amount of outside legislation or Penal Code Amendment will not take us one step further unless the temples are reformed.[1]

Not only has legislation intended to reform the temples failed each time it has been tried, but every attempt has been, and is, fraught with difficulties and dangers. Even in some States of literate America the masses still retain, to no small degree, their religious fanaticism ; how much more, then, the masses in illiterate Hindustan, who are, as were the peoples of mediæval Europe, ignorant, priest-ridden, and violently reactionable to religious excitation.

A handful of devoted individuals are, however, at work endeavouring to rescue innocent devadasi prospects before it is too late. These efforts are led by foreigners. Outstanding among them is a certain English lady missionary, who for over twenty years has devoted her life to this task, and, with her helpers, has saved several hundred Hindu children, boys as well as girls, from temple dedication. This is one of the many tributes paid to her child-sanctuary :

> There was something in the place that could be seen only through prayerful eyes. The three hundred children lived in cottages, each cottage under an Indian girl with about a dozen tiny children in

[1] *Proceedings of the Madras Legislative Council*, official report, November 5th, 1927, p. 513.

> her charge. 'How much do you pay these young women who care for all these children ?' I asked. The lady replied, 'It is very expensive work, for they have to be up at all hours of the day and night – it is too expensive to pay for, so none of us get any salary, we all do it through love.' . . . And love in turn brought forth joy. I have never seen such joy on the faces of people. They shone. . . . .[1]

A few will say : Yes, but how much better if such a woman spent her time, energy, and leadership at home helping our Western girls from becoming public prostitutes, instead of travelling thousands of miles to interfere where she is not wanted, and in a matter which also exists under our very noses in each of our own cities.

It neither can be nor is denied that licensed houses are still maintained even in some parts of the United States, while in London, at eventide, some streets are little better, and in other Western cities such places, if not openly licensed, are frequently only disguised under more innocent names, as massage saloons, baths, dance halls, or manicure parlours. The West, too, has its precocious, nature-offending children, its advocates of free love, and its large number of promiscuous women. We, too, have our white slavers and defilers of young children, among the many stains on our Western civilisation.

But do we defend them ? Defend them in the name of our religion ?

[1] *Christ at the Round Table*, E. Stanley Jones, Abingdon Press, New York, 1928, p. 107.

Does our Christianity demand or commend them?

Bishop Whitehead, with one swift gesture put his finger on the difference between our civilisation and that of Hindu India when he asked: 'What chance would our reformers have of raising or even maintaining the standard of sex morality, if our cathedrals and large churches kept houses of prostitution for the use of priests and congregations?'

As has been shown, it was to the Hindu sacred writings and to the Hindu religious teachers that the members of the Devadasi Association referred Government for the warrant of their calling; and the sending out of 'procurers' to replenish their ranks—the buying of the widow's daughter so that she may be 'married to the gods'—is nothing better than our white slave traffic operating under the protection of a religious cloak.

India, like the West, has men who trade in women and children solely for personal profit, apart from any religious commands.[1] And it may well be asked, as Bishop Whitehead does ask, what hope has she of abolishing this trade so long as the Hindu temples and the Hindu religion set the example and are the site and seal of offence?

Four of the nine books written to controvert *Mother India*, are, for a large part, devoted to sexual immoralities still prevailing in the West, especially in America. But, so long as Hinduism and Christianity

[1] 'The population of Karachi city is 200,000 and out of this 25,000 people might be living on sale of girls.' Dr. G. T. Hingorani, giving evidence before the Age of Consent Committee at Karachi, as reported in *The Indian Social Reformer*, Bombay, October 13th, 1928.

are diametrically opposed in their outlook upon social evils, the *tu quoque* argument upon this matter has no bearing whatsoever.

Those who live by vice in the West recognise themselves as enemies of organised society and exist in perpetual fear of the police.[1] In India, on the other hand, traders in women and children are well known. But, because of the little or no public opinion against their activities, and because of the religious sanction their profession enjoys, these traders proceed openly in their transactions without the slightest social stigma fastening itself to their skirts.

Just here is where we of the West can help. India is extremely sensitive to our opinion. Exactly how far the searchlight of Western knowledge and understanding, turned upon these problems, will rout India's dark shadows has yet to be proved. But no small tribute to its power was paid in November 1927 by Mr. Syed Ibrahim, who, bearing witness to the present tumult in the Hindu ranks occasioned by our Western scrutiny, declared it our duty to hold the beam steady until the wrongs are righted. Said Mr. Ibrahim, addressing the Madras Legislature :

> It is only now when the institution of Devadasis is being tolerated by the Hindu society that the true Hindu religion is in danger of attack, not only by missionary religious bodies in this country but also by mischievous nonentities hailing from far off countries, who pose as reformers of humanity. I am referring particularly to the attacks

[1] *The Road to Buenos Ayres*, Albert Londres, Boni and Liveright, New York, 1928.

of Miss Katherine Mayo against Indian manners, customs and habits of life as recorded in her book *Mother India*. The whole of the Indian nation has with one voice protested, and rightly protested against her infamous attacks. Recording angel only knows how many millions of words have been spoken against her attacks. The moral indignation of the nation rose to the highest pitch. But I now here ask, 'Is the exhibition of such indignation alone sufficient to proclaim the morality and the social purity of the nation ?' I think not. Unless the Hindus with one voice rise to do away with this social canker and social leprosy of the institution of Devadasis, I am afraid the whole world, not merely a Miss Mayo, has got the right, nay, duty to hold the finger of scorn against India, Hinduism and Hindus.[1]

[1] *Proceedings of the Legislative Council of Madras*, November 5th, 1927, p. 523.

CHAPTER XII

THEIR VOICE IS HEARD

ONE evening last winter I was invited to discuss *Mother India* with a few friends in a New York City club. Upon my arrival I found to my surprise that a regular meeting had been arranged, also that some fifteen Indian students, mostly from the International House,[1] had been invited to attend. When I finished my address almost every Hindu in the room sprang to his feet signifying a desire to reply. The chairman gave four of them five minutes each, and during that twenty minutes I listened to many wild stories about India, as well as about myself. The chairman kindly handled the personal attacks, but as nobody in the audience except our Indian friends professed any knowledge of the subject under discussion, I hardly expected support from the floor. When, however, the fourth Hindu proclaimed that no Untouchables exist in India, it was too much for the patience of an Irish auditor, who succeeded in securing the floor shortly after him.

'Why do you come here to insult our intelligence by telling us that Untouchables are unknown in your country?' he inquired in essence. 'Do you deny that there are pariahs in India? Why, man, I have always known, and, I believe, most of this audience have always known of their miserable existence!

'Miss Mayo may be the Saint Patrick of India,' he continued 'She may be driving all the snakes out of

[1] This is a partially self-supporting residential and social headquarters for students at Columbia University, New York City.

your country ; I don't know. But if you are so badly treated by the British, why don't you drive them out yourselves, instead of coming here whimpering to us of your woes and troubles ? Anyway, do not insult us by saying Untouchables don't exist. . . .'

Other critics of *Mother India* have been more guarded than those Columbia College Students. *Unhappy India* says : 'Miss Mayo has devoted some chapters to an account of untouchability in India. The main thesis of the chapters, namely, that untouchability exists in India, is true.'[1] It continues :

> But Miss Mayo would not be her own good self if she stuck to the truth alone. Her training as a yellow journalist and her love of revelling in imaginary melodramatic scenes has led her into wild exaggerations and fantastic inventions. . . .

The Untouchables themselves, however, have, during the past eighteen months, found means of publicly proclaiming in detail the hardships and injustices they are forced to endure under present-day Hinduism. One occasion for this articulation has been the extensive Indian tour of the Indian Statutory Commission, commonly known by the name of its Chairman, Sir John Simon. Not only has this Commission received several interesting testimonials[2] from 'Untouchable' organisations in the various Provinces, but

[1] Page 94.

[2] 'Memorandum from Depressed Classes of Madras,' *The Englishman*, Calcutta, June 18th, 1928. *Memorial to Chairman and Members of Statutory Commission*, from the *Punjab Addharm Mandel*, Kishen Steam Press, Jullundur City. Address to Sir John Simon from the *Sambava Maha Jana Sangham* of South India, High Ground, Palamcottah, Madras. Memorial to the Indian

also it has made opportunities to cross-examine their representatives.

At Calcutta, a joint deputation of Namasudras and others of the class known as 'depressed,' 'outcaste,' or 'untouchable' was heard by the Simon Commission. Its spokesman, Mr. M. B. Mullick, 'detailed the social handicaps inflicted upon the community,' and is thus, in part, reported :

> The population of the depressed classes in Bengal was about two-fifths of the total population [therefore about nineteen million]. Entry to the temples was prohibited for them. If a high caste Hindu was cooking food the mere entry of a depressed class member would pollute him. They lived in separate places in villages and bad names were given to their villages. They had no access to the water of the District Board Wells, but had generally to live on tank[1] water, which was dirty. The children of the depressed classes were given back and separate seats in schools, and were not allowed to touch high caste children. If ever, by some chance, they did so, they were badly beaten. . . . Even the postmen refused to deliver their letters, if their depressed class name or occupation was not written in the address. They had to wait outside to throw their money into the Post Office, when postcards and stamps were thrown to them from a distance by postal clerks.

Statutory Commission by the 'Untouchables of the Bombay Presidency,' *The Pioneer*, Allahabad, June 15th, 1928.

[1] An Indian village tank is the village pond ; for description see *Mother India*, pp. 325-326.

Mr. Hartshorn :[1] Is there no provision in the postal regulations, which would ensure the proper delivery of your ers.

Mr. Mullick : Yes, but caste postmen follow their own regulations. We want an enquiry into this matter.[2]

This of the outcaste's life in Bengal.

The Madrassee 'Adi Dravidas,' in a manifesto, addressed to Sir John Simon, give their number as 8,000,000 souls and explain exactly what they are :[3] 'Although the lower orders of Indian society or the casteless classes are known as the depressed classes, we of the South are known as the untouchables and unapproachables.' Speaking of means of livelihood they say :

> Since a very high percentage of our poor folk living in rural areas have no habitations of their own in most of the districts of the Madras Presidency, but are allowed by sufferance to live on the lands of the landowning higher classes, any demand for wages for work contributed by the depressed classes or any attempt to assert independence is highly resented by their caste masters, which resentment seldom fails to exhibit itself in

[1] Rt. Hon. Vernon Hartshorn, Member of the Simon Commission, Labour Member of Parliament for the Ogmore Division of Glamorganshire.

[2] *Madras Mail*, Madras, January 22nd, 1929.

[3] Printed Appeal addressed to Sir John Simon, Chairman of the Parliamentary Statutory Commission by the *Sambava Maha Jana Sangham*, High Ground, Palamcottah, Madras, May 28th, 1928.

acts of violence against the poor people just to awe them into abject submission.[1]

Again, as to the quality of medical treatment bestowed upon them by Hindu officials, in their time of need :

> As our people are regarded as untouchables, and no better than chattels, medical and sanitary officials treat them as cheap stuff whose lives are not worth much. They invariably exhibit a clear aversion to entering our villages and homesteads to afford the needed help, for fear of pollution, and some of them seem to be obsessed with the idea that we have no right to claim their services. Medicines if asked for may be sent for the use of those stricken with diseases from the caste village where the officials come and halt during their rounds of inspection.[2]

Apparently the quality and supply of drinking-water allowed these Untouchables in Madras parallels the provision made in Bengal. This same appeal states :

> The wells used by the caste people are unapproachable and unavailable to us, and so our people are put to the necessity of resorting to tanks and ponds in the immediate vicinity of their villages. . . . These tanks and ponds . . . are used by all sorts and conditions of men for bathing, for washing their cattle and their clothes, and even the soiled cloths of such as suffer from in-

[1] Printed Appeal addressed to Sir John Simon by the *Sambava Maha Jana Sangham.* [2] *Ibid.*

> fectious diseases are washed in these tanks and ponds.[1]

Finally, in the 'conclusion,' we read :

> Like the dumb driven cattle we have patiently suffered all the wrongs done to us by the higher castes. It is now proclaimed that Hindu Swaraj, Indian millennium, is within sight, perhaps it is going to materialise after all, by and by. . . . So before the British Government make up their mind to bestow Swaraj on 'high caste India,'—the teeming millions have no concern about Swaraj,—we would beg of them to deport us to 'the plantations in America' and Africa rather than leave us to the tender mercies of Indian Swarajists.[2]

Similarly, in the United Provinces, at Lucknow, a deputation from the depressed classes, claiming to represent 12,000,000 outcastes in that one Province, waited upon the Simon Commission, voicing the same general complaint of injustice and oppression, illustrated with specific instances of suffering inflicted.[3]

From Lahore, in the Punjab, comes a like report—a depressed-class deputation waited upon Sir John Simon, declaring :

> They had not even the right to safeguard their individual lives ; this deplorable condition of millions of their depressed community was due to the horrible treatment meted out to them by the high

[1] Printed Appeal addressed to Sir John Simon, Chairman of the Parliamentary Statutory Commission, by the *Sambava Maha Jana Sangham.*

[2] *Ibid.* [3] *The Daily Telegraph*, London, December 7th, 1928.

class Hindus. . . . The deputationists next stated that they did not wish to be called Hindus but Addharmis (protestants) and in the next census, they would write themselves Addharmis. They did not want swaraj in India under the present conditions, as it would mean the monopoly of the caste Hindus.

Two of the eight demands they presented asked for: 'Equal rights of using public wells as enjoyed by the other communities, and, equal rights of ownership of any property, of dwelling houses and common fields, as enjoyed by the other communities.'[2]

Of late years schools have been thrown open to the Untouchables in increasing numbers, but the experiment, so far as can be ascertained, has proved largely fruitless.

I myself saw Untouchable children, both in Bengal and in the United Provinces, sitting outside the thatched schoolhouses, straining to follow the lessons from that distance: and the Rev. J. C. Chatterji, M.L.A., Municipal Commissioner of Delhi and member of the Board of Secondary Education, stated in the course of a memorandum to the Simon Commission that he 'was emphatically of the opinion that the mere throwing open of all educational institutions to the so-called untouchables was a mere farce, as they were either prevented admission into them, or treated very badly even when admitted.'[3]

[1] *The Pioneer*, Allahabad, November 10th, 1928. [2] *Ibid.*
[3] *Madras Mail*, Madras, August 27th, 1928, also *The Hindu* of the same day.

Another memorial, presented to the Indian Statutory Commission, this time by the 'Untouchables of Bombay Presidency,' affirms :

> Though Government have taken special precautions to root out all distinctions of touchability and untouchability, so far as the sacred precincts of Education are concerned, yet the arrogant castefolks (both Brahmins and Non-Brahmins) with their prejudices against our race, are nullifying the objects of Government in a thousand and one ways. They cannot oppose Government openly ; but they lack no means to discourage and debar our children from receiving education in schools side by side with their children. . . They terrorise many illiterate and ignorant parents not to send their untouchable children to the common schools. Why, even threats of setting fire to our huts are hurled in case we went against their will. In many cases, the touchables prevail upon the parents to sign documents and memorials purporting to request Government not to force them to send their children to common schools. If the untouchable parents, taking a bold stand on the orders of Government, persist in sending their children to common schools, the touchables forthwith withdraw their children and thus carry their point.[1]

Regarding those comparatively few teachers who have risen from the ranks of the outcastes, this memorial adds :

[1] As reported and quoted in *The Pioneer*, Allahabad, June 15th, 1928.

When an Untouchable teacher is appointed to any village or town school, the Touchables start a campaign of protest. They not only labour to scandalise the solitary teacher in the eyes of his superior officers, or to justify their protests on grounds of his alleged incompetency, but simultaneously withdraw their children from that school.[1]

The city council of Bombay showed courage in recently resolving that no caste distinctions should be made in the matter of drinking-water arrangements in municipal schools and that caste and outcaste children should sit together.

By way of registering its protest the Bombay Stock Exchange thereupon closed for one whole day.[2]

And Sir Manmohandas Ramji presided over a large public meeting at which resolutions were passed[3] condemning the Corporation's action, and describing it as contrary to the teachings of the Hindu religion.

In February 1928 Mr. M. R. Jayakar, a Hindu member from Bombay City, introduced into the Central Indian Legislative Assembly a resolution recommending that directions be issued to all Local Governments to provide special facilities for the education of the Untouchables and other depressed classes, and also to declare them eligible for all public services.[4]

To the resolution five amendments were offered–

[1] As reported and quoted in *The Pioneer*, June 15th, 1928.

[2] *The Times*, London, October 19th, 1928.

[3] *Ibid.* Also see *Times of India*, Bombay, October 20th, 1928.

[4] *Legislative Assembly Debates*, February 23rd, 1928, p. 686.

none by Government—and the debate upon this simple motion took the best part of one whole day. The discussion shows many divergent opinions among the legislators as to exactly how Government should help the Untouchables. Lala Lajpat Rai, for instance, the author of *Unhappy India*, moved an amendment, part of which read :

> And this Assembly further recommends to the Governor-General in Council to sanction one crore of rupees [£750,000] for the education of the depressed classes. . . .[1]

Disregarding the rather complicated constitutional infringement involved in the spending by the Governor General in Council on a provincial transferred subject of funds derived from central revenues,[2] let us consider, for a moment, whether Untouchability can be abolished simply by educating the Untouchable, or whether Untouchability is not bound to remain just so long as it is willed upon its victim by the majority of his fellow-countrymen.

Here is the view of one speaker in the central Legislature, a man obviously thinking not of the few rebellious and class-conscious Untouchables, but of the great mass of 'untouchable' humanity, too sunk in their ancient misery even to dream of betterment. Says this European member, making himself one with the Hindus among whom he sits :

[1] *Legislative Assembly Debates*, February 23rd, 1928, p. 693. This unconstitutional motion was negatived.

[2] Those desiring information on this point should see the Montagu-Chelmsford Reform Act and the *Legislative Assembly Debate* of February 23rd, 1928, pp. 698-699.

> It seems to me that Untouchability can only be dealt with by attacking the principle and not by making separate provisions for untouchables. How are we to educate and uplift these depressed classes ? What can we do with people who have been taught for generations to believe that if they are touched they themselves commit a sin ? What are we to do with people who are not aware that they have human rights ? . . . I too would like to see a crore of rupees spent. But on what is going to be spent, Sir ? Surely there is only one proper way of spending that money, and that is on educating the oppressors. . . . It has to be solved from the top and not from the bottom. . . . Let us not have people who are outside human charity. It is the conversion of opinion that is wanted. Let us convert opinion, and the education of the untouchables will be solved by itself. When we have realised our human obligation to the untouchable, then there will be no difficulty about lifting him up. He can only be lifted up by recognising his human rights ; he can only be lifted up when we are conscious of him as a human being. . . .[1]

And this speaker, further, definitely objects to the appropriation of public money to provide separate educational opportunities for the Untouchables, on the ground that the act itself would be vicious :

> We must not go on providing special facilities and thereby preserving the principle of untouch-

[1] Mr. Arthur Moore, *Legislative Assembly Debates*, February 23rd, 1928, pp. 698-699.

> ability. Let us have armies of people going about touching the untouchables. Let us have armies of people going about drinking water with them; accepting a glass of water and giving a glass of water. In that way this problem, which must be ripe for solution, can be solved.[1]

Plausible as this sounds, it is too European, too altruistic, to stir the Hindu mind. No Indian rises to agree with it. Rather, the next Indian speaker blames the Government of India for the existence of Untouchability after a hundred years of British rule, and demands that Government, in addition to providing special educational facilities, take on the support of Untouchable children:[2]

> If the Government of India are anxious and if the members of the Legislative Assembly are anxious that the children of the depressed classes should take advantage of the facilities which they keep open, then certainly it is necessary that the school-going children of the depressed classes should be maintained at the public cost. Sir, this is the only way in which the number of the children of the depressed classes can be increased in public schools.[3]

The same speaker, Mr. N. M. Joshi,[4] representing

[1] *Legislative Assembly Debates*, February 23rd, 1928, p. 700.
[2] *Ibid.*, p. 701. [3] *Ibid.*, p. 702.
[4] Narayan Malhar Joshi, Hindu. Educated in India, member Servants of India Society; secretary Bombay Social Service League and Bombay Social Reform Association; sent by Government to Washington, 1920, and Geneva, 1921-22, to represent Indian labour at International Labour Conferences. Nominated member, representing Labour, of Legislative Assembly.

labour, estimates the number of Untouchable children of school age as 10,000,000.[1]

Sir Hari Singh Gour is the next member to secure the floor, demanding that the scope of the resolution be again widened :

> . . . I do not . . . limit the granting of special facilities to the depressed classes and the untouchables. I hope that the Government of India will realise that they owe a larger responsibility to a wider circle of His Majesty's subjects in this country which I have mentioned, namely the backward classes, people to whom on account of social thraldom, on account of age-long custom, or various other reasons facilities for education have not been given to the extent they should have been. . . .[2]

He is interrupted :[3] 'On a point of information, Sir,' says his interrogator. 'Does my honourable friend include women among the backward classes ?' Sir Hari replies :

> I am afraid the women of India are more depressed than the worst of the depressed classes. My friend will remember that in the villages the *pater familias* say, 'I will give education to the boy because he will be able to earn his living and bring back home salary or wages, whereas the girl is good for nothing, she will go into another family and why should I give education ?'[4]

[1] *Legislative Assembly Debates*, February 23rd, 1928, p. 702.
[2] *Ibid.*, pp. 704-705. For biographical note see page 77.
[3] *Ibid.* [4] *Ibid.*

Eventually an amended resolution[1] was adopted.

Now, in view of the anxiety verbally expressed by these Hindu legislators, it is interesting to examine, so far as here possible, the Hindu's active, concrete exertions to help the Untouchables.

That some efforts are being made by the Hindus themselves to rid their country of this scourge is a happy reality. And if a list of these helpful activities were to be compiled, it would appear formidable. Yet it would not alter the fact that, in view of the tremendous, the almost overwhelming needs, their total fruits are microscopic.

The two outstanding Hindu organisations interested in the reduction of untouchability are the Arya Samaj and the Brahmo Samaj. The first of these reformed Hindu sects numbers under half a million members,[2] or about one-eighth of 1 per cent. of India's population, although during the decade 1911-21, it increased in membership 92 per cent. Says the Census Commissioner of its work:

> The majority of the converts are drawn from Brahmanic Hindus, but special efforts are made to secure the reconversion of converts from Hinduism to Christianity and Islam and the reclamation of the depressed classes [Untouchables], to whom the

[1] *Legislative Assembly Debates*, February 23rd, 1928, p. 726. It reads: 'This Assembly recommends to the Governor General in Council to issue directions to all Local Governments to provide special facilities for the education of the untouchables and other depressed classes, particularly by reserving seats in teachers' training classes for them and also for opening all public services to them.'

[2] *Census of India*, 1921, Vol. I, Part I, p. 119.

disregard of caste in the Arya community strongly appeals.[1]

The Brahmos, on the other hand, although they increased their membership 16 per cent. between the two latest Censuses, numbered, in 1921, fewer than 6,400. Yet, we are told, their influence, which should not altogether be measured by their small numbers, lies, for the major part, among the intellectual Hindus of Bengal.[2]

Perhaps a more cheerful sign, from the Untouchable point of view, lies in the reports of Seth Jamnaal Bajaj's action in throwing open the Hindu temple at Wardha to Untouchables,[3] and of Pandit Madan Mohan Malaviya's new movement to purify the outcastes through an initiation ceremony.[4]

But the response of the Untouchables to this somewhat new interest in their well-being, on the part of the caste Hindus, strikes a new note of boldness. As, when opening the All-India Depressed Class Conference in Madras in February 1929 the President, Mr. B. C. Mandal, said :

> The jugglers talk of equality and fraternity but their sympathies are lip deep. They have been giving us bluffs for the last five thousand years. . . . The so-called patriots of India demand political rights, but they are not ready to give social rights to their own countrymen. . . . My friends, do not depend upon any body, try to raise yourselves, have faith in God and in your own selves.[5]

[1] *Census of India*, 1921, Vol. I, Part I, p. 119. [2] *Ibid.*
[3] *The Hindu*, Madras, December 20th, 1928.
[4] *Ibid.*, December 30th, 1928. [5] *Ibid.*, February 25th, 1929.

The real point which concerned *Mother India* is, however, not a matter of theory, but one of practical fact : how do the Brahmans and other high castemen, in the villages, treat the Untouchable element ? For India has 60,000,000 Untouchables and over half a million villages.

The Untouchables have spoken for themselves, but what about the attitude of Brahmans ? Does the following incident shed any light ?

> A case in which nine Brahmins murdered another Brahmin because he had tried to improve the condition of the Depressed Classes came before Mr. Justice Boys and Mr. Justice Bennett in the Allahabad High Court.
>
> Sandar Singh and eight others, high caste Hindus, appealed against a sentence of transportation for life passed on them by the Sessions Judge at Mainpuri, who had found them guilty of the murder of Ramsarup, also a Brahmin. Their victim had annoyed the orthodox Hindus of his village by attempting to raise the Chamars, and other members of the Depressed Classes, whom he allowed to wait on him, fetch his water, and cut his vegetables.[1]

Note his principal sin—to allow the Untouchables to serve his twice-born person. The tale continues :

> When the Chamars complained to him that their offerings had been refused by the Brahmins at the village temple, he advised them to build their own temple and assisted them to do so.

[1] *The Times*, London, April 27th, 1928.

A clear case of mutiny within the ranks of Brahmanism itself ; so :

> This led to legal proceedings by the other side, and it was alleged that the nine appellants had gone to Ramsarup's house and called him out to discuss a compromise. When Ramsarup appeared the appellants had immediately began to beat him with *lathis* (iron-shod staves). Ramsarup's wife, who intervened, was pushed aside, and the appellants had eventually killed him.[1]

Thus ended this village Brahman's efforts to help his Untouchable neighbours ; and the murderers' appeal before the Allahabad High Court in 1928, although it failed, brought out this additional fact showing the pressure brought to bear against even a Brahman who dares to oppose the mind of the orthodox majority :

> Before this attack, Ramsarup had had to separate from his father and other relatives, who had quarrelled with him owing to his behaviour toward the Chamars.[2]

Parting from his family is one of the greatest sacrifices that a Brahman can make, for the paternal tie among Hindus is second only to that of Chinese ancestor-worship.

It may be claimed that this is a single instance, and therefore not typical.

And this is true, for few indeed are the Brahmans who have so far revolted against the evils of their system as to endanger their lives in protest against its continuance.

[1] *The Times*, London, April 27th, 1928. [2] *Ibid.*

CHAPTER XIII

LEGENDS

Gandhi and Tagore are not the only instances of men who have been misrepresented and with whose writings Miss Mayo has taken liberty in a highly improper manner. These two we have known because they are the most pre-eminent personalities and have also cared to reply. Hosts of other gentlemen have been misrepresented and misquoted.—*Sister India*, p. 10.

In examining this statement, typical of many such allegations spread through the numerous attacks upon *Mother India*, it is necessary first to point out certain errors in the book, and, second, to shed light upon the nature of the weapons used and the methods chosen—both familiar in Hindu controversy—in the onslaught upon *Mother India*.

As illustrating the broad charge contained in the final sentence of the above quotation, let us take the case concerning the late Lord Sinha, which has appeared in several 'replies.' This gentleman is mentioned only once in *Mother India*, and then to draw attention to one of his good works. The passage speaks of 'Lord Sinha's society for the help of the outcastes of Bengal and Assam.'[1] Unfortunately, Lord Sinha died in March 1928. No sooner had he passed beyond human reach and reference than a letter from 'a personal friend and close associate' appeared in the Indian

[1] Page 153.

press.[1] The object of this communication was to expose beyond all shadow of doubt one of *Mother India*'s 'deliberate misrepresentations.'

The letter in question charged that a conversation, printed in *Mother India*, with a person therein designated as 'a respected Hindu nobleman,'[2] whom 'it would be a graceless requital of courtesy to name,'[3] was in fact a conversation with the late Lord Sinha. This idea, it states, was 'confirmed by him,' whereupon a denial of *Mother India's* slander was forthwith prepared for the press ; but, the letter continues, on being presented with the denial, the Indian peer refused to sign it. The actual words of the letter-writer, Mr. Sicar, read :

> When Miss Mayo's book was published in London I happened to be there. Lord Sinha's attention was drawn to the gross injustice done to him by Miss Mayo—and in fact a contradiction, for publication in the Press, had been drafted for him, but Lord Sinha refused permission for its use.[4]

Apparently it never occurred to Mr. Sicar to ask how Lord Sinha recognised anonymously quoted words as being his own except by recalling them ; nor how, having recalled them, a man of his character could do otherwise than refuse a repudiation. For most people Lord Sinha's refusal to sanction the publishing

[1] *The Englishman*, Calcutta, March 6th, 1928; *The Hindu*, Madras, March 8th, 1928 ; *Madras Mail*, Madras, March 10th, 1928 ; *Unhappy India*, p. lv., etc.

[2] *Mother India*, p. 195.

[3] *Ibid.*, p. 196.

[4] *The Englishman*, March 6th, 1928, etc.

of the prepared denial will, in itself, constitute conclusive evidence.[1]

Another fable has been built around *Mother India's* account of a luncheon party given to Miss Mayo in Delhi by an Indian friend, in order that she might privately hear the opinions of certain Home Rule politicians. 'They had spoken at length on the coming expulsion of Britain from India,' this passage reads, 'and on the future in which they themselves would rule the land.

' "And what," I asked, "is your plan for the princes?"

' "We shall wipe them out!" exclaimed one with conviction. And all the rest nodded assent.'[2]

Unhappy India 'exposes' this 'misstatement.' Here is the method :

> In the absence of any names it was not easy to get a clue for verification. But from inquiries from all the possible people who could have arranged such a party or who could have attended it, I learned that Mr. K. C. Roy of the Associated Press arranged a luncheon to which a number of Indian gentlemen were invited.[3]

Then follows a letter from Mrs. K. C. Roy, saying, 'We gave a luncheon party to Miss Mayo. . . I do

[1] *Unhappy India* (pp. 497-498) reports that Lord Sinha was interviewed by a representative of the *Indian Daily Mail*, in 1927, and was asked to point out passages from *Mother India* which he held to be false : 'Lord Sinha replied that he just remembered one statement made by Miss Mayo which was a lie, namely, that Indian mothers taught their children unnatural vice.' It might be supposed that if Mr. Sicar's accusation were correct Lord Sinha would also have remembered it.

[2] *Mother India*, p. 284.

[3] *Unhappy India*, pp. xlviii-xlix.

not recollect whether the position of the Indian princes was discussed. At any rate, I know that there was no discussion as to their being "wiped out."' Yet other parties, attended by other Bengalis, were given in Delhi to Miss Mayo, who joins Mrs. Roy in affirming that the latter lady's luncheon was not the occasion of the conversation in question.

A more interesting incident concerns the well-known actress, Madame Alla Nazimova.

One day during the winter 1927-28 the author of *Mother India* was surprised to receive, from a prominent producing company in New York, an invitation to attend the opening performance of a new playlet, with Madame Nazimova heading the bill, entitled *India*. A second surprise came when she read that its author, Edgar Allen Woolf, acknowledged that his sketch was based on her book. Whether Miss Mayo approved the production or resented it, she was helpless in the matter, because Hindu customs are uncopyrightable, and because *Mother India*, although it purports to portray Hindu customs within a certain limited field, can claim no monopoly of the topic.

The Russian actress's playlet, nevertheless, was the subject of many questions in the Central Indian Legislature and of newspaper comments up and down the country, all assuming Miss Mayo's responsibility in the matter. Thus, the *New Empire* of Calcutta, under date of February 29th, carried a despatch, 'from our own correspondent, New York, February 27th,' under the headlines '*Mother India* Explained,—Miss Mayo's Misrepresentation On The Stage.' Yet the 'story' itself, when divorced from its misleading headlines, is identical with that printed by the London *Daily Mail* on February 3rd.[1]

In Delhi, Mr. B. Das took the Assembly's time to ask :

> Has the attention of the Government been drawn to a letter of Sreemati Rangini Devi from the United States in the *Hindustan Times* and other papers that Miss Mayo's book *Mother India* is being presented on the American stage as a one-act play depicting the inhuman cruelty of an Indian husband to his wife ?
>
> Have Government taken any action so far to stop misrepresentation of Indian life to the American people ? If not, are Government prepared to take any action ?[2]

The heavily burdened Government of India, continually bombarded by just such questions, was prepared. Its spokesman, Sir Denys Bray, replies : 'Steps were taken to initiate such action as may be possible the day the article came to my notice.'[3]

So somewhere in the India Office and, perhaps, even in the State Department at Washington—although it is to be hoped London showed more judgment than to push the matter forward to that extreme—rests a file of papers, daily collecting more dust, relating to Madame Nazimova and her one-act playlet. Meanwhile,

[1] This is a clear-cut instance of an Indian-owned newspaper 'lifting' a despatch from a London contemporary ; changing the headlines, and representing that the despatch was sent by its own staff in New York.

[2] *Legislative Assembly Debates*, official report, March 10th, 1928, Delhi, p. 1,128.

[3] *Ibid.*

by political Indians it is generally believed that the Russian tragedienne's sketch was a part of some deep-laid plot to belittle their country in American eyes.

Mr. K. Natarajan's behaviour is of real significance to the social reform movement in India, for he is one of its few outstanding leaders and edits *The Indian Social Reformer*, an influential weekly. This paper has sought opportunities to attack both *Mother India* and its author, as well as to reprint in detail many of the onslaughts of others. This social reform editor also wrote one of the first 'replies' to be published in book form, which volume says of *Mother India* :

> The book, in the most charitable view, is the product of a fanatic frenzy for the superiority and supremacy of the whites.[1]

Approximately half of his work is an attempt to discredit one of the 109 authorities that *Mother India* presents. The Abbé Dubois, to whose work *Mother India* refers nine times among its 269 quotations,[2] is classified by Mr. Natarajan's as 'an impostor from first to last' ;[3] the following typifies his general manner :

> Many of the Abbé Dubois' 'observations' on Hindu religion are merely his reading into it of the things he had known of the religions in his own country. The story of childless wives going to temples to be visited at night by God in the person of

[1] *Miss Mayo's Mother India, a Rejoinder*, by K. Natarajan, editor of *The Indian Social Reformer*, G. A. Natesan, Madras, 1927, p. 12. [2] See *ante*, pp. 75-76.

[3] *Miss Mayo's Mother India, a Rejoinder*, p. 60.

a priest, is distinctly a reminiscence from the Abbé's Seminary days.[1]

Before the advent of *Mother India* few Hindus, if any, thought of questioning this authority, whose book, *Hindu Manners, Customs and Ceremonies*,[2] was re-translated by Henry K. Beauchamp, a man of wide Indian experience, in 1897, at which time Mr. Beauchamp attempted to bring it up to date. The first few editions of *Mother India*, however, failed to make clear in the bibliographical footnote that the book was first completed in 1821. This oversight the author acknowledged by a correction in later impressions. Yet Natarajan is not content to state this plain fact, but proceeds to twist it into a conclusive untruth. 'The deliberate disingenuousness of Miss Katherine Mayo,'[3] he writes, 'is clear from the fact that in all her several references to the Abbé Dubois' book, she not once tells the reader that the manuscript of the book was submitted to the East India Company in 1807[4] and that the account in it relates to a period separated from our time by a century and a quarter.'

Against this statement of the Hindu social reform leader may be set these passages from *Mother India*, first edition: 'The observations on this point made by the Abbé Dubois a century since' (p. 85). Writing

[1] *Miss Mayo's Mother India, a Rejoinder*, p. 60.

[2] *Hindu Manners, Customs and Ceremonies*, Abbé J. A. Dubois, 1821, re-translated and edited by Henry K. Beauchamp, 1897, Clarendon Press, Oxford, 1924.

[3] *Miss Mayo's Mother India, a Rejoinder*, p. 73.

[4] Mr. Beauchamp states that the Company purchased the first manuscript in 1807, but the 'finally corrected' copy was not sent to the Madras Government until 1821.

in the beginning of the nineteenth century, the Abbé Dubois said' (p. 123). 'Says the Abbé Dubois again, writing in the beginning of the nineteenth century' (p. 179), while several phrases used in presenting the other six quotations from the Abbé (pp. 154, 225) call attention to the period of his writing.

Not only does Natarajan ignore these instances where Miss Mayo clearly shows her intention not to mislead; but in his eagerness to dishonour not only the American author, but also the French writer, he totally disregards this important section of Mr. Beauchamp's preface to the third edition of Dubois, written in 1905, at which time the book had long been a familiar classic in India:

> . . . by the Indians themselves the [Dubois's] work has been received with universal approval and eulogy. The general accuracy of the Abbé's observations has nowhere been impugned; and every Indian critic of the work has paid a warm tribute to the Abbé's industry, zeal and impartiality. Perhaps I may quote in conclusion here the opinion expressed by one of the leading Indian newspapers, *The Hindu*, which in the course of a long review of the book, remarked: 'It is impossible to run through the immense variety of topics touched in this exceedingly interesting book; but we entirely agree with Mr. Beauchamp in his opinion that the book is as valuable to-day as it ever was. It contains a valuable collection of information on a variety of subjects, including ceremonies and observances which might pass as trifles in the eye of many an ordinary person. The Abbé's

description might be compared with the experience of the modern Hindu, who will find that while the influence of English education is effecting a quiet and profound change and driving the intellectual and physical faculties of the people into fresh grooves, the bulk of the people, whom that influence has not reached, have remained substantially unaltered since the time of the French Missionary.'[1]

In December 1927, Mr. Natarajan presided over the annual meeting of the Indian National Social Conference, at Madras, where delegates had collected from all over the country. This conference, his journal tells us, was attended by 'a large and representative gathering of ladies and gentlemen interested in social reform movement.'[2] On this occasion several of the speeches were strongly reminiscent of *Mother India*; for example: 'If we want to grow into a robust, strong and self-respecting nation, if we want to reach our full physical and mental height, the system of child marriage must go.'[3] And 'Again our marriage laws which render women a chattel or piece of furniture in the hands of her husband, the vilest sinner and hardened criminal as he may be, need revision according to the changed conditions of modern life.' And Mrs. Sarojini Naidu, who spoke on Hindu temple prostitutes, is thus reported: 'This was a social and spiritual cancer and

[1] For further information compare Mr. Natarajan's book with Mr. Beauchamp's third edition, used by Miss Mayo.

[2] *Indian Social Reformer*, K. Natarajan, editor, January 7th, 1928, p. 293.

[3] *Ibid.*, January 14th, pp. 310-312, speech by Dr. S. Muthulakshmi.

how, she asked, dared they to ask for freedom when these malpractices existed in them which they did not fight and remove.'[1]

Yet, when another speaker, Mr. Surendranath Arya, dared actually to name *Mother India* and to declare openly that the book was true, his act turned the whole conference into a pandemonium :

> He said that the women were much ill-treated by men and in spite of all their condemnation, what was said by Miss Mayo on that subject was true. (At this there was great uproar among the audience and cries of 'shame, shame,' 'sit down' and 'we do not want to hear you' and so on were raised.) The speaker went on to speak amidst those cries which were kept up till he finished his speech.[2]

How any one knew he had finished his speech, amidst all that noise, the Natarajan account does not tell us, but an eye-witness has related that Mr. Arya continued speaking until he was actually dragged down by a woman delegate seizing upon his coat tails.

The president's own paper gives these details of the next morning's proceedings :

> Mr. Natarajan, at the outset, referred to the unpleasantness caused at Tuesday's meeting when Mr. Surendranath Arya in speaking on the resolution regarding women's rights made some observations regarding Miss Mayo's book which raised a storm of protest. . . The speaker said he had

[1] *Indian Social Reformer*, January 7th, 1928, p. 296.
[2] *Ibid.*, p. 294.

since had an interchange of views with Mr. Arya who said that it was not his intention to justify Miss Mayo's book as a whole and that his observations about the truth of her charge, applied only to the treatment of Hindu women.[1]

Exactly fifty-one weeks later Mr. Natarajan editorially explained his attitude toward *Mother India*: 'The resentment provoked by the book is not due to the truth or otherwise of the facts stated in it, but to the broad inferences reflecting on the Indian and particularly the Hindu race and religion.'[2]

Rabindranath Tagore, once winner of the Nobel prize, has written two letters indicting *Mother India*; to both of these many legendary properties have been attached.

The first, addressed to the *Manchester Guardian*, was written before Mr. Tagore had read the book, and like the resolution tabled in the Legislative Assembly, was based solely upon a review of *Mother India* which Mr. Tagore happened to see while travelling in the Dutch East Indies. His opening paragraph comprises an appeal for space in the paper to vindicate an 'unjustifiable attack'; in the second paragraph we read these words:

> While travelling in this island of Bali I have just chanced upon a copy of the *New Statesman* of July 16th containing the review of a book on India written by a tourist from America.[3]

[1] *Indian Social Reformer*, January 7th, 1928 p. 294.
[2] *Ibid.*, December 1st, 1928, p. 209.
[3] *Manchester Guardian*, Manchester, October 11th, 1927.

As Mr. Tagore tacitly acknowledges he had not read the book that he attacks, it is hardly necessary to give further notice to this communication.

His second letter, addressed to the New York *Nation*, opens with a lengthy paragraph which makes general war upon both British and American authors :

> I came to know from the advertising columns of your paper that Miss Katherine Mayo's *Mother India* has been lauded by Arnold Bennett as 'a shocking book, in the honourable sense.' Unfortunately, for obvious reasons, there is a widely prevalent wish among the race that rules India to believe any detraction that may bring discredit upon India, and consequently the kind of shocks that Miss Mayo has manufactured offers them a delicious luxury of indignation. The numerous lies mixed with facts that have been dexterously manipulated by her for the production of these shocks are daily being exposed in our journals ; but these will never reach the circle of readers which it is easy for Miss Mayo to delude. Along with other Eastern victims of lying propaganda we in India also must defencelessly suffer mud-besmearing from unscrupulous literature ; for your writers have their machinery of publicity which is cruelly efficient for raining slanders from a region usually unapproachable by us, shattering our fair name in an appallingly wholesale manner.[1]

In fairness to Mr. Tagore it should be added that he inscribed these lines before the publication of eight of

[1] *Nation*, New York, January 4th, 1928.

the nine 'replies' from the hands of his fellow countrymen; also, before his friends and associates began their extensive American lecture tours to counteract the so-called offending volume.

Mr. Tagore, however, makes a specific charge in his third paragraph. 'For my own defence,' he says, 'I shall use the following extract from a paper written by Mr. Natarajan, one of the most fearless critics of our social evils. He has incidentally dealt with the incriminating allegation against me deliberately concocted by Miss Mayo out of a few sentences from my contribution to Keyserling's *Book of Marriage*—cleverly burgling away their true meaning and shaping them into an utterly false testimony for her own nefarious purpose.'[1]

Tagore's readiness to impute motives again rather obviates the need of attention. Here, however, are the facts in the case.

Introducing a quotation from Tagore's essay in Keyserling's *Book of Marriage*, *Mother India* says:

> The frank give-and-take of the Indian Legislature, between Indian and Indian, deal with facts. But it is instructive to observe the robes that those facts can wear when arrayed by a poet for foreign consideration. Rabindranath Tagore, in a recent essay on 'The Indian Ideal of Marriage,' explains child marriage as a flower of subliminated spirit, a conquest over sexuality and materialism won by exalted intellect for the eugenic uplift of the race.

[1] *Nation*, New York, January 4th, 1928.

His *conclusion*,[1] however, logically implies the *conviction*, simply, that Indian women must be securely bound and delivered before their womanhood is upon them, if they are to be kept in hand.[2]

In reproducing the following quotation from Tagore's essay, the first several editions of *Mother India* omitted the three words italicised below and printed elision marks in their places:

'The "desire," *however*, against which India's solution of the marriage problem declared war, is one of Nature's most powerful fighters; consequently, the question of how to overcome it was not an easy one. There is a particular age, *said India*, at which this attraction between the sexes reaches its height; so if marriage is to be regulated according to the social will [as distinguished from the choice of the individual concerned], it must be finished with before such age. Hence the Indian custom of early marriage.'[3]

In later editions, however, the two words, 'said India,' were restored. Their omission doubtless gave emphasis to the idea that Tagore did not dissociate himself from the Hindu custom of early marriage, which idea, it is safe to say, will continue to be imbibed by many readers of his full text as found in Count Keyserling's volume. And by changing 'his conclusion'

[1] In later editions the word 'conclusion' reads 'explanation,' and 'conviction' is changed to 'assumption.'

[2] *Mother India*, p. 50.

[3] *Mother India*, p. 51, and *The Book of Marriage*, Count Keyserling, Harcourt, Brace and Company, New York, 1926, p. 112.

to read 'his explanation,' and 'conviction' to read 'assumption,' in the text of *Mother India*, the author further acknowledged her mistake.

A personal associate of Mr. Tagore, Mr. C. F. Andrews, later advanced the information that in certain books, which, however, Mr. Andrews was unable to name, and which, he said, have never been translated from Bengali into English, Tagore has vehemently denounced the practice of child marriage. Furthermore, Mr. Andrews stated that the poet still favours ridding his country of the child marriage blight.[1]

However, my readers are left to decide for themselves whether or not the author of *Mother India* 'deliberately concocted' the 'incriminating allegation,' as Mr. Tagore asserts.

And perhaps it is pertinent to note here the general absence of Tagore's name from the roster of to-day's active fighters on behalf of Hindu child brides. That his championship for this cause, so deeply in need of the support of every prominent Indian, should lie buried in Bengali, hidden from the non-Bengali-speaking Hindu majority, or should be shrouded in an ambiguous phrase, or should be conspicuous only to those familiar with his personal life, is difficult to reconcile with the idea of championship worthy of the name.

Tagore's letter to the *Nation* makes one additional charge :

> Let me in conclusion draw the attention of your readers to another amazing piece of false state-

[1] Statement made in the presence of the author.

ment in which she introduces me, with a sneer, as a defender of the 'Aruvedic' system of medicine against Western medical science. Let her prove this libel if she can.

Those who have been side-tracked from the main issue of *Mother India* by this challenge will remain on their siding. Miss Mayo objects to making public, even to-day, the name of an international health expert whose signed statement is in her files, and which statement I give below :

> In the spring of 1924 Rabindranath Tagore was making a public speaking tour through the Far East. The newspapers were filled with reports of his criticisms of western culture. As I could not believe that he really meant that Ayurvedic medicine was superior in its achievements to modern medicine and fearing that the cause of science, which is nothing but truth, might be damaged, I called upon him in May 1924, while he was in Peking. He said that Ayurvedic medicine had much that should be preserved and was undoubtedly superior to other systems of medicine for many diseases, but that the regular medical profession was too bigoted to admit it.
>
> I asked him how he knew that Ayurvedic medicine was superior. As he made no answer I asked him whether he had ever visited a modern medical laboratory. He said he had never been in one. I then explained that a medical laboratory is a place for ascertaining the truth and that the regular medical profession was ready to use any drug or

method for the alleviation of suffering that promised success, provided it was first ascertained that no harm would come to the patient. I also pointed out that Ayurvedic medicine had not contributed anything toward the prevention of disease and that modern medicine had brought under control such terrible diseases as plague, yellow fever, cholera, smallpox and many others, in a scientific way. I said that laboratories such as he had been criticising were places that could test the value of Ayurvedic drugs and that before continuing his condemnation of them, he ought to visit one and acquaint himself with their work.

Perhaps Mr. Tagore will recall the occasion—his visitor was far too eminent to be forgotten easily; in any case, to-day we have his own implication that he is not in favour of India's ancient Ayurvedic code as opposed to Western medical science.

The fact is both important and encouraging. Important, because with such leaders as Gandhi condemning Western medicine, it stands in need of the counterbalancing support of such outstanding Indians as Rabrindranath Tagore; encouraging, because, of all countries in the world, India most needs scientific medical help, and, in her need, most endangers the rest of human society.

CHAPTER XIV

A CALF IS KILLED

'ONE of the most intolerably painful chapters in Miss Mayo's book is that which describes the conditions of confinement in the orthodox Hindu home. I remember that at my first reading of this I slammed the book and pitched it away—resolved to bear no more. Yet no part of the book is more elaborately documented, and on turning up her authorities, chapter and verse can be found for practically every horrible detail.'[1]

Miss Rathbone's revulsion must have been experienced by many another reader, yet, curious as it may seem, not a single one of the 'replies' attempts to deny the truth of the dreadful details in *Mother India's* chapter on the Hindu *dhais*.

'These conditions are due not to ignorance but to religious traditions,' says a recent Governor of Bengal. 'The act of child-birth being in the eyes of the Hindu an unclean act, nothing must come in contact with it which is not already defiled.'[2] Or, as a missionary doctor with many years of Indian experience puts it: 'The belief that the woman at this time is unclean and a source of defilement to others determines the whole entourage of the confinement.'[3]

[1] 'Has Katherine Mayo Slandered "Mother India"?' Eleanor F. Rathbone, *Hibbert Journal*, January, 1929, p. 203. For biographical note see pages 59-60.

[2] 'India Seen and India Served,' the Earl of Lytton, *The Review of the Churches*, London, January, 1929, p. 51.

[3] *Tuberculosis in India*, Arthur Lankester, M.D., Butterworth and Company, London, 1920, p. 150.

No layman could write of the details involved in this Hindu custom, first of all because no man is allowed to witness them. Passing them by, then, we may turn to their results. These are clearly shown in the infant mortality records.

Infant mortality (deaths in the first year of life per 1,000 *births)*

[1] U.S.A., average 1921-25	74
[2] England and Wales, average 1921-25	76
[2] New Zealand, average 1921-25	43
[3] India, average 1922-25	178

Average infant mortality (per 1,000 *births) for various cities,* 1922-25

[1] New York	69	[3] Madras	276
[1] London	68	[3] Bombay	298
[3] Calcutta	306	[3] Cawnpore	461
[3] Poona	827		

It is a strange circumstance that Poona, where the headquarters of two of the leading Indian social reform societies[4] are established, and where the National Christian Council has its centre, should contribute such a particularly appalling record.

'Special causes,' says the Indian Census, 'contribute to the high mortality of infants in India. Owing to the custom of early marriage cohabitation and child-birth commonly take place before the woman is physically mature and this, combined with the primitive and insanitary methods of midwifery, seriously affects the

[1] Figures compiled by Committee on Administrative Practice, American Public Health Association, New York, 1929.

[2] *The World Almanac*, New York, 1929, p. 308.

[3] *Annual Report of the Public Health Commissioner with the Government of India for* 1925, Vol. I, Calcutta, 1927, pp. 12-13.

[4] Servants of India and Poona Seva Sedan Society.

health and vitality of the mother and through her of the child.'[1]

Grounds for hope, however, are to be found in the facts that during the decade 1916-25, the average infant mortality in British India has been reduced from 202 per 1,000 births to 174; similarly, the general death rate has been lowered from 32.72 per 1,000 in 1917 to 24.72 in 1925.[2] And in the city of Simla, where an active Maternity and Infant Welfare Organisation functions, the deaths among infants during their first year of life has been decreased 50 per cent. in the past five years, or from 424 in 1920 to 211 in 1925,[3] thereby showing what is possible.

Mother India quotes an American public health expert, 'now in international service,' to the effect that when other countries know the real conditions of public health in India they 'will turn to the League of Nations and demand protection against her.'[4] This quotation has aroused wide and varied comment. Hindu politicians such as the one who wrote *Unhappy India* admit its truth to argue that their country will remain a menace both to international health and to peace so long as Britain retains the reins of Government.[5]

[1] *Census of India*, 1921, Vol. I, Part I, p. 132.

[2] *Statistical Abstract for British India*, His Majesty's Stationery Office, London, 1928, pp. 358 and 371. England and Wales during the decade 1916-25 averaged 13.31 per thousand. (*The Registrar-General's Statistical Review of England and Wales*, 1926, Tables, Part I, p. 2; His Majesty's Stationery Office, 1927.)

[3] *Annual Report of the Public Health Commissioner with the Government of India for* 1925, p. 25.

[4] *Mother India*, p. 329. [5] *Unhappy India*, p. 469.

Colonel J. D. Graham, Chief Public Health Officer with the Government of India, when recently speaking in Calcutta, 'stated that India was one of the world's reservoirs of infection for plague and cholera and that in matters of health she was an international offender and a dangerous one as well.'[1] In reporting this speech and in commenting upon it *The Hindu* of Madras, an Indian-edited newspaper, once again turns to politics :

> No one will deny the element of truth which exists in that accusation but in the general context of present day European criticism of India, it is a little difficult to avoid the suspicion of a political argument. Col. Graham does not go so far as to say that it is an irrefutable reason for not transferring to India the control of her own destinies. . . . But the implication is there beyond a doubt. . . .[2]

Mother India itself, however, discredits political argument in this sentence :

> . . . the only power that can hasten the pace of Indian development toward freedom, beyond the pace it is travelling to-day, is the power of the men of India, wasting no more time in talk, recriminations, and shiftings of blame, but facing and attacking, with the best resolution they can muster, the task that awaits them in their own bodies and souls.[3]

Another section of the book almost completely

[1] *The Hindu*, December 9th, 1927. [2] *Ibid.* [3] Page 25.

avoided by its antagonists is the four chapters concerning the Hindus' cruelty to dumb animals. Here again, conditions in the West, even in bygone ages, cannot be compared with those in Hindu India to-day, for the simple reason that no matter how cruel our forefathers may have been, their cruelty was never induced by their religion. And although it can be denied that Hinduism literally commands cruelty to animals, its effect in producing willingness to witness or to inflict any torture, yet forbidding the direct taking of life, amounts to a religious edict authorising, even creating, cruelty. Thus any animal may be deliberately tormented, or may suffer torture, without stirring the Hindus' compassion, and this as a logical outcome of his religious code. But no matter how terribly maimed an animal may be, no matter if it is half eaten away by disease, or almost starved to death, no matter what its condition or suffering, orthodox Hinduism forbids the taking of its life.

In September 1928 a maimed and suffering calf, in Mr. Gandhi's establishment, was put out of its misery with Mr. Gandhi's consent.[1]

Immediately a storm arose from many quarters, public meetings[2] to condemn the act of kindness were organised, resolutions of 'disgust' were passed. At the meeting held under the auspices of the Humanitarian League in Bombay, the secretary, Mr. Jayanthai Mankar, pointed out that 'about three years ago he had consulted Mr. Gandhi in regard to methods of

[1] *Young India*, November 22nd, 1928.

[2] *The Statesman* (weekly edition), Calcutta, October 18th and 25th, 1928.

carrying on humanitarian propaganda on the lines adopted by American organisations. Then Mr. Gandhi warned him not to imitate the activities of the West.' Now, in defence of his present action, Mr. Mankar continued, behold Mr. Gandhi openly stating that he derived some of his ideas of non-violence from the West! And so the body of the meeting demanded the deletion of 'Mahatma'—'Saint'—from before Gandhi's name, which was accordingly done.[1]

This controversy indicates two important facts: first, that the humane act constituted an event in Gandhi's life; and, second, that the orthodox are not prepared to follow a leader who dares to transgress the Hindu code even for the relief of a helpless dumb creature. But alas for the hope that Gandhi, once started, will go fearlessly forward in the name of mercy! In the same paper in which he speaks of the calf incident he prints this letter addressed to himself:

> I am the manager of. . . *goshala* [cow asylum]. There are in my charge some 500 head of cattle. They are all utterly useless for any purpose and are simply eating their head[s] off. Out of these from 350 to 400 animals on the average are constantly at death's door, destined to die off one by one in the long end every year. Now tell me what am I to do?[2]

To this direct appeal for leadership, Mr. Gandhi made a vague evasive reply throwing the blame back upon the management. This one sentence summarises the whole:

[1] *The Statesman* (weekly edition), Calcutta, October 25th, 1928.

[2] *Young India*, November 22nd, 1928, p. 391.

> It is incumbent upon them [the management] and upon the organisers of all similarly placed institutions to devise the most effective means of nursing and ministering to the needs of diseased and ailing cattle.[1]

Less than a month previous to this episode Gandhi printed a letter from another correspondent, part of which read :

> I am much distressed and perplexed by the habitual torture of bullocks by the inhabitants of this country, chiefly Hindus, who call themselves protectors of the cow ! . . . The way the hands of the drivers, made filthy by cruelty, grasp and twitch the very backbone of the shrinking creatures at the tail-socket, when the tail itself is a broken, twisted abomination, is a sight which brings shame on the Hindu religion. . . .[2]

Since *Mother India* deals with this identical point, but perhaps in greater detail,[3] Mr. Gandhi's comment is additionally interesting. Having scolded his correspondent for indulging in a hasty generalisation, he adds :

> There is no doubt that some drivers in the cities are guilty of the practice referred to in the letter, and there is no doubt also that the passer-by goes his way totally oblivious of the torture. . . . We would be agitated if a rabid dog was shot, but we

[1] *Young India*, November 22nd, 1928, p. 391.
[2] *Ibid.*, August 30th, 1928, p. 293. [3] *Mother India*, p. 220.

are indifferent, if not willing witnesses to the cruelties such as are mentioned in the letter I have reproduced.[1]

Personally, I have ridden inside bullock carts, though never in a city, and my own observations were of worse things than tail twisting.

Yet the one book which attempts to explain away *Mother India's* animal chapters does so by shifting the blame, closing with these words :[2] 'The " quality of mercy" is not altogether independent of economic factors and of government action and inaction.'

[1] *Young India*, August 30th, 1928, p. 293.
[2] *Unhappy India*, p. 300.

ONE SUCCESSFUL METHOD

Some few Indians will take plain speech as it is meant – as the faithful wounds of a friend ; far more will be hurt at heart. Would that this task of truth-telling might prove so radically performed that all shock of resentment were finally absorbed in it, and that there need be no further waste of life and time for lack of a challenge and a declaration ! – Final paragraph of *Mother India*, p. 363.

THE few Indians who took the plain speech as it was intended have with some exceptions kept their own counsel. In like manner most of those who were 'hurt at heart' have kept their wounds to themselves. But, as has been shown, the politicians, both Hindu and Christian, non-white and whites, organised protest meetings, wrote refutations, passed resolutions, stormed, agitated, and writhed under the Western searchlight that *Mother India* threw upon Hindu social evils.

With perhaps two exceptions, all of the books written in refutation have declared *Mother India's* object to be political. Says *Sister India*[1] 'It is impossible to doubt that the main object of Miss Mayo's book is political.' And *Unhappy India*[2] ' All these facts leave no doubt in the mind of an Indian that the real motive behind the book is political and racial.' Mr. K. Natarajan in his *Rejoinder*[3] uses such phrases as 'If Miss Katherine Mayo was not a purblind propagandist but an honest inquirer. . .' And *Father India* confidently

[1] By 'World Citizen,' p. 4. [2] By Lajput Rai, lxiii.
[3] *Miss Mayo's Mother India, a Rejoinder*, p. 37.

informs us : 'Her mission is to prove that coloured people are not fit for freedom.'[1] Those Christian missionaries who have written denunciatory articles show the same readiness to attribute political motives and the same uneasiness as to the political effect of the book. Mr. C. F. Andrews connects *Mother India* with a general campaign : 'There has been all along, quite unconcealed, a definite political motive behind it.'[2] And Bishop Fred B. Fisher states of the book that '. . . in effect it says, "see what degraded people these Indians are." And whites immediately say, "Certainly. they should be rigidly governed !" '[3]

It is quite natural for those whose minds are primarily fixed on politics to view their world through political spectacles, and if *Mother India* is, as they seem to fear, a powerful argument against further extension of home rule, until raised social standards shall have secured the interest of the masses of the people, that is sufficient, in their eyes, to prove its political purpose. Many laymen, however, agree with *A Son of Mother India Answers* when it says :

[1] Ranga Iyer, p. 12.

[2] *Young India*, May 17th, 1928. As this book goes to press *Young India* for March 21st, 1929, comes to hand, bearing a retraction from Mr. Andrews written after a visit to Miss Mayo : '. . . . it seemed clear to me that she had gone out independently without a conscious political motive. But this only drives the problem of her grossly unfair book still deeper.' In printing this Mr. Gandhi remarks : '. . . . in spite of Dinabandhu Andrews' retraction, I am not shaken in my opinion that the book bears in it patent evidence of a political bias. It contains falsehoods which the authoress must have known to be such. She has since written things which too are probably false. In the face of such patent facts, evidence to the contrary must be held to be irrelevant.'

[3] Interview in *Post Standard*, Syracuse, N.Y., April 9th, 1928.

Anyone who has read the book more than once will be convinced that what hurt Miss Mayo's feelings most in India was the suffering of (1) women, (2) children and (3) animals.[1]

Or, the opinion expressed by Basil Mathews, International Literature Secretary of the World Committee of the Y.M.C.A., will find many echoing minds :

> . . . Miss Mayo again and again reiterates her praise of and affection for Indians. What she is fighting is that vast immemorial social and religious system which creates the social horrors and manifold cruelties ; the emasculation and the paralysis of initiative in so many millions of India's people. She wants to help to free India, or to help India to free itself. She may sound brutal, superior, disgusting and all the rest. But she is not a dog in a dustbin just kicking up rubbish in order to find offal ; but a sanitary inspector seeking evils with a view to their cure.[2]

The cure, *Mother India* said, lies in the hands of the Hindus themselves. To some this declaration is too bold, to others entirely unnecessary, even objectionable, as, they believe, every country, including India, and no matter what misery of the helpless is involved thereby, should be left alone to conduct its own affairs. But Basil Mathews retorts :

> . . . If anyone says that is India's business and not hers, the answer is twofold : first, in the inter-

[1] By Dhan Gopal Mukerji, p. 81.

[2] 'Mother India,' by Basil Mathews, *The Review of the Churches*, London, January, 1928, p. 117.

dependent world of to-day India's well-being is the interest of all just as our well-being is the interest of India; and secondly, that, so far, no one has exposed these realities in a way that yields social reform.[1]

To this final point it may be added: with few but creditable exceptions, no Hindu attention was paid to the Hindu 'drains' until the West began to scrutinise them. Just as Mark Twain found ridicule a weapon of curative power in America, so 'sensitiveness,' to-day, is opening the way to constructive force in the East. 'I have lived and wandered in foreign countries for many years,' writes a Hindu Master of Arts: 'I have boasted very often of our ancient civilisation, and our art, literature, ethics and philosophy. But, —but I have not talked so often of other things that also appertain to our India. . . . And why? Because it makes us *ashamed* to speak of those things in foreign countries. A feeling of shame ties up our otherwise so voluble tongues.'[2]

Mother India, by suddenly laying these 'other things' bare to the world, has loosened many Indian tongues to acknowledge them at home, even while 'shame' or 'sensitiveness' still produces vehement denials of the same fact abroad.

Recent Hindu visitors to America, whose declared purpose has been to 'offset' *Mother India*, steadfastly deny that Western scrutiny can stimulate Hindu reform.

[1] 'Mother India,' by Basil Mathews, *The Review of the Churches*, London, January, 1928, p. 117.

[2] Har Dayal, M.A., 'The Shame of India,' *Modern Review*, Calcutta, September, 1926, p. 243.

Nevertheless, the fact remains that since the book was published Hindus in India have talked more, and with greater anxiety, about their problems of child marriages, enforced widowhood, temple prostitution, and Untouchability than ever before; similarly, the Indian press is now carrying endless articles and correspondence upon these same questions.

The villages of the Gurgaon District, in the Punjab, have of late become conspicuously bright spots in the entire peninsula. In less than seven years amazing results have been achieved: more sanitation, better health, larger crops, greater prosperity. The author of this extraordinary effort, Mr. F. L. Brayne, the local Deputy Commissioner, explains his success in a short volume written in the hope that it 'will prove of use to other workers in this vast and neglected, but fascinatingly interesting field of enterprise.'[1] From Mr. Brayne's account it appears that the method pursued has been ruthlessly to tell the villagers the unvarnished facts; to this single point is laid a large measure of the accomplishment:

> We have learnt that to call a spade a spade and make no attempt to beat about the bush or employ refinements of speech is far the easiest way to provoke that discussion in a village audience which is the only way to ensure a complete understanding of the matter in hand. . . . If the village audience maintains a stony silence the lecturer can cut no ice, but once the villager can be drawn into an

[1] *Village Uplift in India*, F. L. Brayne, Pioneer Press, Allahabad, 1927, p. v.

argument or made to laugh at himself the battle is won.[1]

The propaganda leaflets used in this campaign could not possibly have been more candid ; yet, together with lectures and examples, they form its backbone. Take, for instance, these extracts from a leaflet on village cleanliness :

> When you lose your way in Gurgaon district you find your way by your nose. The greater the stink the nearer the village.
>
> Even the animals clean their young and do not foul their nests by insanitary habits. Why are Gurgaon villagers worse than animals ?[2]

Of the state of the women, another pamphlet reads :

> From their birth they are taught that they are an inferior creation, they are treated as such and therefore they *are* inferior. Release them from their degradation and slavery, bring them up as the equals of the boys and they *will be* equal. . . .
>
> *Don't allow children to marry.* Wait till they grow up and are properly developed physically and mentally. Child marriage means sickly children, unhappy homes, and infinite misery.
>
> Insist on all marriages and *karewas* being properly entered up in a register. This will save litigation and trouble. Unregistered marriages are just like the mating of birds. The only reason for not registering marriages was that women had no position or status and were hardly regarded as

[1] *Village Uplift in India*, p. 1. [2] *Ibid.*, p. 11.

human beings, being chattels owned by their parents and bartered away to become the property of their husbands, SO REGISTER ALL MARRIAGES AND ACKNOWLEDGE THE RIGHTS OF WOMEN.[1]

Such methods have worked wonders in one district. And some witnesses testify that in like manner *Mother India* is helping the whole sub-continent—helping the Hindus to rid themselves of the religious and social customs whose deadly consequences it arrayed before their eyes.

In addition to those Indians already quoted as 'taking plain speech as it was meant,' some have gone so far as to welcome the disputed volume. In a letter addressed to the Press at the height of the protest campaign organised by Hindu castemen, the secretary of an outcaste organisation said :

> Sir,—We are thankful to Miss Mayo for having expressed her sympathy with the depressed and backward classes of India. The tyrannies of the high class Indians over the poor Achuts are so innumerable that they may cover hundreds of such volumes as *Mother India*. We are trying to translate the book in the vernacular languages and distribute it free throughout India.
>
> [Signed] QUDRAT ULLAH.
>
> Secretary, Dawat-i-Islam Aborigines Tract and Book Society, Lucknow, November, 15th, [1927].

[1] *Village Uplift in India*, pp. 21, 23.

[2] *The Pioneer Mail*, Allahabad, November 18th, 1927.

And another Muhammadan, this time in Lahore, took the same stand two days later:

> Altogether 'Mother India' is a book the perusal of which I most earnestly commend to all Muslims as a first lesson in healthy introspection and the facing of facts—exercises the faculty of which a thousand years of association with Hindus has robbed us of. The book is one that should be translated into every vernacular of India and I sincerely trust that a Muslim Anjuman—or, failing that, the Government—will see that this is done. 'Mother India' is a brave book which should be made a text-book in the Muslim Universities of Aligarh and Hyderabad, both for the courageous truth in it and for the simple beauty of its style.[1]

High-caste Hindus have replied to the welcome that some Muhammadans have given the book by insinuating[2] or definitely stating that the English edition had deleted from its pages certain passages derogatory to Muhammadan customs, which passages appear in the American text:

> In the American edition of *Mother India* Miss Mayo had many uncomplimentary things to say about Indian Muslims which were omitted in the English editions, evidently under advice from certain quarters.[3]

[1] *Light*, Lahore, November 17th, 1927.

[2] See Appendix 1, p. 236.

[3] *Indian National Herald*, March 4th, 1929; *The Hindu*, March 4th, 1929; *Bombay Daily Mail*, March 4th, 1929; *Ceylon Morning Leader*, March 7th, 1929.

I, personally, have checked the American edition with that published by Jonathan Cape in London, and the only differences I have been able to find lie in the substitution of equivalent terms for words not common to both countries; as, dollars and cents for pounds, shillings and pence. Furthermore, the English publishers inform me that they actually set up *Mother India* from the American proofs.

It is often stated that *Mother India* was an unfortunate title to choose. The reason guiding that choice is explained by the author herself in an address to 'The Women of Hindu India':

> By the title of an earlier book some of you have been offended. *Mother India*, you say, is to you and yours a sacred figure—the embodiment of your Hindu race-loyalty, your Hindu race-idealism; and its name has now been rudely affixed to a bald statement of your Hindu cultural defects.
>
> That title was chosen with an object. Its purpose was to awaken your intelligent patriotism and the consciences of your men, by making inescapable contrast between, on the one hand, florid talk of devotion and 'sacrifice' poured out before an abstract figure, and, on the other hand, the consideration actually accorded to the living woman, mother of the race.[1]

[1] *Slaves of the Gods*, Katherine Mayo, Jonathan Cape, London, 1929, pp. 211, 212.

CHAPTER XVI

SOME RESULTS

We believe that with all its faults of over-statement and exaggeration MISS MAYO'S first book [*Mother India*] did definite and traceable service. It provoked a vast torrent of indignation, but it gave strength to all the reformers who are endeavouring to change conditions in India. It shocked people out of complacency. Indians saw how they were presented to Western eyes. . . . Nobody could longer blind himself to the fact that child marriage, the prevention of the remarriage of widows, the treatment of the outcaste and cruelty to animals outraged the Western peoples. . . . Reform must come from within. Happily there is evidence on all hands that Indian opinion is changing and that the new movement is finding leaders. When it has triumphed, India itself will be able to take a more charitable view of those who first uttered the thoughts of the West. –Editorial, *The Statesman*, Calcutta, April 11th, 1929.

IT will be years, probably decades, before a comprehensive estimate of *Mother India's* fruits can be drawn and balanced. Yet certain results are already ripe for record. Amongst these is an increasing readiness on the part of both Indians and Europeans resident in India to acknowledge and make public the existing status of India's womanhood. Where before, whether from a pessimistic disbelief in the efficacy of protests, or from a natural dislike of becoming the butt of Hindu resentment, private citizens shrank from public mention of the horrors they daily saw, now, following *Mother India's* lead, they begin to come forward into print, and over their own names bear witness to the truth. For example, in the *Times of India* for February 28th, 1928, the following testimony appeared:

> On Saturday morning, the 25th February, when I was coming from Matheran to Neral by rickshaw, I passed a group of people on the road. A girl of perhaps 15 years was being driven along by men armed with sticks with which they prodded her periodically. She was entirely naked and subjected to the gaze of every passer-by. Her arms were tied behind her in such a way as to cause dislocation unless she were double-jointed. I tried to find out what the trouble was, but my rickshaw coolies were not anxious to stop and merely said 'jungli peoples,' and hurried on. The girl's screams and groans were pitiful, but I was powerless to help her, and could not speak the language.
>
> It seems incredible that such a thing could happen; a dozen men torturing (for it was nothing less) a wretched girl. Is there no way of meting out punishment to these people, or are they able to treat their women as they like? Can Government do nothing in a matter of this sort?
>
> After such an experience I can believe anything I have read in *Mother India*. . . .
>
> (Mrs.) A. KEEGAN, Bombay.

Another case brought to public attention because of *Mother India* came to light in the *Pioneer Mail* of May 11th, 1928:

> Yesterday I was compelled from my room and my chair, in the early morning of a very hot day

while doors and windows were still open by the sound of incessant and loud weeping—a young voice in distress—it is a cry which is unmistakable—and I was not surprised to see on the road a small cart, springless and rough, moving slowly along, carrying a burden all tied up in cloth, secured all round with string, and successfully excluding all air and light—and from which same bundle the cries were coming.

I stopped the cart, which was driven by a boy of perhaps 20, whose face was as expressionless as that of his bullock and asked 'what is the matter?' It was the usual story—a poor little girl-wife being taken from her village to join her husband and *his* mother. Her age? Eleven.

A little crowd of wayfarers gathered round us as I talked. They were all sympathetic—she *was* too young. But—it was the custom "and"—added an old man, who must have years of experience—'it happens every day at this time of year.'

No help for the poor little girl—no comfort in her sorrow—unbreakable custom.

Surely these things, and the remark of the Health Officer of Calcutta Corporation in a recent report 'for every boy who dies of tuberculosis between the ages 16–20, six girls die'—help to confirm Mother India and how many little hearts are broken?

All honour to Katherine Mayo who tries to help these poor little girls.

IDA MARY WILLMORE, New Capital,
Patna, May 1st.

The *Behar Herald* tells us that Mrs. Willmore, who signs this letter, is the wife of the Inspector-General of Civic Hospitals in Behar and Orissa. Then, without a word of denial of her statement, without a word of hope or sympathy for these girl-wives, it editorially attacks the lady who has dared to express compassion for this victim of Hindu culture :

> Mrs. Willmore's letter is indiscreet for more reasons than one. Lately she has been interesting herself in one or two humanitarian institutions, notably the Blind School at Patna. Her praise of Miss Mayo at the present moment is not calculated to increase her usefulness in these activities. . . . Another reason why Mrs. Willmore's letter is indiscreet is that on account of a different culture Europeans are unable to appreciate Indian customs and view points. . . .[1]

In this one editorial, the *Behar Herald* largely explains why both Indians and Europeans, if working to relieve the suffering in India, have resisted the temptation to corroborate *Mother India* in public speech or print. Westerners will, however, find it difficult to appreciate a point of view which holds that a European lady living in India can endanger her usefulness in such humanitarian work as a school for the native blind by the simple act of calling attention to an apparently common Hindu custom. Yet that is the fact.

Or, again, it is a Hindu who writes to the native-owned *Indian National Herald*, under date of June 28th, 1928:

[1] *Behar Herald*, Patna, May 12th, 1928.

Sir,—Miss Mayo—some people believe—has written half truths but she has rightly condemned some horrible customs prevalent among Indians in general and Hindus in particular.

Every one has a right to do particular thing provided he does not trespass on the moral code of society.

But when a man of above 75 years of age—with one foot in "Nanashankersheth's Wadi"—marries a tender girl of sixteen or so and the girl in her approaching widowhood is strictly forbidden to remarry according to prevalent custom, she has to lead a miserable life.

Such a marriage is the subject of much talk and comment in my Bhatia community, since one rich old man has married for the sixth time.

Reformers, I hear, tried to prevent this marriage seeking legal help, but there is no law to do it and this horrible marriage after all is an event of the past.

Will not some legislator with prevalent human feelings move in the matter for the general good of Hindus?

[Sd.] DHANJI LAXMIDAS.[1]

180 Bazaaragate Street,
Bombay, June 28th.

If it had not been for the advent of *Mother India* would this letter have been written, would it have been printed? Or would Rai Sahib Harbilas Sarda have read the following story to the assembled legislators in Simla?

[1] *Indian National Herald*, Bombay, July 2nd, 1928.

> The driver of No. 16 passenger train stated that while examining his engine near the water tank at Narayanpet Station, he noticed a girl get down from the third class bogie carriage and running to station well to jump into it.
>
> The father of the girl told the police that his daughter Bhingoobai had been married to one Luxmon, four years back when she was about six years old. In accordance with the custom, she was sent to her husband's house two months after marriage. After remaining there two months, she returned to her parent's house, was sent back by the latter, but returned again.
>
> This happened several times. Her father taking advantage of one of his relations named Yedoo going to Shahabad determined to send his daughter back to her husband with this relation and himself took her to the station and saw her entrained. While he and Yedoo were engaged in conversation on the platform he was informed his daughter had fallen in a well. He ran to the well with others and a cultivator, named Samboo, jumped into the well and brought the girl out still alive but senseless. She expired soon after.[1]

The horrors this little child must have experienced at the hands of her lawful husband! Yet her parents may have loved her with that curious Hindu love which only sees *her* duty to her husband. Were the gods kind in giving her sufficient courage to commit suicide? Or, did that act need less courage than to face her husband again?

[1] *Legislative Assembly Debates*, September 15th, 1927, p. 4,411.

The narrator himself added, "Sir, this is not a solitary incident of its kind in this country."[1]

It is not denied that similar items, with much greater detail, could be culled from newspapers and reports in the West. Indeed, American and British editors would probably spend large sums in collecting such 'stories' for their 'news value.' But therein lies the difference and the point. To our editors they would constitute startling news-stories, to be sought, written up, and 'splashed.' To Indians they are commonplace, everyday occurrences, seldom published except when addressed to the papers in the form of letters from Indian social reformers and from Europeans.

If, however, *Mother India* had done no more than stir Indian opinion by throwing a searchlight upon the wrongs done Hindu women, room for debate might still exist, from certain points of view, as to the wisdom of its having been written.

But more has been accomplished.

Since the summer of 1927, when first the book reached the peninsula, and in spite of the ensuing deluge of criticism, a few individuals have taken the message to heart. Of these few, a handful who are in a position to take immediate action have done so.

The Princes of India rule over one-third of the area of the whole peninsula.[2] Within the limits of their own

[1] *Legislative Assembly Debates*, September 15th, 1927, p. 4,411.

[2] The Indian States and Agencies cover 711,032 square miles with almost 72,000,000 inhabitants, or some 101 persons per square mile, as compared to a mean density in British India of 226. (*Census of India*, 1921, Part I, Vol. I, pp. 5 and 57). Sir Sidney Low informs us that these states, principalities, and lordships not under the direct control of British India number 448. (*The Indian*

territories these rulers have complete autocratic powers, although some have recently instituted partially elected assemblies. Since *Mother India* appeared, edicts, orders or decrees either prohibiting child marriages or raising the age of consent for married children, within the jurisdiction of their states, are reported to have been promulgated by the Princes of Baroda, Bikaner, Gondal, Indore, Kashmir, Kotah (*sic*), Mandi, and Rajkot (*sic*).[1]

In Mysore the Legislative Council has adopted a resolution raising the age of consent for girls to sixteen, and has agreed to fix the marriageable age for boys and girls at twenty and fourteen respectively.[2] These are the more advanced principalities.

Too much hope, however, must not be placed upon such decrees being actually enforced. Take, for instance, the history of compulsory education in the first native state to legislate on it—Baroda. Here 'compulsory education has been enforced since the year 1906';[3] yet, in 1912, fifteen years later, only 105 out of every 1,000 females between the ages of fifteen and twenty were literate.[4]

On the other hand, while, as we have seen, the Government of India is not to be stampeded into supporting laws which are almost certainly not enforceable, it seized the opportunity created by *Mother India* pub-

States and Ruling Princes, Sir Sidney Low, Benn's Library, London, 1929, p. 11.)

[1] *The Modern Review*, Calcutta, January, 1928, June, 1928; *Behar Herald*, Patna, April 28th, 1928; *Statesman*, Calcutta, September 13th, 1928. This list is probably incomplete.

[2] *Civil and Military Gazette*, Lahore, December 24th, 1928.

[3] *Census of India*, 1921, Vol. I, Part I, p. 179.

[4] *Ibid.* p. 187.

licly to open, examine, and ventilate the subject of child marriage, for the education of public opinion.

To this end, as we have seen, it appointed an Age of Consent Committee, under the chairmanship of Sir Moropant Joshi, to take evidence all over British India. When this fact became public property, the Simla correspondent of Mrs. Besant's paper, *New India*, remarked:

> It may be mentioned that rarely has an announcement of the Government found such a ready echo in the columns of the world press as this announcement of Mr. Crerar. The reason is that the publication of *Mother India* has directed the western world's attention to the social ills in India.[1]

Yet the elected members of the Legislative Assembly refused the necessary appropriation for this committee to carry out its work of investigation. Here is the *Manchester Guardian's* report :

> The Standing Finance Committee of the Legislative Assembly has rejected entirely the application of one lakh of rupees for the expenses of the Committee to investigate the question of the age of consent in India on the ground that the explanation of Mr. Haig, Secretary Home Department, is unsatisfactory on the point why members of the Central Legislature should be excluded from membership of the Committee.[2]

As the London *Times* observed when the personnel

[1] Quoted in the *Bombay Daily Mail*, May 16th, 1928.
[2] September 4th, 1928.

of the Committee was first announced, 'The absence of any member of the Assembly from the committee at first seems curious, but all the unofficial members of the House who have shown interest in the subject have deeply committed themselves to particular views.'[1] Thus the question was whether to appoint legislators who took no interest in the matter to be investigated; to appoint legislators previously and publicly wedded to a theory, which they might attempt to lead the Committee to approve; or, leaving the Central Legislature entirely aside and turning to other outstanding figures, to appoint a committee of interest but uncompromised persons.

This third was the choice of the Government; an 'Age of Consent Committee' was set up, consisting of five Indian members and one European. These comprised legislators from Provincial Councils, a High Court Judge, a Chief Judicial Officer, a woman superintendent of a Government hospital, and an outstanding Hindu lady.[2]

Fortunately Government did not allow the Finance Committee's refusal of funds to choke off the Committee's work, which is steadily proceeding throughout India. The final report is due to be made public late in 1929.

[1] *The Times*, London, June 26th, 1928. [2] *Ibid.*

CHAPTER XVII

MOTIVES

MANY and varied are the motives adduced in explanation of *Mother India*. Most of the 'replies' have either ignored or repudiated the book's declared purpose as stated in its first chapter, where the author furthermore declares, 'In shouldering this task myself, I am fully aware of the resentments I shall incur: of the accusations of muckraking; of injustice; of material-mindedness; of lack of sympathy; of falsehood perhaps; perhaps of prurience.'[1]

Easily she might have added: Of being British-born; of bearing malice and hatred against the British; of being backed by Moscow; of having sold my soul to Britain; of writing a dime novel; even of loving pornography and courting riches through pandering to my fellow Americans' depraved tastes. For each of these accusations, and many others, equally fantastic, have in turn been made.

Following the additional imputations in the order in which they are suggested, we find the Rev. Reuben F. Porter, in Wabash, Indiana, recently informing his congregation that 'Miss Mayo is English[2] and travelled around India under the supervision of the British Government.'[3] Because he had recently returned from

[1] *Mother India*, p. 26.

[2] Miss Mayo was born in Ridgeway, Pennsylvania, the tenth in descent from American parentage. (*Who's Who in America*, 1918 *et seq.*, and Records Massachusetts Society of Mayflower Descendants.)

[3] *Plain Dealer*, Wabash, Indiana, November 30th, 1928.

India, and because of the cloth he wears, this gentleman's words presumably carry weight with his hearers.

A leading Canadian journal adds its contribution, an equally well-founded, though antipodal, suspicion:

> Who sent this United States woman out to India to stir up the caste stench which has been so successfully kept down by the astute, humane and skilful handling of John Bull? Was it Moscow? [or] Was it the same body of officials who sent General Reilly of the United States army over to Europe to discover to what extent that nation won the Great War?[1]

From Australia, again, comes the assertion, 'In this book I seem to discern two motives, one of which is envy, hatred and malice against the British. . . .'[2]

Less wonder, therefore, that a Hindu politician should declare, 'We have reason to believe that Miss Mayo's visit was not a spontaneous one, and that she was urged to come to India by those Britishers with vested interests, who think that the development of self-government in India is a menace to them and their pockets.'[3] And the Indian-owned newspapers go only a step further when they name the sum received from British merchants or the British crown, in such headlines as these: '£5,000 For Miss Mayo—Official Subsidy—Author Engaged by a Syndicate—Startling

[1] *Daily Mail and Empire*, Toronto, Canada, September 24th, 1928.

[2] A. M. Pooley, in *The Evening News*, Sydney, N.S.W., December 22nd, 1927. See also *The Hindustan Review*, Allahabad, January-March, 1929, p. 82.

[3] *Unhappy India*, p. xx.

Revelations.'[1] Or '£5,000 for "Drain Inspector"—Govt. of India Reported to have Subsidised *Mother India*.'[2]

Mr. Gandhi sets afloat the 'dime novel' idea by insinuating that *Mother India* is a 'shilling shocker.'[3]

And as to the final count, American audiences pay to hear Dhan Gopal Mukerji tell them that 'sex, not life, rules American literature and drama.' In my books,'[4] he is reported as announcing 'I have talked about the soul of India these many years. But I notice that books on sex and Indian pornography are mostly read nowadays. For instance in *Mother India*, Miss Mayo talks of nothing but the most abnormal sex cases, and because of that people buy the books in large quantities.'

However, this did not prevent the speaker from writing *A Son of Mother India Answers*.

Even in the British House of Commons Mr. Rennie Smith, the Labour Member from Penistone, asked the Under Secretary of State for India 'whether Miss Mayo was assisted in the production of this book by the India Office or the Government of India?'[5] eliciting this reply:

> Miss Mayo received no assistance in the production of her book, either from the India Office or from the Government of India, beyond the supply

[1] *Forward*, Calcutta, November 6th, 1927.

[2] *Indian National Herald*, Bombay, November 5th, 1927.

[3] 'Drain Inspector's Report,' *Young India*, M. K. Gandhi, September 15th, 1927.

[4] *Tribune*, Des Moines, Ia., October 18th, 1927.

[5] *Parliamentary Debates*, House of Commons, extracts relating to Indian Affairs, Session 1927, Part IX, p. 706.

of official information on matters of fact which is afforded to any member of the public who asks for it.[1]

That was on November 14th, 1927. Ten days later Lord Birkenhead, the then Secretary of State for India, took occasion thus to challenge the statement of another member of the House of Commons:

> I saw it stated in another place,[2] by a member of the House of Commons, that a book which has created wide public attention, called *Mother India*—it was written by Miss Mayo, I think—was inspired either by the Government of India or by the Government of this country. I should not deal with this matter if I were not so struck by the complete irresponsibility which would enable a member of another place to make a statement so absolutely false, without putting forward a vestige of evidence. I most expressly invite that lady [Miss Ellen C. Wilkinson, Member of Parliament for Middlesbrough] either to withdraw that charge or to produce the evidence upon which she founded herself.[3]

But these pronouncements have never received the wide publicity enjoyed by the more accusatory ones. The rumour that *Mother India* was inspired by some governmental or political body persisted. So widely was

[1] *Parliamentary Debates*, House of Commons, extracts relating to Indian Affairs, Session 1927, Part IX, p. 706.

[2] In the British Parliament it is customary for the members of both Houses to refer to the other House as 'another place.'

[3] *Parliamentary Debates*, House of Lords, extracts relating to Indian Affairs, Session 1927, Part IV, p. 184.

it believed in Europe during 1928 that the English publisher, Mr. Jonathan Cape, found it necessary to set the legend at rest once and for all so far as he was concerned, by issuing this public statement over his own signature:

> I first heard of *Mother India* in January 1927, in New York, where I met Miss Mayo, who told me that a book on India which she had been engaged upon for some time was nearly finished. She offered it to me for publication. I brought the manuscript back with me and read it on board ship. I felt the book could not fail to attract attention, but before being accepted it was read in manuscript by several distinguished persons competent to judge of its value and substantial accuracy.[1]

The letter goes on to point out that the book was accepted in the ordinary course of business, was advertised as its merits deserved, and 'at no time did the publishers have any communication, official or unofficial, in reference to the book with any political or other organisation.'[2]

Meanwhile few opportunities seem to have been lost, by those considering themselves hurt or offended, to pump new life into this old legend. Hindu politicians have fairly rained questions on the All-India Legislative Assembly in an endeavour to tie the Government to the book. The first shower occurred at Simla in September, 1927, the second at Delhi in March of the

[1] *The Times*, London, March 28th, 1928. [2] *Ibid.*

following year, and the last storm in the Assembly, reported at this writing, took place during the September session, again at Simla, in 1928. In the Council of State further questions were asked in March, 1929.[1] Apparently the home-rule politician is vowed not to let the matter rest despite the author's, the publisher's and the officials' repeated statements of the facts.

[1] See *Legislative Assembly Debates*, printed in the Appendix I, September 19th and 20th, 1927, and March 7th, September 4th, 1928. Also *Council of State Debates*, March 4th, 1929.

CHAPTER XVIII

CONCLUSION

THE material presented in these pages is but a fractional part of the evidence that has come into my hands, from Indian sources, substantiating the paramount thesis of *Mother India*. Perhaps, however, sufficient has been presented to prove beyond doubt these two facts: First, that the worst religious and social customs of the Hindus of India prevail to a wide degree; and, second, that Western public opinion to-day is a real power for correcting those Hindu customs most to be deplored.

Time and time again, during the past two years, the Hindu in India has used the argument that America and Europe are watching and that, therefore, something must be done to retrieve the Hindu position before the Western world. Thus, in the most recent Central Indian Legislative Debate to hand, we find an ardent exponent of the child marriage bill using these words:

> People in England and America are watching how we deal with this Bill. Writers like Miss Mayo, and politicians like Mr. Winston Churchill have declared that India cannot be granted self-government so long as she tolerates and commits acts of oppression against girls of tender age.[1]

It is immaterial that no such statement is to be found in *Mother India*, for the book has obviously developed

[1] *Legislative Assembly Debates*, January 29th, 1929, Delhi, p. 196. Speech by Rai Sahib Harbilas Sarda.

that conclusion in the speaker's mind. Nor is it pertinent to say that a desire for social betterment which is spurred on only by foreign eyes, or by fear of criticism from other countries, or by desire for political power, is built on foundations of sand. The needs of Hindu India are dire—so dire that if by the simple process of facing the facts, of scrutinising those needs and their causes, we of the West may speed up a rescue, we can hardly deny our obligation to apply that scrutiny.

If a Hindu should produce a book on the slums of England which would so prick the Englishman's conscience as to start a national movement for the abolition of slums, it is safe to forecast that few thinking Englishmen would be anything but grateful for the book. Similarly, it is not too much to say that if an Indian presented the United States with a volume so powerful as to start a new and constructive policy toward the settlement of the American negro problem, few Americans and no true leaders would feel anything but gratitude toward its author.

Even from Mr. Natarajan's *Indian Social Reformer*, whose bitterness from the first has been followed in these pages, is wrung this reluctant testimony to the good already achieved by *Mother India*:

> It must be admitted, too, that, while her [Miss Mayo's] poisonous generalisations about Indians, and especially, Hindus as a class aroused resentment, her book has stimulated action which otherwise would not have come so soon. Indian opinion is almost morbidly sensitive to Western criticism,

> and Miss Mayo's bittingsgate [*sic*] has gone home more effectively than the long and patient propaganda of social reformers in many circles hitherto but slightly responsive to their reasoned arguments.[1]

The primary object of *Mother India*, as the author makes clear in its first chapter, was, however, not to reform but to *inform*. The reforming power since developed by the book as toward the Hindu social status, has been bestowed upon it by those hundreds of thousands of Western readers who have grasped its message.

But if for any reason whatsoever its issues are allowed to be blurred over, confused, or twisted, then, perhaps, the greatest impulse for reform in Hindu India's history may be frittered away.

[1] *Indian Social Reformer*, K. Natarajan editor, Bombay, March 9th, 1929, p. 433.

APPENDIX I

LEGISLATORS AND 'MOTHER INDIA'

EXCERPTS from the Central India Legislative Assembly Debates of questions and answers concerning *Mother India* and its author.

Legislative Assembly Debates, September 19th, 1927, Vol. IV, No. 64, pp. 4544–4547.

MISS MAYO'S BOOK 'MOTHER INDIA.'

1128. * Mr. M. S. Aney: (*a*) Has the attention of the Government been drawn to the following special message first published in *The Hindustan*, a Gujrati daily of Bombay and since published in all the prominent Indian newspapers:

'Many of the British M.P.'s have been provided with a free copy of Miss Katherine Mayo's book *Mother India.*'

(*b*) Will the Government be pleased to state whether free copies of the same book have been supplied to any officials and the Anglo-Indian publicists in India also?

(*c*) Will the Government be pleased to say whether the Publicity Department of the Government of India has been supplied with a copy of the book or not?

The Honourable Mr. J. Crerar: (*a*) Government have seen the report, and have ascertained from the Secretary of State that no copies of the book have been distributed by the India Office or at public expense.

(*b*) Not so far as Government are aware.

(*c*) No.

Mr. A. Rangaswami Iyengar: May I know if Government are aware that Miss Mayo is connected with the British Library of Literature in New York?

The Honourable Mr. J. Crerar: Will the Honourable Member kindly repeat the question?

Mr. A. Rangaswami Iyengar: May I know if Government can tell us what connection Miss Mayo has with the British Library of Literature in New York?

The Honourable Mr. J. Crerar: I am afraid I have no information on the point. If the Honourable Member will put down the question, I shall endeavour to answer it.

The Honourable Sir Basil Blackett: I will answer the question. The answer is that she has none.

Mr. B. Das: Do I take it that Miss Mayo was not at all helped by any of the Provincial Governments or the Government of India in the matter of collection of materials for her book, or that she was not at all helped by the Secretary of State by the supply of any materials?

The Honourable Mr. J. Crerar: Miss Mayo received no more assistance from any officials of Government than would be accorded to any other private person.

Lala Lajpat Rai: The question is whether she *was* given any assistance. The question I wish to ask is, did the Publicity Department of the Government of India give any assistance to Miss Mayo in connection with the materials for her book?

The Honourable Mr. J. Crerar: I am not aware that the Government of India gave any assistance of any sort to Miss Mayo, but if she did get any assistance, it was no more than would ordinarily be extended to any other member of the public.

Mr. A. Rangaswami Iyengar: May I ask if the Government of India's Publicity Department supplied Miss Mayo with any photographs that are published in her New York edition?

The Honourable Mr. J. Crerar: I have no information on the point, but shall inquire.

The Honourable Sir Basil Blackett: The answer is in the negative.

Mr. K. Ahmed: In view of the fact that the Honourable Member has admitted that no more than ordinary courtesy was shown to Miss Mayo and no more materials were supplied than would ordinarily be supplied to a member of the public, do Government propose to supply us with the precise extent of the help accorded ?

The Honourable Mr. J. Crerar: I did not say that any materials were supplied to Miss Mayo. If ordinary courtesy was extended to her, I think there would be no reasonable objection on that ground.

Mr. A. Rangaswami Iyengar: May I know exactly what assistance was given to her, whether by way of courtesy or by way of departmental accommodation?

The Honourable Mr. J. Crerar: Miss Mayo spent some months in the country. I am afraid I cannot give all the details the Honourable Member requires.

Lala Lajpat Rai: Are Government aware that Miss Mayo was a guest of a Superintendent of Police in Lahore and got information from the Head of the Publicity Department of the Government of India?

The Honourable Mr. J. Crerar: No, Sir.

Mr. K. C. Neogy: Has the Honourable Member read the book himself, and has the Honourable Member read both the editions, American and English?

The Honourable Mr. J. Crerar: I have only read one edition.

Mr. K. C. Neogy: Is it a fact that there is some difference between the two editions, and that things uncomplimentary to Muhammadans were left out in the English edition?[1]

The Honourable Mr. J. Crerar: So far as I am aware, there is no difference in the letterpress.

Mr. M. S. Aney: Is it a fact that Miss Mayo was furnished by some officials with materials before they were actually published, and that the materials were checked by some officials before they were actually published?

The Honourable Mr. J. Crerar: No, Sir.

Mr. K. C. Neogy: Has the Publicity Department compared the two editions?

Mr. President: I am prepared to let Mr. Coatman answer the question.

Mr. K. C. Neogy: We would like to hear Mr. Coatman.

[1] The only difference this author has been able to discover between the American and English editions of *Mother India* lies in the substitution of equivalent terms for words not common to both countries ; as, dollars and cents for pounds, shillings, and pence.

Mr. J. Coatman: I have read both the editions, Sir, but I cannot say that I have compared them as one would compare two different texts; and I am not conscious of any material difference between the two editions.

Mr. K. C. Neogy: Has the Honourable Member been supplied with complimentary copies of both the editions?

Mr. J. Coatman: No, Sir.

Lala Lajpat Rai: Is the Honourable Member aware that a statement has been made in the Press that a C.I.D. Inspector asked an Indian gentleman in Lahore to see Miss Mayo?

The Honourable Mr. J. Crerar: The statement was made in the Press, but my information is that it is not correct.

Mr. B. Das: Will the Honourable Member verify it?

The Honourable Mr. J. Crerar: I have already made an inquiry on the subject.

Mr. M. R. Jayakar: Having regard to their present experience, will the Government consider the advisability of being more careful in future about extending such courtesies to American tourists?

The Honourable Mr. J. Crerar: I cannot agree that the Government has been in any respect careless in the matter.

Lala Lajpat Rai: Are Government aware that Mahatma Gandhi and Miss Bose[1] of the Victoria Girls School in Lahore have entirely repudiated the statements Miss Mayo put into their mouths in her book?

[1] See *ante*, pp. 136-137.

Munshi Iswar Saran: Will the Honourable Member kindly state the nature of the courtesy they extended to Miss Mayo?

The Honourable Mr. J. Crerar: I have already answered that question.

Munshi Iswar Saran: As I am at a distance, I could not hear it fully.

The Honourable Mr. J. Crerar: I said Miss Mayo spent some months in India and I am not in a position to give the complete details asked for.

Munshi Iswar Saran: I do not want details; I want to know the broad features of the courtesy.

The Honourable Mr. J. Crerar: I have already answered the question.

* * *

Legislative Assembly Debates, Tuesday, September 20th, 1927, Vol. IV, No. 65, pp. 4641–4643.

STAY OF MISS MAYO, AUTHOR OF "MOTHER INDIA," AS A GUEST OF A SUPERINTENDENT OF THE C.I.D.[1] AT LAHORE

1190. *Mr. Gaya Prasad Singh: (*a*) Is it a fact that Miss Mayo, the author of *Mother India*, was the guest of a Superintendent of the C.I.D. at Lahore during her visit to this country, and that an Inspector of the C.I.D. was deputed to help her in making enquiries and acquaintances?

(*b*) Is it a fact that an official of the Intelligence Department, Government of India, arranged for her stay in Lahore, with the Superintendent of the C.I.D., or helped her in any other way?

[1] Criminal Investigation Department.

(*c*) Do Government propose to institute an enquiry, and place the facts before the House? If not, why not?

The Honourable Mr. J. Crerar: (*a*) No.

(*b*) No.

(*c*) I have placed the facts before the House and no enquiry is necessary.

MISS MAYO'S BOOK "MOTHER INDIA"

1191. *Pandit Hirday Nath Kunzru: (*a*) Has the following telegram from Bombay published in the *Leader* of the 7th instant come to the notice of Government: 'A special message to the *Hindustan*, a local Gujrati daily, says that many of the British Members of Parliament have been provided with free copies of Miss Katherine Mayo's book *Mother India*.'

(*b*) If the information contained in the message is correct, will Government state whether free copies of *Mother India* have been distributed by or at the instance of the British Government? If so, have the British Government made themselves responsible for the statements made in the book?

(*c*) Are Government aware that *Mother India* is regarded by Indians as a malicious and filthy libel on the people of this country?

(*d*) Have Government informed the British Government that a free distribution of this book by them would create deep and universal resentment and indignation in this country?

The Honourable Mr. J. Crerar: (*a*) and (*b*): I invite attention to the answer I gave to Mr. M. S. Aney's question on the subject on the 19th September, 1927. The British Government have neither caused the book to be distributed nor made themselves responsible for any statement contained in the book.

(*c*) Government have seen articles on the subject in the Public Press.

(*d*) The fact is obvious and it is unnecessary to bring it to the British Government's notice.

Mr. K. C. Neogy: Is the Honourable Member aware that this publication has accentuated racial feeling in India to a very great extent?

The Honourable Mr. J. Crerar: That, Sir, is a matter of opinion.

Pandit Hirday Nath Kunzru: May I ask the Honourable Member, Sir, whether the British Government have borne any portion of the cost involved in the distribution of the book?

The Honourable Mr. J. Crerar: Not a penny, Sir.

Mr. Gaya Prasad Singh: May I know, Sir, if the Publicity Bureau of the Government of India have received any complimentary copies of the book?

The Honourable Mr. J. Crerar: No, Sir; they have not.

Mr. Sarabhai Nemchand Haji: Will Government kindly inquire as to who it is that has distributed these copies to the Members of Parliament in London?

The Honourable Mr. J. Crerar: That, Sir, is not the concern of the Government of India.

Pandit Hirday Nath Kunzru: Are Government prepared to contradict the distorted statements contained in the book in view of the racial feeling that has been accentuated by it in India?

The Honourable Mr. J. Crerar: I think that matter could better be dealt with by a non-official agency.

Pandit Hirday Nath Kunzru: Do not Government think it worth their while to correct the mis-statements and exaggerations contained in that book in view of the fact that it has been circulated in other countries and is being used as a sort of propaganda against this country?

The Honourable Mr. J. Crerar: As I have already replied, Sir, that is a matter which can be much more effectively dealt with by a non-official agency and by those who have the most direct knowledge of the matters dealt with in the book.

Mr. K. C. Neogy: Does the Honourable Member admit that this book contains untruths and exaggerations?

The Honourable Mr. J. Crerar: That, Sir, is asking for an expression of opinion.

Mr. K. C. Neogy: Is not the good name of the people of India a matter of concern for the Government?

The Honourable Mr. J. Crerar: Certainly the matter is one in which the Government of India naturally take interest.

Mr. N. M. Joshi: Do not the Government of India maintain a propagandist in countries like America who could be asked to correct the mis-statements contained in Miss Mayo's book?

The Honourable Mr. J. Crerar: We have no propagandist agencies in America.

Mr. Varahagiri Venkata Jogiah: May I know, Sir, if the Government of India propose to proscribe the book?

Mr. A. Rangaswami Iyengar: May I know, Sir, whether the Government of India do expend some money out of the revenues of India on propaganda work in America?

The Honourable Mr. J. Crerar: No, Sir.

Mr. K. Ahmed: Are Government aware that the *Manchester Guardian* has made the observation and has given the advice to the people of India that it is better for them to counteract the effects of the book and that it is good for the English people to forget them?

The Honourable Mr. J. Crerar: I remember seeing something in the *Manchester Guardian* somewhat vaguely and remotely resembling what the Honourable Member has said.

Dr. A. Suhrawardy: Will the Honourable Member kindly inquire as to how many Members of this House have read Miss Mayo's book, *Mother India*?

The Honourable Mr. J. Crerar: I suggest that that question should be addressed to other Members of this House and not to myself.

Dr. A. Suhrawardy: Is the Honourable Member aware that Miss Mayo's book contains extracts from the debates of this House?

The Honourable Mr. J. Crerar: Yes, Sir.

Dr. A. Suhrawardy: Will the Honourable Member kindly inquire whether Mr. Coatman was responsible for supplying the appalling statements and figures to the Honourable Member who moved the Bill regarding Hindu child marriages?

The Honourable Mr. J. Crerar: I do not think, Sir, that question arises.

Mr. Ram Narayan Singh: Are Government prepared to proscribe the book?

The Honourable Mr. J. Crerar: Quite apart from any legal considerations that might arise, I think that it would be very ill advised from the Honourable Member's own point of view to proscribe the book.

Mr. K. C. Neogy: Are Government taking any legal opinion in the matter?

The Honourable Mr. J. Crerar: No, Sir.

Mr. M. Ruthnaswamy: Are the Honourable Members opposite in favour of proscribing the book?

Mr. Ram Narayan Singh: Are Government prepared to take legal opinion in the matter as to whether the book is fit to be proscribed or not?

The Honourable Mr. J. Crerar: The legal position is so clear that it is unnecessary to do so.

* * *

Legislative Assembly Debates, September 20th, 1927, Vol. IV, No. 65, pp. 4655–4656.

OFFICIAL ASSISTANCE TO MISS MAYO IN COLLECTING MATERIALS FOR HER BOOK "MOTHER INDIA"

1163. *Mr. M. S. Aney: (*a*) Has the attention of the Government of India been drawn to Miss Mayo's book *Mother India* and the numerous statements regarding India and Indian people contained therein?

(*b*) Is it a fact that Mr. Coatman, Head of the Publicity Department of the Government of India, was associated with Miss Mayo in collecting materials for her book?

(*c*) Is there any truth in the rumour that Miss Mayo was in some way or other subsidised by the Scout Service Funds?

(*d*) Is it a fact that Mr. Coatman saw the proofs of the book?

(*e*) Will the Government find out and disclose the names of such officials as helped Miss Mayo in the collection of materials of that book or in writing it?

The Honourable Mr. J. Crerar: (*a*) Government have seen the book. (*b*), (*c*) and (*d*). There is no truth whatever in these suggestions and I should like to repudiate them emphatically. I would also refer the Honourable Member to the Foreword to the book itself, in which the author expressly states that she submitted the manuscript of the book to no one connected with official life.

(*e*) Government have no reason to suppose that any official gave Miss Mayo any assistance beyond what is given to any member of the public.

ISSUE OF A CONTRADICTION TO THE NUMEROUS ALLEGATIONS CONTAINED IN MISS MAYO'S BOOKS "MOTHER INDIA" AND "ISLES OF FEAR"

1164. * Mr. M. S. Aney: (*a*) Will the Government be pleased to state whether they have issued any instructions to the Head of the Publicity Department to promptly issue any book or pamphlet to give an authoritative contradiction to any of the numerous allegations contained in the two books of Miss Catherine Mayo (*sic*) *Mother India* and *Isles of Fear*?

(*b*) If not, will the Government be pleased to say whether they propose to do so hereafter?

(*c*) If not, why?

The Honourable Mr. J. Crerar: (*a*) and (*b*). Government have not given and do not propose to give such instructions.

(*c*) They do not consider that such instructions would serve any useful purpose.

Mr. K. C. Neogy: Do Government attach any importance to the resentment that has been caused among the public by this book.

The Honourable Mr. J. Crerar: Government have naturally observed that with interest and concern.

Mr. K. C. Neogy: Are Government in sympathy with the statements that have appeared in this book?

The Honourable Mr. J. Crerar: That, Sir, is rather too general a question for me to reply to either affirmatively or negatively.

Mr. M. R. Jayakar: Does that book represent the opinions of Government on the culture and traditions of Indians?

The Honourable Mr. J. Crerar: I have already explained that Government accept no responsibility for what has appeared in this book.

Mr. K. C. Neogy: Is the Government attitude one of neutrality in this matter?

(No answer.)

Mr. K. C. Neogy: Do Government possess any opinion on the statements contained in the book?

The Honourable Mr. J. Crerar: The Honourable Member is asking for an opinion.

Mr. K. C. Neogy: Do Government possess any opinion at all? That is not a question of opinion, but of fact.

Mr. B. Das: Are Government going to proscribe that book?

Mr. K. Ahmed: In view of the fact that there is great commotion and disorder in the House and in the country, do Government propose. . . .

Mr. President:[1] Order, order.

Mr. K. Ahmed: The question arises, Sir, and I am entitled to put supplementary questions. May I know under what rule or standing order the Chair rules me out of order?

Mr. President: Order, order.

* * *

Legislative Assembly Debates, Wednesday, March 7th, 1928, Vol. I, No. 22, p. 1059.

PURCHASE BY THE INDIA OFFICE OF COPIES OF "MOTHER INDIA"

194. Mr. R. K. Shanmukham Chetty: Will Government be pleased to state, whether the India Office purchased copies of the book called *Mother India* by Miss Mayo, and if so, how many copies?

The Honourable Mr. J. Crerar: I have no information, but invite the Honourable Member's attention to the answers given by me in the House on.

[1] The President, Mr. Patel, is a Hindu.

the 19th and 20th September, 1927, to questions 1128 and 1191 which make it clear that the India Office purchased no copies for distribution.

* * *

Legislative Assembly Debates, Tuesday, September 4th, 1928, Vol. III, No. 1, p. 25–26.

GOVERNMENT'S DISAPPROVAL OF THE ALLEGATIONS MADE BY MISS MAYO IN HER BOOK "MOTHER INDIA" AGAINST INDIANS

39. *Mr. Lalchand Navalrai: (*a*) Will the Government be pleased to state whether any steps have been taken by Government to express their disapproval of the allegations made by Miss Mayo in her book *Mother India* against Indians?

(*b*) If not, do Government propose to take any such steps?

The Honourable Mr. J. Crerar: I would invite the Honourable Members' attention to the answers given by me in this House on the 20th September, 1927, to the questions asked on the subject.

Mr. Lalchand Navalrai: That was only an advice given at that time. Will the Government take any steps to express its own approval or disapproval? That was only an advice given to local agencies to pronounce condemnation of the book. But my further question is, whether Government is prepared to take upon itself to express its condemnation or disapproval of this scurrilous book.

The Honourable Mr. J. Crerar: On the occasion to which I have referred I answered a very large number of questions at very great length and I defined the position of the Government on that occasion. I regret that I have nothing further to add on the present occasion.

Mr. K. Ahmed: I take it that it is not the duty of the Government of India to express disapproval.

Mr. Lalchand Navalrai: My supplementary question, Sir. Does the Government approve of that book?

The Honourable Mr. J. Crerar: The Honourable Member is asking for an opinion. I am not prepared to express any opinion.

Mr. Gaya Prasad Singh: You are not prepared to express disapproval also?

* * *

Extract from the *Council of State Debates*, Monday, March 4th, 1929, Vol. I, No. 9, p. 156.

ISSUE OF FREE RAILWAY PASSES BY SOME OF THE GOVERNMENT-MANAGED RAILWAYS TO MISS KATHERINE MAYO.

32. The Honourable Mr. G. A. Natesan (on behalf of the Honourable Sir Phiroze Sethna) : Will Government please state :

(*a*) if it is a fact that free railway passes were issued by some of the Government-managed Railways to Miss Katherine Mayo when she visited India ?

(*b*) if the reply be in the affirmative, the names of the railways that issued such free passes, and whether such free passes were given with the knowledge and permission of the Railway Board ?

(*c*) if other than Government-managed Railways also issued such free passes, and, if so, which ?

The Honourable Sir Geoffrey Corbett : No passes

were issued by any of the State or Company-managed Railways.

* * *

Extract from the *Punjab Legislative Council Debates*, Vol. X, No. 21, of November 22nd, 1927, p. 1198.

*702. Raizada Hans Raj: Will the Honourable the Finance Member please state—

(*a*) whether it is a fact that Government officials in the Punjab, especially of the police department and the Information Bureau, helped Miss Mayo in the collection of materials for the publication of her book *Mother India*?

(*b*) whether the Government is aware that this book has been bitterly resented by the Indian public;

(*c*) whether the Government intends to take steps to proscribe its entry into the Punjab;

(*d*) whether in the American edition of the book, there were certain things written against Muhammadans but were removed in the English edition;

(*e*) whether the Punjab Government had anything to do in the matter?

The Honourable Sir Geoffrey de Montmorency: (*a*) Government understands that during her visit to the Punjab Miss Mayo met and conversed with a number of officials and non-officials. No official help was given to her in the Punjab towards the collection of material.

(*b*) Yes.

(*c*) No.

(*d*) Government has no information on this point.

(*e*) No.

APPENDIX II

'THE TIMES' EDITORIAL

The following editorial appeared in the London *Times* dated March 27th, 1928, under the heading:

THE LEGEND OF "MOTHER INDIA"

The article which a well-informed Correspondent contributes to our columns this morning—some personal experiences of the progress achieved in the last twenty years by the women of India—suggests a brief reminder of the treatment accorded by *The Times* last summer to MISS MAYO's remarkable book on certain aspects of the same problem. A reminder is necessary because of the extraordinary legend which has grown up about it, not only in India but in this country, and more recently in the United States. To judge from a whole series of speeches, newspaper articles, and even published volumes, it seems by now to have become almost an accepted fact that *The Times* gave extraordinary publicity to *Mother India* when it first appeared, used it (with some mysterious object) as 'propaganda,' refused altogether to hear the other side of such questions as it raised, and violated the most elementary canons of controversy by 'suppressing' informed criticism.

The actual truth is so different from the legend that it only requires restatement. When *Mother India* made its appearance it was treated precisely like any other serious volume received from the publishers. It was reviewed by experts, according to custom, both in *The Times* itself and in the *Literary Supplement* of *The Times*. The reviews were printed on the pages ordinarily devoted to this purpose. They were not unusually conspicuous in appearance. They were detached and judicial in substance. Thus, while paying tribute to the author's courage and carefulness, they called attention to 'signs of overstatement' and 'dangerous generalities,' recognised that the book would meet with a mixed reception, and expressed in particular a hope that it would find Indian readers to recognise its points of value. At no time (until this morning) has any reference been made to it in a leading article or other editorial comment. It would be impossible, in fact, to imagine anything less like an attempt to use *Mother India* for propagandist purposes. In the course of last August, the month after these notices had appeared, a letter criticising the book at large was received from SIR CHIMANLAL SETALVAD, who happened to be in England, and other distinguished signatories. This letter was declined with a courteous explanation that it was an established rule of *The Times* to decline all letters criticising publications other than those for which *The Times* itself was responsible. That is a rule for which there are very obvious practical reasons, for there would literally be no end to the correspondence demanding insertion if once it came to be recognised that anyone interested in, or aggrieved by, some volume or pamphlet or newspaper, in any part of the world, might look as a matter of right for space to challenge it in these columns. If MISS MAYO's book had in any sense been fathered by *The Times*, or if exception had been taken to *The Times*' reviews of it, the case, of course, would have been entirely different. There remain on record, as anyone may recall, innumerable instances in which room has instantly been found for criticism of this character. No doubt every rule of the kind admits of variation, and it might be argued that the appearance of *Mother India* was an event of such overriding importance as to call for the immense advertisement of a protracted newspaper controversy in England. But is this really what the critics desired?

APPENDIX III

A SHORT BIOGRAPHY OF KATHERINE MAYO

Miss Katherine Mayo was born at Ridgeway, Pennsylvania, of ancestry for ten generations American. After her education at private schools in Boston and Cambridge, she turned to historical research as a hobby. As early as 1896, in the *New York Evening Post*, under the *nom de plume* of 'Katherine Prence,' appeared her historical articles on colonial, Revolutionary, and mid-century topics, mainly in the setting of Monmouth County, N.J. At this period of her life Miss Mayo was living in New Jersey, and, as these contributions show, she spent much labour in patient research, delving deeply into county records, old journals, and obscure documents, and in collecting from the oldest inhabitants the traditions and memories of a community rich in colonial history. A little later we find in the *Atlantic Monthly* and *Scribner's Magazine* portrayals, from her pen, of living incidents, in the Guianas. For, at the beginning of this century, she resided for eight years in that Dutch colony in South America where over one-third of the population is British East Indian.

After this, for some years, she devoted herself exclusively to historical research, and in 1910, in Oswald Garrison Villard's preface to his *John Brown*, we read:

> The author also gladly records his lasting indebtedness to Miss Katherine Mayo, whose journeys in search of material for his use have covered

a period of more than two years and many thousands of miles. But for her judgment, her tact and skill, and her enthusiasm for the work, it could hardly have approached its present comprehensiveness.[1]

Again, in 1913, the late Mr. Horace White,[2] distinguished publicist, one-time editor of the *Chicago Tribune* and the *New York Evening Post*, paid a similar tribute to Miss Mayo's work in his *Life of Lyman Trumbull*[3] when he wrote: 'Miss Katherine Mayo has lightened my labours greatly by her intelligent and indefatigable search of old letters and newspaper files and by interviews with persons still living.' The only value of such research work must rest upon its accuracy.

Miss Mayo's first book was inspired by a particularly brutal murder, committed almost under her eyes, upon one whose class was thereby revealed as largely without protection. This murder laid bare a piece of public work crying to be done. In the foreword to *Justice to All* she tells the story:

> This book is the fruit of a tragedy.
>
> Three years and more ago, with simple devotion and with courage beyond all praise, a young American labouring man laid down his life for his trust. . . . Samuel Howell was an Iowan farmer's son. . . On the day of his death he had charge of

[1] *John Brown*, Oswald Garrison Villard, Houghton Mifflin Company, Boston, 1910, p. ix.

[2] See *New York Evening Post*, September 18th, 1916.

[3] *The Life of Lyman Trumbull*, Horace White, Houghton Mifflin Company, Boston, 1913, p. vii.

an important piece of construction in a rural part of the State of New York.

Early one Saturday morning, on his way to his work, Howell was ambushed by four men who demanded the week's pay-roll. The four brandished revolvers. Howell was alone and unarmed. But, no matter what the odds, it was impossible to that boy to surrender a charge. So he drove his motorcycle straight through the gang, who emptied their revolvers into his body from a distance of two paces.

Bleeding from seven mortal wounds, Howell guided his machine over a thousand yards of rough road, to the construction site. There he kept grip on his consciousness until he had turned over the heavy pay-roll to a responsible man; . . . and until, by name and by number, he had positively identified two of his murderers as labourers who had been employed for a month on the job.

Then he collapsed. Three days later he died.

A clearer case of identification, an easier case to handle, will never occur in the history of crime. . . .

This statement I make without qualification for the reason that I spent the entire day of the murder on the spot, and was personally cognisant of all that was done and left undone.

I saw the complete breakdown of the sheriff-constable system. Both county sheriff and village constables, present on the scene, proved utterly unrelated to the emergency, and for reasons perfectly clear. . . .

'We earn our living on country jobs, among men like these,' said the carpenter-boss, nodding towards the listening foreigners. 'Knives and guns are their playthings and when they want me they'll get me, just as they got poor Howell. We have to think of our families. We can't afford to earn gunmen's ill-will. There is no protection in the country districts. Sheriffs and constables don't help us at all. *Howell was only a working man. You'll have forgotten him in a month.*'[1]

These bitter words appear to have sunk deep into the hearer's mind—perhaps they became a driving power. For she sought and found a State which gave to its rural population police protection; she lived with that State's protective force, studied its history, its work, its enemies and its friends. Then she compiled the book of which the late President Theodore Roosevelt writes in introduction:

> This is the Force which Katherine Mayo describes in a volume so interesting, and from the standpoint of sound American citizenship, so valuable that it should be in every public library and every school library in the land. In the author's foreword the murder of gallant young Howell, and the complete breakdown of justice in reference thereto under our ordinary rural police system, makes one's blood boil with anger at the folly and timidity of our own people in tamely submitting to such hideous conditions. . . .[2]

[1] *Justice to All*, Katherine Mayo, Putnam, New York, 1917, p. xv. [2] *Ibid* p. ix.

This single volume did more than any other one thing to secure a similar force in New York. In the spring session of 1917 the New York Legislature passed the New York State Police Bill. Yet the Bill was not passed without a fight. At first labour, organised labour, mistaking motives, opposed the legislation.

Shortly after publishing this, her first book, Miss Mayo wrote a volume of short stories on the same subject, which she christened *The Standard Bearers*. In a review of this book the *New York Evening Post* remarks:

> Katherine Mayo's work has already accomplished great things. The author of these stories was in fact largely responsible for the recent organisation of the New York State troopers.[1]

And a leading paper in the largest city of the State in which the stories are laid says:

> These are genuine records of events, giving real names of troopers and actual localities. Occasionally, at the request of the police, the names of innocent persons and of criminals have been changed; but otherwise the stories are transcripts of absolute fact.[2]

Search through the reviews of these books for a critic who might throw doubt upon Miss Mayo's will and ability to set forth the facts as they actually happened proves abortive. A third State Police volume, *Mounted Justice*, was welcomed by the *New York World* in this fashion:

[1] *New York Evening Post*, August 17th, 1918.
[2] *Philadelphia North American*, August 17th, 1918.

Like its predecessors this book is filled with true stories of the performances of brave men having a special assignment for the good of a great State. These tales are told with care, simplicity and a vividly graphic pen. They do not need verbal embroideries.[1]

But to the somewhat austere *North American Review*[2] is left the credit of first connecting the word 'propaganda' with Miss Mayo's name:

> One is inclined to think that no better propaganda work has ever been done than that which Miss Mayo has performed for the Pennsylvania State Police. It is all the more effective because it is not, after all, propaganda in any ordinary sense but genuine story-telling undertaken from a true literary impulse and backed by a sincere belief. The Union of the two motives amounts to inspiration.

Between her second and third State Police volumes Miss Mayo's work, like that of many another, was interrupted by the World War. She was urged by friends to accompany the American Expeditionary Force overseas, there to make an impartial, unofficial, and independent investigation of the Y.M.C.A.'s work, which was then under heavy fire of criticism, while, among other duties, running the entire army canteen service in France.

It was of this work—*That Damn Y*—that the Y.M.C.A.'s official organ proclaimed:

> The best perspective and survey of the Association's part in the war work has been produced in

[1] *New York World*, May 28th, 1922. [2] August, 1922.

> a recent book by Katherine Mayo. . . . It is the most complete, the fairest, and most readable study of the war service yet produced. Miss Mayo is a trained correspondent and a keen analyst. She went over with a decided prejudice against the Association and has not entirely gotten over it. . . . People who jumped at conclusions from partial and hasty reports will read her book with a new vision.[1]

Her fifth book, *Isles of Fear*, resulted from a close personal study of the Philippine Islands, and again Miss Mayo definitely states the object and terms of her investigation in the first chapter:

> . . . being myself free to go, and having some previous experience in field investigation, I determined to make an attempt to serve my fellow countrymen by collecting for their use the material that their own obligations preclude their collecting for themselves. . . . I could accept no medium through which to get my facts, whose whole value must rest on their first-hand quality. In accordance with which principle I made it a rule, throughout to see all witnesses privately, and to choose my own roads and times and places, independent of any guidance. I used no Government conveyances, and received no Government favours. . . .[2]

Notwithstanding these facts, Lajpat Rai, in a book stamped by some critics as the best reply[3] to *Mother*

[1] *Association Men*, New York, July 1920. See *ante*, pp. 122-123.

[2] *The Isles of Fear*, Katherine Mayo, Faber and Gwyer, 1925, pp. 3 and 5.

[3] *Unhappy India*, p. xix.

India, describes Miss Mayo's fifth book as her first appearance in print, and with these words: 'Her first début into the realm of authorship was made by the publication of a volume of her "researches" into the conditions of the Filipinos. . . .'

But it was left to an Englishman writing in the *New Republic*[1] to stigmatise *Isles of Fear* as a 'propagandist volume.' And another Englishman, Mr. C. F. Andrews, felt the need of no further authority than that of his compatriot to warrant the charge: '*Isles of Fear*, as Mr. Ratcliffe has stated, was directed against Philippine Independence.'[2]

On the other hand, American journals fail to agree with these foreign imputations. They believe the work to be an exposition of certain defects of the American administrations and a plea for justice to the Filipino masses, rather than class propaganda against them. Thus we find the *New York Evening Post* writing editorially:

> Not since Edmund Burke's indictment against Warren Hastings has so strong an indictment been drawn against the misgovernment of a subject people as that which Katherine Mayo in her articles on *The Isles of Fear* draws against our administration of the Philippines during the years 1916–1921.[3]

And the *Saturday Review of Literature* in the course of an article states:

[1] S. K. Ratcliffe in *The New Republic*, New York, September 21st, 1927, p. 127.

[2] *Facts about India, A Reply to Miss Mayo*, C. F. Andrews, *Young India*, Ahmedabad, May 17th, 1928, p. 160. See *ante*, p. 206.

[3] *New York Evening Post*, editorial, November 29th, 1924.

> '*The Isles of Fear* is a sincere, straightforward, conscientious, and truthful exposition of the human factors in our Philippine problem. Its writer has rendered a courageous and needed public service, and in doing so has produced a literary work of no mean order.[1]

The *Brooklyn Eagle* says of the book: 'No better luck could befall the Philippines than that it [*Isles of Fear*] should become a best seller.'[2] And the *Times of Manila*[3] expresses the opinion that '. . . the real target of Miss Mayo's attacks is America as represented by both Democratic and Republican administrations at Washington.'

It should be borne in mind, however, that both British critics, Messrs. Ratcliffe and Andrews, made their accusations against *Isles of Fear* in articles attacking *Mother India*, while the American journals expressed themselves when the Philippine book was still fresh from the presses.

In *Mother India* Miss Mayo again declares her reasons for undertaking the inquiry, namely, discontent with what 'the average American actually knows about India,'[4] adding:

> It was dissatisfaction with this status that sent me to India, to see what a volunteer unsubsidised, uncommitted, and unattached, could observe of common things in daily human life. . . . I would try to determine, for example, what situation

[1] July 4th, 1925, p. 873. [2] George Currie, in April 5th, 1925.
[3] Editorial, April 14th, 1925. [4] *Mother India*, pp. 20-21.

would confront a public health official charged with the duty of stopping an epidemic of cholera or of plague; what elements would work for or against a campaign against hookworm; or what forces would help or hinder a governmental effort to lower infant mortality, to better living conditions, or to raise educational levels, supposing such work to be required.

None of these points could well be wrapped in 'eastern mystery,' and all concern the whole family of nations in the same way that the sanitary practices of John Smith, of 23 Main Street, concern Peter Jones at the other end of the block.

In March, 1929, Miss Mayo's seventh book was published, *Slaves of the Gods*, presenting twelve short stories of the sombre side of Hindu life, together with over a hundred substantiating quotations from present-day Indian sources. Chapter Fourteen of this volume is an appeal 'To the Women of Hindu India' and closes with these words:

> Let us of the West, then, be your friends, with frankness and with honesty, and not with a veil of deception between us. We believe that nothing good is hurt, while much evil is cured, by the broad light of the sun.
>
> Sympathy won by misrepresentations is little worth. Let us have mutual truth. Its wounds are honourable and make, in the end, for mutual respect. We have each our weaknesses, each our strengths. Let us know and help each other.[1]

[1] *Slaves of the Gods*, pp. 246-247.

APPENDIX IV

LORD NORTHCLIFFE'S STATEMENT

A written statement by the late Viscount Northcliffe concerning the murder of William Francis Doherty, dated Bombay, January 21st, 1922, and published in *The Daily Mail*, London, January 25th, 1922, and in *The Over-Seas Daily Mail* of January 28th, 1922.

' . . . I reprint details of the absolutely unprovoked murder of Mr. Doherty, an able young American engineer, whose death, reported in *The Daily Mail*, is now being investigated at Bombay.

'William Francis Doherty was an American citizen born in Texas, the brother of Benjamin Doherty, a well-known resident at Galveston, in that State. Most of his life, however, was spent in California, where both he and his wife were students at the Leland Stanford University. He had recently come to Bombay as a partner with Richard Brenchley in engineering contracts connected with the work of the Bombay Improvement Trust.

AMERICAN VICTIM

'Owing to the scarcity of housing in the city he was living in a bungalow some distance out at Persik, in the Thana district. On the morning of November 19th he came into the city with his wife by train, parting from her at the station to walk to the workshop and agreeing to meet again in a certain train the same afternoon. He was entirely unarmed; he had not even a stick. He was an innocent unofficial person, not even English, going quietly about his business.

'Many witnesses saw what followed. He was walking with a man companion when a mob of 50 or 60 people, apparently all Mohammedans, poured out of the by-streets and attacked him with *lathis* (heavy sticks). His companion escaped by running up an alley but not till he had been badly hurt. Mr. Doherty, an athlete and a very strong man, kept up a running fight with the mob for a quarter of an hour or more until another mob from another direction closed on him.

'Twice he was beaten to the ground and twice he got to his feet again and went on fighting. At last he fell with a fractured skull and otherwise horribly injured. The mob beat him on the ground, trampled on his face, stripped off his clothes, boots, and valuables, and left him, still breathing, to lie under the hot sun for nearly two hours before he was picked up by a military lorry and taken to hospital, where he died immediately.

'I have given this story in some detail because it is typical of the kind of crimes which the followers of Mr. Gandhi [the Extremist Non-Co-Operation leader] commit and to which they are incited by his so-called non-violent propaganda. This case was worse because the victim was an American quite unassociated in Mr. Gandhi's quarrel with the British Government. Apparently the peaceful speeches of Mr. Gandhi, who has lately become careful to appear at, but to take little part in, meetings, have the direct effect of stirring up the natives to crime, while the Indian native newspapers, in language well understood by the natives, urge the removal of white men from India.

GANDHI'S MOTOR-CAR

'Reuter's chief correspondent informs me that fresh extremist newspapers are being started here with great rapidity. In regard to Indian crimes, Mr. Gandhi's defenders have several defences: first, that the crimes are committed by those who have gone beyond his control. But I suggest that newspapers at home carefully reprint his speeches as reported in his myriad newspapers. You can then judge their effect.

'Others of his defenders liken these outrages to events in the French Revolution, asserting that they are the usual road to freedom. Gandhite newspapers claim that Indian progress is entirely due to native ability and that the British Empire was saved by the efforts of Indian troops. These newspapers defy the British Government to arrest Mr. Gandhi.

'Mr. Gandhi urges what he calls the "complete Indianisation" of India, by which natives would return to native simplicity. But he personally uses fully modern methods, such as trains, telegraphs, telephones, posts, and, particularly, a rapid motor-car. As in 1857 and 1897, the Indian Government is showing extreme patience. Civilised Hindus and Mohammedans, who are loyal to a stable government, who are themselves threatened by extremists, and who decline to wear the white caps worn by Mr. Gandhi's supporters, ask me how long the Government will tolerate their intimidation and the murders such as that of Doherty.'

APPENDIX V

MEETINGS FAVOURABLE TO THE SARDA CHILD MARRIAGE BILL

List of meetings, with dates, places, auspices, and descriptions, wherever procurable, which passed resolutions in favour of the Sarda Child Marriage Bill, between April and December, 1928, together with the source of information. This list does not pretend to be complete. It was secured by a close following of the Indian press.

Date	*Place*	*Description of Meeting*	*Source of Information*
Apr. 29th	Lucknow	Conference of Purdah Ladies	*Times of India*, May 5th
May 21st	Madras	Pachiyappa's Hall, auspices of Standing Com. Ind. Nat. Social Conference	*Hindu*, May 22nd.
May 30th	Arni	Arni Hindu Youths' League	*Hindu*, June 2nd
July 17th	Calcutta	Bengal Presidency Council of Women	*The Pioneer*, July 22nd, etc.
July 17th	Triplicane	Hindu Dharma Paripalana Sabha in the Mani Aiyar Hall	*Hindu*, July 18th
July 23rd	Simla	Child Marriage Prohibition League, in the Indian Association rooms	*The Pioneer*, July 28th *Hindu*, July 27th, etc.
July 29th	Narsannapet	Citizens in the premises of Sri Venkateswara temple	*Hindu*, Aug. 3rd

Date	Place	Description of Meeting	Source of Information
Aug. 11th	Bombay	Citizens under auspices of Tarun Maharashtra Mandal in the Prarthana Samaj Hall	*Bombay Daily Mail*, Aug. 16th
Aug. 26th	Kalyan	Andhras met under the auspices of Kalyan Andhra Association	*Indian Social Reformer*, Sept. 22nd
Sept.	Calcutta	'Women of Bengal' met at Albert Hall	*Statesman*, Calcutta, Sept. 13th
Sept.	Allahabad	Under auspices of Women's Indian Association	*Hindu*, Sept. 3rd
Sept. 23rd	Peshawar	'Ladies of Peshawar,' premises of Ayra Putri Patasala	*Stri Dharma*, October, 1928
Nov.	Ajmer	Rajput women, conference of	*Simla Times*, *Dec.* 20th *The Pioneer*, Dec. 1st
Dec.	Calcutta	Indian National Social Conference	*The Pioneer*, Dec. 28th

A report from Simla, printed in the *Hindu*, September 4th, states that public meetings have been called to support the Bill under the auspices of the following organisations: Bombay Presidency Women Council, Women's Indian Association, Gujrat Stri Mandal, Arya Mahila Samaj, Rashtriya Stri Sabha, Stri Zarthosti Mandal, Beni Israil Stri Mandal, Salvation Army, Bombay Seva Sadan, Bhagini, Samaj, Shravika Ashram and Indian Medical Relief; adding that the following have also accorded their support to the measure: All-India Jat Mahasabha, All-Indian Sudhi Conference, Bans Muldia Sabha, All-India Khandelwal Mahasabha, All-India Jadav Mahasabha, All-India Shinchare Mahasabha, All-India Gulheri Vaisha Mahasabha, All-India Kurna Kshatriya Conference, All-India Iyagi Brahmin Mahasabha, the Executive Committee of the Shromani Gurudwara Prabandhak Committee, Bengal Provincial Sabha, Bombay Presidency Social Service Conference.

APPENDIX VI

MEETINGS PROTESTING AGAINST THE SARDA CHILD MARRIAGE BILL

List of meetings, with dates, places, auspices and description, wherever procurable, held to protest and pass resolutions against the Sarda Child Marriage Bill between April and December, 1928, together with the source of the information. This list does not pretend to be complete. It was secured by following the Indian press.

Date	*Place*	*Description of Meeting*	*Source of Information*
Apr. 22nd	Cocanda	Public meeting in hall attached to Venugopala Swami Temple	*Hindu*, Apr. 27th
Apr. 22nd	Madurantakam	Public meeting in the Hindu High School Hall under auspices of Taluk Hindu Association	*Hindu*, May 2nd
Apr. 27th	Palghat	Public meeting of the Brahmins in the 'Amity Hall'	*Hindu*, May 2nd
May 14th	Kodavasal	'Well attended meeting' where resolutions were passed	*Hindu*, May 25th
May 15th	Sengalipuram	'Well attended meeting' where resolutions were passed	*Hindu*, May 25th
May 17th	Kovilvermi	Mass Meeting	*Hindu*, May 22nd
May 19th	Mannargudi	Public meeting in the local Ahobila Mutt	*Hindu*, May 22nd
May 20th	Cuddalore	The South Arcot District Child Marriage Protest Conference	*Hindu*, May 22nd

Date	*Place*	*Description of Meeting*	*Source of Information*
May 20th	Conjeeveram	'Monster meeting' in Devarajaswami temple, auspices of the Ahobila Mutt	*Hindu*, May 24th
May 22nd	Mayavaram	Northern bank of the Cauvery under auspices of Brahmana Samajam	*Hindu*, May 24th
May 22nd	Sriperumbudur	Public meeting in front of Sri Audikesava Perumal and Bashyakaraswami temple	*Hindu*, May 30th
May 27th	Cocanda	Meeting in the Sri Seetharamaswami temple	*Hindu*, June 5th
May 29th	Kumbakonam	Public meeting in the local temple	*Hindu*, June 1st
May 29th	Srirangam	Hindu citizens in Sri Ranganadhaswami temple	*Hindu*, June 4th
May 30th	Tirupattur	Hindu public meeting in the Municipal Elementary School	*Hindu*, June 2nd
May 31st	Royapuram	Meeting of Hindu inhabitants	*Hindu*, June 2nd
June 1st	Alwartirunagari	Meeting of citizens held in Alwar temple	*Hindu*, June 7th
June 3rd	Tinnevelly	Public meeting of citizens at Kailasapuram	*Hindu*, June 7th
June 4th	Vellore	Public meeting in New Agraharam, Vellore	*Hindu*, June 7th
June 4th	Vellore	Similar meeting at Sankar Mutt, Saidapet, Vellore	*Hindu*, June 7th
June 4th and 5th	Kumbakonam	Meetings held at Ethakudi, Kurichi, Rajagopalapuram and Radhanarasimhapuram villages of Mannargudi taluk	*Hindu*, June 14th
June 6th	Kumbakonam	Meeting of Brahman residents of Senangulum in Mannargudi taluk	*Hindu*, June 14th

Date	*Place*	*Description of Meeting*	*Source of Information*
June 7th	Mannadi-mangalam	Meeting of Hindu citizens of Mannadimangalam, Madura District	*Hindu*, June 13th
June 8th	Cocanada	Public meeting of the women of Cocanada held in Jagannaickpur	*Hindu*, June 13th
June	Karuku-richi	Public meeting	*Hindu*, June 11th
June 12th	Vellore	Conference of orthodox Hindus of district in the Sankar Mutt, Vellore	*Hindu*, June 15th
June 13th	Tuticorin	Citizens of Alwartiruna-gari in the Swami Sam-dhi	*Hindu*, June 15th
June 15th	Rander	Muhammadans of Ran-der, auspices of Rander Mehefile Islam Kutbhana	*Bombay Daily Mail*, June 18th
July 22nd	Madura	Public meeting of citizens of Madura in the Vic-toria Edward Hall	*Hindu*, July 28th
Aug. 10th	Kumbako-nam	Public meeting of ortho-dox Hindus in the Pill-ayar temple	*Hindu*, Aug. 10th
Oct. 2nd	Kumbako-nam	Local Brahmans in Sri Sarangapaniswami tem-ple, auspices Hindu Tract Society	*Hindu*, Oct. 5th
Oct. 9th	Turaiyur	Public meeting of citizens	*Hindu*, Oct. 17th

Notices of lectures against the Sarda Child Marriage Bill are commonly reported in *The Hindu*, while *The Englishman* (Calcutta, September 18th, 1928) reports a memorial said to be signed by 20,000 Marwaris protesting against the Bill. Another general meeting of about 200 women of Georgetown, Madras, protesting against the proposed legislation, was held in January, 1929, according to *The Hindu* of January 8th, 1929.

BIBLIOGRAPHY

Butler, Clementina: *Pandita Ramabai Sarasvati.* Fleming H. Revell Company, New York, 1922.

Brayne, F. L.: *Village Uplift in India.* The Pioneer Press, Allahabad. 1927.

Collet, Sophia Dobson: *Life and Letters of Raja Rammohun Roy,* edited by Hem Chandra Sarkar. A. C. Sarkar, Calcutta. 1913.

Dubois, Abbé J. A.: *Hindu Manners, Customs and Ceremonies,* 1821, re-translated and edited by Henry K. Beauchamp, 1897. Clarendon Press. 1924.

Encyclopædia Britannica, 11th ed. 1910-11.

Gandhi, M. K.: *Indian Home Rule.* Ganesh and Company, Madras. 1924.

Gandhi's Letters on Indian Affairs. V. Narayanan and Company, Madras. 1923.

Indian Year Book, 1926 and 1928. The Times Press, Bombay.

Jones, E. Stanley: *Christ at the Round Table.* Abingdon Press, New York. 1928.

——*The Christ of the Indian Road.* Abingdon Press, New York. 1925.

Keyserling, Count Hermann: *The Book of Marriage.* Harcourt, Brace and Company, New York. 1926.

Lankester, Arthur: *Tuberculosis in India.* Butterworth and Company, London. 1920.

Londres, Albert: *The Road to Buenos Ayres.* Boni and Liveright, New York. 1928.

Low, Sir Sidney: *The Indian States and Ruling Princes.* Benn's Library, London. 1929.

Mayo, Katherine: *Isles of Fear.* Faber and Gwyer. London. 1925.

——*Justice to All.* Putnam. New York. 1917.

——*Mother India.* Jonathan Cape and Company, London. 1927.

——*Mounted Justice.* Houghton Mifflin, Boston. 1922.

——*Slaves of the Gods.* Jonathan Cape and Company, London. 1929.

——*The Standard Bearers.* Houghton Mifflin, Boston. 1918.

——*That Damn Y.* Houghton Mifflin, Boston. 1920.

Phadke, N. S.: *Sex Problem in India.* D. B. Taraporevala Sons and Company, Bombay. 1927.

Smith, Vincent A.: *The Oxford History of India.* Clarendon Press, Oxford. 1923.

Sumati Bai, G.: *Woman Awakened,* Foreword by Dr. Annie Besant. Tagore and Company, Madras. 1928.

Thompson, Edward: *Suttee.* George Allen and Unwin, Ltd., London. 1928.

Villard, Oswald Garrison: *John Brown.* Houghton Mifflin, Boston. 1910.

Van Tyne, Claude H.: *India in Ferment.* D. Appleton and Company, New York. 1923.

The World Almanac, 1929. The New York World, New York.

White, Horace: *Life of Lyman Trumbull.* Houghton Mifflin, Boston. 1913.

Zimand, Savel: *Living India.* Longmans, Green and Company, New York. 1928.

OFFICIAL DEBATES, REPORTS AND DOCUMENTS

Annual Report of the Public Health Commissioner with the Government of India for 1925, Vol. I. Government of India Central Publication Branch, Calcutta. 1927.

Census of India, 1921, Vol. I, Parts I and II. Superintendent, Government Printing, Calcutta. 1924.

The Gazette of India, March 31st, 1928. Published by Authority, Delhi.

Government of India Act, 1919. His Majesty's Stationery Office, London.

Health Organisation in British India. League of Nations Publication. 1928.

India in 1927-28, A Statement prepared for presentation to Parliament, by J. Coatman. Government of India Central Publication Branch, Calcutta. 1928.

Legislative Assembly Debates, Official Reports. Government of India Press, Delhi and Simla. 1922, 1927, 1928 and 1929.

Opinions on the Hindu Child Marriage Bill, Paper No. 1. Government of India Legislative Department. February, 1928.

Parliamentary Debates, Extracts Relating to Indian Affairs, House of Commons. His Majesty's Stationery Office, London. 1927.

Parliamentary Debates, Extracts Relating to Indian Affairs, House of Lords. His Majesty's Stationery Office, London. 1927.

Proceedings of the Legislative Council of the Governor of Madras, Official Reports. Superintendent, Government Press, Madras. November, 1927.

BIBLIOGRAPHY

Punjab Legislative Council Debates, Official Report. Superintendent, Government Printing, Lahore, Punjab. 1927.

Report of the Royal Commission on Agriculture in India. His Majesty's Stationery Office, London. 1928.

Statistical Abstract for British India. His Majesty's Stationery Office, London. 1928.

CHRONOLOGICAL LIST OF 'REPLIES' TO 'MOTHER INDIA'

Ranga Iyer, C. S.: *Father India, A Reply to Mother India.* Selwyn and Blount, Ltd., London. November 1927.

Natarajan, K.: *Miss Mayo's Mother India, A Rejoinder.* G. A. Natesan and Company, Madras. December, 1927.

Mukerji, Dhan Gopal: *A Son of Mother India Answers.* E. P. Dutton and Company, New York. February, 1928.

Chapman, J. A.: *India, Its Character,* 'A Reply to *Mother India.*' Basil Blackwell, Oxford. 1928.

'World Citizen' (S. G. Warty): *Sister India, A Critical Examination of and a Reasoned Reply to Miss Katherine Mayo's 'Mother India.'* Sister India Office, Churchgate Street, Bombay. (No date, first received May 1928.)

Lajpat Rai *Unhappy India, Being a Reply to Miss Katherine Mayo's 'Mother India.'* Banna Publishing Company, Calcutta. 1928.

Lakhanpal (Mrs.), C.: *Mother India Ka Jawab.* Gurukula Press, Dehradun, India. 1928.

Miss Mayo's Grandhakhandanamu: edited by Pandit Puranam Suryanarayana Thirthulu. G. L. Sastri and Company, Madras. 1928.

Nehru, Srimati Uma: *Mother India Aur Uska Jawab.* Kashinath Bajpai, Allahabad. 1928.

PERIODICALS, NEWSPAPERS AND PAMPHLETS

[*Address*] *to Sir John Simon;* from the Sambavar Maha Sangham of South India. High Ground, Palamcottah. May, 1928.

All-India Women's Conference on Educational Reform. Scottish Mission Industries Company, Poona. 1927.

Amrita Bazar Patrika. Calcutta. 1927.

Andrews, C. F.: 'The Basis of Inter-religious Fellowship,' in *Young Men of India, Burma and Ceylon.* June 1928. Calcutta.

Andrews, C. F.: 'The Facts About India, A Reply to Miss Mayo,' in *Young India,* June 21st, 1928, *et al.* Ahmedabad.

Association Men, Official Organ of the Y.M.C.A. in the U.S.A., 1920. New York.

Biennial Survey of Occupation and Directory of Christian Missions in India, Burma and Ceylon. Scottish Mission Industries Company, Ajmer. 1926-27.

Baptist Missionary Review, 1928. Editorials and article on 'Development of Indian Leadership.'

Behar Herald, 1928. Patna.

Bombay Daily Mail, 1927-28. Bombay.

The Brooklyn Eagle, April 5th, 1925. Review of *Isles of Fear* by George Currie.

Ceylon Morning Leader, 1929. Colombo.

The Christian, 1928. London.

The Civil and Military Gazette, 1928. Lahore.

Clark, Alden H. : 'Is India Dying ?' in *Atlantic Monthly*, February, 1928, Boston, and *Young Men of India, Burma and Ceylon*, March, 1928. Calcutta.

Daily Express, 1927. London.

The Daily Mail, January 25th, 1922, and February 3rd, 1928. London. Statement by The Right Honourable Viscount Northcliffe, and despatch on *India*.

Daily Mail and Empire, 1928. Toronto, Canada.

The Daily Telegraph, 1928. London.

Daily Times, 1928. Victoria, B.C.

Dayal, Har : 'The Shame of India,' in *The Modern Review*, September 1926. Calcutta.

The Dedication Bill, Manifesto to the Madras Government by the Members of the Devadasi Association. Aurora Press, Madras. December 1927.

The Englishman, June 18th, 1928. Calcutta. Memorandum to the Simon Commission from the Depressed Classes of Madras.

The Evening News, 1927. Sydney, N.S.W.

Forward, 1927. Calcutta.

Gandhi, M. K. : 'The Drain Inspector's Report,' in *Young India*, September 17th, 1927. Ahmedabad.

The Hindu, 1927, 1928, 1929. Madras.

Indian National Herald, 1927, 1928. Bombay.

Indian Social Reformer, 1927. Ed. by K. Natarajan. Bombay.

The Indian Witness, 1927. Ed. by J. Waskom Pickett, Lucknow.

Life Prospectus for India. Phœnix Assurance Company Ltd., Calcutta, 1927.

The Leader, 1927. Allahabad.

Light, 1927. Lahore.

Lytton, the Earl of: 'India Seen and India Served,' in *The Review of the Churches*, January 1929. London.

The Madras Mail, 1928. Madras.

Mallik, Surenda Nath: 'On the Causation of the High Mortality Among Children and Mothers in India,' in *The Journal of State Medicine*, May 1928. London.

The Manchester Guardian: 1927, 1928, 1929.

Mathews, Basil: 'Mother India,' in *The Review of the Churches*, January 1928. London.

Mayo, Katherine: 'India,' in *Liberty Magazine*, January 14th, 1928. New York.

Memorial to Chairman and Members of Statutory Commission, from the Punjab Addharm Mandel. Kishen Steam Press, Jullundur City, India. [1928.]

The Nation, 1928. New York.

The Modern Review, 1928. Calcutta.

New Empire, 1928. Calcutta.

New India, edited by Dr. Annie Besant, 1927, 1928. Madras.

The New Statesman, 1927. London.

New York Evening Post, 1896, 1918, 1924.

The New York Times, 1927, 1928.

New York World, 1922, 1928.

North American Review, 1922. New York.

O'Dwyer, Sir Michael: 'Mother India—Swaraj and Social Reform,' in *Fortnightly Review*, February 1928. London.

Over-Seas Daily Mail, January 28th, 1922. London.

Philadelphia North America, August 17th, 1918.

The Pioneer, 1928. Allahabad.

The Pioneer Mail, 1927, 1928. Allahabad.

Plain Dealer, 1928. Wabash, Indiana.

Post Standard, 1928. Syracuse, N.Y.

Ratcliffe, S. K.: 'Impossible India,' in *The New Republic*, September 21st, 1927. New York.

Rathbone, Eleanor F.: 'Has Katherine Mayo Slandered Mother India,' in *The Hibbert Journal*, January 1929. London.

San Francisco Chronicle, January 23rd, 1929.

Sastry, N. Yagnesvara, article in *Stri-Dharma*, July 1928. Madras.

Saturday Review of Literature, July 4th, 1925. New York.

The Statesman (daily and weekly editions), 1927, 1928, 1929. Calcutta.

Stri-Dharma, the official organ of the Indian Women's Association, 1927, 1928. Madras.
The Sun, October 30th, 1928. New York. Esther Norton's interview with Mrs. Naidu.
The Times, 1928. London.
The Times of India, 1927, 1928. Bombay.
The Times of Malaya, 1927. Ipoh.
Times of Manila, editorial, April 14th, 1925. Philippines.
The World, 1922. New York.
Tribune, October 18th, 1927. Des Moines, Ia.
Young India, edited by M. K. Gandhi, 1927, 1928, 1929. Ahmedabad.

INDEX

Acharya, M. K., on Hindu Child Marriage Bill, 116-117

Addharmis, Untouchable 'Protestants,' 169

Adi Dravidas, of Madras, 166. *See also* Untouchables

Age: method of determining, 52, 66-67; single women understate, 58; young wives overstate, 58; Indian reticence regarding, 66; guessing at, 66-67

Age of consent, 111; difficulties of enforcing the law, 85-88; Native States, 221. *See also* Hindu Child Marriage Bill; Marriage, consummation of

Age of Consent Committee: evidence before, 53, 68-71, 88, 160; member of, on prevalence of child marriage, 64; *New York Times* on, 73; Hindu Child Marriage Bill postponed until report is in hand, 120; appointment of, 73, 222-223; Legislative Assembly Standing Finance Committee on, 222-223

Agricultural classes: marriage ages, 64-65

Agriculture: *Report of the Royal Commission*, 127-129; crops in Gurgaon, 209

Ahmed, Mr. K.: on assistance given Miss Mayo, 235

Ali Khan, Lieutenant Kunwar Jamshed: on Age of Consent Law, 88

Aligarh University, 212

All-India Depressed Class Conference, Madras (1929), 177

All-India Legislative Assembly. *See* Legislative Assembly

All-India National Social Conference (1928), 64

All-India Women's Conference on Educational Reform (1927), 91-92

Allahabad High Court: trial of Sandar Singh for murder of Brahman who helped Untouchables, 178-179

Ambala, district and sessions judge on Hindu Child Marriage Bill, 101-102

American Expeditionary Force, Miss Mayo and, 122-123

American Marathi Mission, Ahmednagar, 135

American Public Health Association, 198

Amrita Bazar Patrika, Calcutta, National Christian Council's statement published in, 138

Andrews, C. F.: on age of puberty, 70; quotes Gandhi on spirit of International Fellowship Council, 145-146; quotes Tagore on child marriage, 194; states *Mother India* is propaganda, 206; retracts charge against Miss Mayo, 206; on *Isles of Fear*, 260

Aney, M. S., on *Mother India*, 233 *et seq.*

Animals: cruelty to, 16, 25, 201-204, 214; feeding of, 126-129; killing of, 201-203

Annual Report of the Public Health Commissioner with the Government of India for 1925, 198-199

Archibald, Mrs. C. H., supports *Mother India*, 147-148

Arya Samaj, on child marriage, 102, 176-177

Arya, Surendranath, declares *Mother India* true, 189

Association Men, review of *That Damn Y*, 123, 258-259

INDEX

Atlantic Monthly: 'Is India Dying?' 126-132; articles by Katherine Mayo, 253
Ayurvedic medicine vs. Western medicine, 26, 31-33, 195-196

Babies, weight of, 77, 85
Baby widows, 94-95, 100. *See also* Widows
Backward classes. *See* Untouchables
Bai, G. Sumati, author of *Woman Awakened*, on child marriage and puberty, 66, 72, 91
Bajaj, Seth Jamnaal, opens Wardha temple to Untouchables, 177
Balfour, Dr. Margaret I.: widely quoted, 23, 49; hospital statistics on motherhood, 49-54; quoted in *A Son of Mother India Answers*, 74; on Age of Consent Law, 88
Baptist Missionary Review, The: editorial on Dr. Balfour's hospital statistics, 52; analyses *Mother India's* quotations, 75-76; on Dr. Stanley Jones, 124-125; on Dr. Alden H. Clark, 130-131; quotes Dr. (Mrs.) Muthulakshmi Reddi on evils of child marriage, 132-134; on Miss Bose's statement as printed in *Mother India*, 137; on National Christian Council, 140-141; reports Kodaikanal Missionary Union's Annual Conference (1928), 144; on Gandhi and International Fellowship Council, 146
Bar Library Club of Calcutta High Court, The Honorary Secretary of, on child marriage, 99-100
Baroda, reforms in, 221
Baroda, Her Highness the Maharani Chimana Saheb Gaekwar of, on child marriage, 91-92
Basis of Inter-religious Fellowship, The, by C. F. Andrews, 145-146
Bastardy: 'A Bill for the promotion of bastardy in India,' 101
Beauchamp, Henry K., translator of Dubois' *Hindu Manners, Customs and Ceremonies*, 186-188
Behar Herald, reports Mrs. Naidu on betrothal, 48; attacks Mrs. Ida M. Willmore, 217; reforms in Native States, 221
Belvi, D. U., on orthodoxy and child marriage, 83-84
Bengal: marriage age in, 59; treatment of Untouchables in, 165
Bennett, Arnold, on *Mother India*, 191
Bennett, Mr. Justice, 178
Bentinck, Lord William: declares suttee to be culpable homicide, 105-106; thuggee stamped out, 107-108
Besant, Dr. (Mrs.) Annie: editor of *New India*, 19, 222; writes foreword to *Woman Awakened*, 66, 72, 91; and J. Krishnamurti, 92
Betrothal: Mrs. Naidu on, 48; marriage confounded with, 60-61, 79; Mr. Acharya on, 116-117; Hindu Child Marriage Bill does not forbid, 117
Bhagat Ram. *See* Ram, Bhagat
Bhat, Mrs., on puberty and consummation of marriage, 71
Biennial Survey of Occupation and Directory of Christian Missions in India, quoted, 144
Bikaner, reforms in, 221
Birkenhead, Lord, on alleged Government responsibility for *Mother India*, 227

INDEX

Blackett, The Hon. Sir Basil, on Miss Mayo's alleged Government connection, 234, 235
Blind, school for, Patna, 217
Bole, S. K., on age of consent, 88
Bombay, city of: ovation to Prince of Wales, 26-28, 30, 39-40, 43; William Francis Doherty killed by rioters, 39-46; maternity statistics, 49; India's second city, 50; Parsis in, 50; equal rights for Untouchables, 171; infant mortality in, 198
Bombay Daily Mail: on *The New Statesman* review of *Mother India*, 18; Dr. Campbell on early marriage, 53; Mitra Mandal on marriage age, 69; Mr. S. K. Bole on Age of Consent, 88; Dr. Balfour on infringement of Age of Consent Law, 88; Mrs. F. S. Talyarkhan on child marriage, 92; publishes letter on 'horrors' of widowhood, 95; publishes National Christian Council, 138; American *Mother India* said to omit anti-Muslim material, 212; quotes *New India* on Age of Consent, 222
Bombay Presidency, Untouchables' memorial to Indian Statutory Commission, 165, 170
Bombay Presidency Social Reform Association, 68-69
Bombay Stock Exchange, closes in protest against Untouchables, 171
Book of Marriage, Keyserling's, 192-193
Bose, Miss Mona, *Mother India* accused of misquoting, 76, 136-137
Boy Scouts, 130-131
Boys, Mr. Justice, 178
Brahman, murdered for helping Untouchables, 178-179
Brahmans, and Christianity, 143-144
Brahmo Samaj, 176-177
Bray, Sir Denys: Government action on *India*, 184
Brayne, F. L., author of *Village Uplift in India*, 209-211
Brenchley, Richard J., partner of W. F. Doherty, 40, 42-43, 263
British Library of Literature, New York, Miss Mayo no connection with, 234
Brooklyn Eagle, The, on *Isles of Fear*, 261
Brown, Dr. Edith, on truth of *Mother India*, 148
Buddhists, proportion of, in Burma, 103
Bullocks, cruelty to, 203-204
Burma, favours abolition of Hindu child marriage, 103
Butler, Clementina, author of *Pandita Ramabai Sarasvati*, 95

Calcutta: meeting to denounce *Mother India*, 21; Untouchables' deputation to Indian Statutory Commission, 164-165; infant mortality in, 198; Corporation Health Officer on tuberculosis in, 216
Calcutta High Court: Honorary Secretary of the Bar Library Club on child marriage, 99-100
Campbell, A. Y. G., on rape of girl-wife by husband, 86-87
Campbell, Dr. G. E., on early motherhood, 53
Cape, Jonathan, public statement on *Mother India*, 228
Caste system, 16; disregard of, 176-177; tyrannies of, 211
Cattle, feeding of, 126-129; cruelty to, 201-204
Cawnpore, infant mortality in, 198
Census of India, 1921, marriage statistics, 57-61; *Living India*

misquotes, 60-61 ; and *A Son of Mother India Answers*, 60-61 ; on marriage age, 59, 65 ; on birth horoscopes, 66 ; on age of Hindus, 66-67 ; on infant marriage, 86 ; on widows, 94, 109 ; on infanticide, 108-109 ; statistics of widows, 109 ; on disregard of caste, 176-177 ; on infant mortality, 198-199 ; area and population of Native States, 220-221 ; Baroda, literate females, 221

Ceylon Morning Leader, alleged omission of anti-Muslim material in American *Mother India*, 212

Chamars, 178. *See also* Untouchables

Chand, R. B. Diwan, on child marriage, 87

Chapman, J. A., author of *India : Its Character, A Reply to 'Mother India,'* 22

Chatterji, Rev. J. C., on schools for Untouchables, 169

Chattiar, M. R. Ry. T. A. Ramalingam, on Age of Consent Act, 87

Chetty, R. K. Shanmukham, on *Mother India*, 246

Childbirth : maternity statistics, 49-54 ; terror during, 55 ; infant mortality, 64, 198-199 ; unclean act, 197 ; conditions of, 197

Child-marriage : evils of, 54-56, 62, 78-84, 90-93, 132-134, 210-211, 215-219 ; same as betrothal, 48, 61, 79, 117 ; not practised by Parsis, 50 ; not objectionable so long as not consummated, 61-62 ; prevalence of, 64 ; alleged not consummated, 74 ; as a mark of social respectability, 94 ; not practised in Burma, 103 ; Government attitude towards, 115-116 ; in Native States, 220-221. *See also* Marriage

Child-marriage, statements on : *The New Statesman*, 16 ; Gandhi, 25 ; Dr. (Mrs.) Muthulakshmi Reddi, 53-56, 132-134 ; Dr. Kugler, 54 ; Professor Phadke, 62-63, 90 ; Surenda Nath Mallik, 64 ; Mrs. B. Nehru, 64 ; Sir Hari Singh Gour, 77 ; Rai Sahib Harbilas Sarda, 78-79, 86, 114-115, 219-220 ; Dr. Lankester, 80 ; Mr. Kumar Ganganand Sinha, 80-81 ; Munshi Iswar Saran, 81, 117 ; Lala Lajpat Rai, 82 ; Pandit Madan Mohan Malaviya, 82, 89 ; Sir Purshotamdas Thakurdas, 82-83 ; Mr. D. U. Belvi, 83-84 ; Mr. J. Manjiah, 84 ; R. B. Diwan Chand, 87 ; H. H. the Marharani of Baroda, 91-92 ; Mrs. Jelal Shah, 92 ; Mrs. F. S. Talyarkhan, 92 ; J. Krishnamurti, 93 ; Principal, Sanskrit College, Benares, 96-97 ; Justice Venkatasubba Rao, 97 ; Rai Bahadur, T. M. Narasimhacharlu, 98 ; Marwari Association of Calcutta, 99 ; Bar Library Club, High Court, Calcutta, 99-100 ; Advocate General of Madras, 100 ; Rai Bahadur B. Vikramjit Singh, 100-101 ; Vice-Chancellor M. M. Dr. Ganganatha Jha, 101 ; Arya Samaj, 102, 176-177 ; Burmese, 103 ; Mr. Taw Sein Ko, 103 ; *The Gazette of India*, 113-114 ; Mr. M. K. Acharya, 116-117 ; C. V. Visvanatha Sastri, 117-118 ; Dr. Clark, 131-132 ; Rev. James Smith, 139-140 ; *The Indian Witness*, 141 ; Tagore, 192-194 ; F. L. Brayne, 210-211 ; *The Statesman*, 214 ; Ida Mary Willmore,

216; Dhanji Laxmidas, 218; Princes of India, 221
Child Marriage Bill. *See* Hindu Child Marriage Bill
Child-sanctuary, for devadasis, 158-159
Children's Protection Bill, The, 77
Cholera, India as source of, 200
Christ at the Round Table. *See* Dr. E. Stanley Jones
Christ of the Indian Road. *See* Dr. E. Stanley Jones
Christian, The, quotes statement on truth of *Mother India*, 148
Christianity and conversion of Untouchables, 143
Christians, Indian, statistics, 144
Churchill, Rt. Hon. Winston, and Swaraj, 230
Cities, percentage of population in, 50
Civil and Military Gazette, reports Mysore Legislative Council, 221
Civil law, Roman, on age at puberty, 68
Clark, Rev. Dr. Alden H., signs letter of protest, 121, 125, 135; on *Mother India*, 126; on fodder crops in India, 126-127; on cattle, 128-129; on sports, 129-130; on child marriage, 131-132; his action when *Mother India* was published, 134-135; his views on *Mother India* for America, 135; letter to Miss Mayo, 135
Coatman, J., author of *India in 1927-28*; effect of *Mother India*, 5; on different editions of *Mother India*, 237; on complimentary copies of *Mother India*, 237
Cohabitation, immediately after puberty, 59; follows early marriage, 63; effect of, 63; age of, 132. *See also* Marriage, consummation of
Collet, Sophia Dobson, *Life and Letters of Raja Rammohun Roy*, 106
Columbia University, New York City, 163
Compulsory education, results of in Baroda, 221
Concubines, 102
Council of India, London: S. N. Mallik on child marriage, 64-65
Council of State, The, question concerning *Mother India*, 229, 248-249
Cow asylum, 202
Cows, feeding of, 126-129; cruelty to, 201-204
Crerar, The Hon. Mr. J., as Home Member, 115-116; appointment of Age of Consent Committee, 222; on *Mother India*, 233 *et seq.*
Currie, George, on value of *Isles of Fear* to the Philippines, 261

Daily Express, Mr. Iyengar demands ban on *Mother India*, 18
Daily Mail, The (London): Lord Northcliffe's statement on William Francis Doherty, 42, 263-266; on *India*, 183-184
Daily Mail and Empire (Toronto), on Miss Mayo, 225
Daily Telegraph, The (London), deputation of Untouchables in United Provinces to Indian Statutory Commission, 168
Daily Times (Victoria, B.C.), D. G. Mukerji left India when eighteen, 22
Das, Mr. B.: on *India*, 184; on Government aid given Miss Mayo, 234
Dayal, Har, 'The Shame of India,' 208

INDEX

Dawat-i-Islam Aborigines Tract and Book Society, Lucknow, 211
De Montmorency, Sir Geoffrey, on Government and Miss Mayo, 249
Death rate, India compared with England and Wales, etc., 198
De Boer, John J., signs protest to *Mother India*, 121, 135
Dedication Bill, Manifesto to the Madras Government by the Members of the Devadasi Association, The, 155-157
Delhi Municipal Commissioner, schools for Untouchables a farce, 169
Depressed classes. *See* Untouchables
Desai, Mahadev, Gandhi's 'Boswell,' 36
Devadasi Association of Madras, manifesto, 155-157, 160
Devadasis, 151-162, 209; Bishop Whitehead on, 149-150, 160; sanctuary for, 158-159; Mrs. Naidu on, 188-189
Devi, Sarojini. *See* Naidu, Mrs. Sarojini
Devi, Sreemati Rangini, letter on *India*, 184
Dholakiya, Lalbhai D., on child widowhood, 95
Dhais, native midwives, 52, 197
'Dime novel,' *Mother India* as, 224, 226
Dispensaries, number of, 51
Doherty, Annette H., visited by Mrs. Naidu, 39, 42-45; statement, 42-45; visits Gandhi, 45
Doherty, Benjamin, resident of Galveston, Texas, 263
Doherty, William Francis, killed by rioters in Bombay, 39-45, 263-265
'Drain Inspector's Report, The,' 24-38. *See also* Gandhi, M. K.
Dubois, Abbé J. A.: author of *Hindu Manners, Customs and Ceremonies*, 185-188; K. Natarajan calls 'impostor from first to last,' 185; *The Hindu* reviews his work, 187-188
Duncan, Jonathan, 108

East India Company, The, 186
Education: and child marriage, 82-83; Native States, 221
Edye, Mr., on age of Indians, 66-67
Egypt, fodder crops, 127
Englishman, The: 'Memorandum from the Depressed Classes of Madras,' 164; Mr. Sicar's letter regarding Lord Sinha, 181
Encyclopædia Britannica: on age of maturity, 68; on suttee, 106; on thuggism, 107; on infanticide, 109
England, slums, 231
England and Wales: percentage of widows in, 109; infant mortality in, 198-199
Evening News (Sydney), alleges Miss Mayo hates British, 225
Expectation of life, 53, 77

'Facts About India, A Reply to Miss Mayo,' by C. F. Andrews (q.v.), 70
Father India, by C. S. Ranga Iyer: reply to *Mother India*, 22; on prostitutes, 152-153; Miss Mayo as propagandist, 205-206
Fellowship Council, The International, 145-146
Fisher, Bishop Fred B.: signs letter of protest, 121, 135; *Mother India* as propaganda, 206
Fodder crops, 126-129; comparison of Indian and Egyptian, 127

INDEX

Forward (Calcutta): on *Mother India*, 21; reports meeting to denounce *Mother India*, 21; on Miss Mayo as Government agent, 226
Fortnightly Review, on protest letter to *The Times*, 20

Games, 129-131
Gandhi, Mohandas Karamchand: review of *Mother India*, 'The Drain Inspector's Report,' 23, 25-37, 226; operation for appendicitis, 26, 31-35; on Ayurvedic vs. Western medicine, 31-35, 196; Miss Mayo's visit to, 26-29, 36; 'Message to America,' 27-29; opinion on hospitals, 31, 33, 51; attempts to conserve American public opinion, 38-48; Bombay riots (1921), 39; Mrs. Doherty's visit, 45-46; on spirit of International Fellowship Council, 145-146; on government reforms; 105, 112; alleged misquoting of, 180; calf killed, 201-202; title of 'Mahatma' deleted, 201-202; on killing of animals, 201-204; on C. F. Andrews' retraction of statement about *Mother India*, 206; *Mother India* as 'dime novel,' 226; urges complete Indianisation, 265-266
Gandhi's followers: applaud Prince of Wales, 30; typical crimes, 264-266
Gandhi's Letters on Indian Affairs, acknowledge his responsibility for Bombay riots of 1921, 39
Gazette of India, The, on Hindu Child Marriage Bill, 113-114
Girl mothers, ages of, 49-50, 53-54, 57, 131-133
Girl wife, suicide of, 219-220
Girls: unmarried at puberty, stigma attached to, 58; married ages of, 59-61; kidnapping of, 102; cruelty to, 215-216, 219
Gondal, reforms in, 221
Goshala, 202
Gour, Sir Hari Singh: debility of Indians due to child marriage, 77; on education of Untouchables, 175
Government of India: asked to ban *Mother India*, 18; and Reforms, 105-120, 222; Miss Mayo as agent of, 225-229; no unusual help given Miss Mayo, 226-227, 233-249
Government of India, Public Health Commissioner, Annual Report (1925), 198-199
Graham, Colonel J. D., India as source of plague, 200
Grant, J. P., on widow remarriage, 110-111
Gurgaon District, village uplift in, 209-211

Haji, Mr. Sarabhai Nemchand, on free copies of *Mother India*, 240
Hartshorn, Rt. Hon. Vernon, member of Indian Statutory Commission, quoted, 166
'Has Katherine Mayo Slandered "Mother India"?' by Eleanor F. Rathbone, 59, 197
Health Organisation in British India, on hospital statistics, 51
Hibbert Journal, 59, 197
Hindu, The: criticism of *Mother India*, 17-18; age of puberty in Malabar, 69; Government sounds public opinion on Hindu Child Marriage Bill, 118; Resolutions on Hindu Child Marriage Bill, 119-120, 270-272; American missionaries' protest letter, 121; Dr. Jones on *Mother India*, 122;

INDEX

Dr. Clark on *Mother India*, 135; Wardha temple open to Untouchables, 177; All-India Depressed Class Conference, Madras (1929), 177; initiation ceremony to purify outcastes, 177; Mr. Sicar's letter and Lord Sinha, 181; Colonel Graham on plague, 200

Hindu Child Marriage Bill, The, 78, 84, 92; objects of, 96-97; opinions on, 96-104, 112-120; 267-272; public discussion, 118-120; Government attitude towards, 115-116; meetings in favour of, 119, 267-269; protest meetings, 119-120, 270-272

Hindu Manners, Customs, and Ceremonies, by Abbé Dubois, 185-188

Hindu Widow Remarriage Act of 1856, The, 94, 109-110

Hindustan Review, alleges Miss Mayo hates British, 225

Hindustan Times, letter from S. R. Devi on *India*, 184

Hingorani, Dr. G. T., on prostitution in Karachi, 160

Home Rule. *See* Swaraj

Hooton, Major-General A. (Surgeon-General of Bombay): on Gandhi's operation, 32-34; conversation with Gandhi, 35

Horoscope, at birth, 66

Hospitals: number of, 51; Gandhi on, 31, 33, 51; inadequate, 75

House of Commons: statement of weight of Indian babies, 77; questions on *Mother India*, 226-227

Howell, Samuel, circumstances of his murder, 254-256; 'only a working man,' 256

Humanitarian League of Bombay, deletes Gandhi's title of 'Mahatma,' 201-202

Hyderabad University, 212

Ibrahim, Syed, on devadasis, 161-162

Illiteracy. *See* Literacy

Incorporated Law Society of Calcutta, on child marriage, 100

'India,' by Katherine Mayo, 35

India, playlet based on *Mother India*, 183-185

India in Ferment, by Claude H. Van Tyne, quoted, 39-40

India in 1927-28, quoted on effect of *Mother India*, 5

India: Its Character, A Reply to 'Mother India,' by J. A. Chapman, 22

India Office, London, 64, 184; no regulation on medical treatment of prisoners, 34; no unusual help given Miss Mayo, 226-227; and *Mother India*, 234-238

'India Seen and India Served,' by the Earl of Lytton, 197

Indian Daily Mail: Rev. Stanley Jones on *Mother India*, 122; interviews Lord Sinha, 182

Indian Home Rule: Gandhi on Western medicine, 31; Gandhi on hospitals, 51

'Indian Ideal of Marriage, The,' by Rabindranath Tagore, 192

Indian Medical Service, Gandhi operated on by officer of, 32

Indian National Herald, announces Mrs. Naidu's visit to America, 46, 47; National Christian Council's statement, 138; letter by Dhanji Laxmidas, 217-218; alleges Government subsidised *Mother India*, 226

Indian National Social Conference, The, Madras, 188-190

Indian Penal Code: on age of consent, 85-86, 111; on prostitution, 157-158

Indian Social Reformer, The: on child marriage, 64, 68-69, 70; on age of puberty, 64; on widow remarriage, 110-111; letter from Dr. Clark, 134-135; National Christian Council's Statement published, 138; reprints article in *Madras Law College Magazine* on legislation against prostitution, 157; reports Indian National Social Conference, Madras, 188-190; states *Mother India* has stimulated action among Hindus, 231-232. *See also* Natarajan, K.

Indian States: and Swarajists, 182; number, area, and population, 220-221; reforms in, 221

Indian States and Ruling Princes, The, by Sir S. Low, 221

Indian Statutory Commission: Untouchables heard, 163-171

Indian Witness, The: article by Y.M.C.A. secretary on misquotation of Miss Mona Bose, 135-137; on evil customs, 141-142; letter from Bhagat Ram, 143

Indian Women's Association, on widowhood, 107

Indian Year-Book, The, on Boy Scouts, 231

Indore, reforms in, 221

Infant marriage. *See* Child marriage

Infant mortality: in India, 198-199; in U.S.A., 198; in England and Wales, 198-199; in New Zealand, 198; in various cities, 198

Infanticide, 105, 108-109, 120; statistics of, 108-109

Institute of Plant Industry, Indore, director of quoted, 127

Intercourse, Indian Penal Code on, 85. *See also* Age of consent

International Fellowship Council, The, 145-146

International House, New York City, 163

'Is India Dying?' Alden H. Clark, 126-134

Islam, and the Arya Samaj, 176. *See also* Muhammadans

Isles of Fear: reasons actuating author of, 259; Lajpat Rai on, 260; S. K. Ratcliffe on, 260-261; C. F. Andrews on, 260-261; *N. Y. Evening Post* on, 260; *Saturday Review of Literature* on, 261; *Brooklyn Eagle* on, 261; *Times of Manila* on, 261

Iswar Saran, Munshi: on decay of Hindu race, 81; on courtesy shown Miss Mayo, 238

Iyengar, A. Rangaswamy: tables resolution to ban *Mother India* in Legislative Assembly without having read it, 18; on Miss Mayo's activities in New York, 234 *et seq.*

Iyer, C. S. Ranga. *See* Ranga Iyer, C. S.

Jains, practise child marriage, 61

Jayakar, M. R., *Living India* misquotes, 113; on education of Untouchables, 171; on American tourists, 237 *et seq.*

Jha, M. M. Dr. Ganganatha, on child marriage legislation, 101

Jogiah, Mr. Varahagari Venkata, on the banning of *Mother India*, 242

John Brown, in which Oswald Garrison Villard pays tribute to Miss Mayo's judgment, 254

Jones, Rev. Dr. E. Stanley, author of *Christ at the Round Table*, etc., on *Mother India*, 122; on *That Damn Y*, 122-123; gives one-sided picture in *Christ of the Indian Road*, 125;

signs letter of protest, 121, 135; describes child-sanctuary, 158-159
Joshi, Narayan Malhar: on education of depressed classes, 174-175; on Government propaganda, 241
Joshi, Sir Moropant, chairman Age of Consent Committee, 222
Journal of State Medicine, The, quoted, 64
Justice to All: reason actuating author of, 254-255; late President Theodore Roosevelt in introduction to, 256

Kaestha, Moti Lal, on age of puberty, 69-70
Kali, the Hindu goddess of destruction, 107-108
Karachi, prostitution in, 160
Kashmir, reforms in, 221
Keegan, (Mrs.) A., letter to *Times of India* on Hindu cruelty to girls, 215
Keyserling, Count Hermann, *Book of Marriage*, 192-193
Ko, Taw Sein, on child marriage, 103-104
Kodaikanal Missionary Union's Annual Conference (1928), 144
Kotah, reforms in, 221
Krishnamacharya, D. P., on religion and early marriage, 66
Krishnamurti, J.: on evils of Hindu customs, 93; on *Mother India*, 93
Kugler, Dr., on early motherhood, 54
Kunzru, Pandit Hirday Nath, on *Mother India*, 239 *et seq.*

Lady Hardinge Medical College, Delhi, principal quoted, 53
Lajpat Rai, Lala: author of *Unhappy India*, 22; on child marriage, 82; on Hindu Child Marriage Bill, 112; alleges *Mother India* misquotes Miss Bose, 136; Miss Mayo as yellow journalist, 164; on education of Untouchables, 172; on Mr. Sicar's letter regarding Lord Sinha, 182; on India as source of plague, 199; on cruelty to animals, 204; on *Mother India* as propaganda, 205; alleges Miss Mayo Government agent, 225; on assistance given Miss Mayo, 234 *et seq.*; on *Isles of Fear*, 259-260
Lakhanpal, Mrs. C., author of *Mother India Ka Jawab*, 23
Laxmidas, Dhanji, letter to *Indian National Herald*, 218
Lankester, Arthur, author of *Tuberculosis in India*, 80, 197
Leader, The, Allahabad, on letter to *The Times*, 20
League of Nations, 199
Lecture tours in the U.S.A. to counteract *Mother India*, 38, 48, 192
'Legend of "Mother India," The,' editorial in *The Times*, 250-252
Legislative Assembly: resolution to ban *Mother India*, 18; on child marriage (q.v.), 96 *et seq.*; on education of Untouchables, 171-176; questions on *India*, 184; Finance Committee refuses appropriation for Age of Consent Committee, 222-223; questions on *Mother India*, 228-229, 233-249
Legislative Assembly Debates: Sarda and Miss Mayo, 78; on marriage statistics, 79; on child marriage, 79-84 *et seq.*; on widows, 95; number of widows, 110; on Age of Consent Bill, 111; on Hindu Child Marriage Bill, 112-120; on

girl wife's suicide, 219; Sarda on Hindu Child Marriage Bill and western opinion, 230; questions on *Mother India* and its author, 233-248
Liberty Magazine, quoted, 35
Life and Letters of Raja Rammohun Roy, by Sophia D. Collet, 106
Life of Lyman Trumbull, The, by Horace White, quoted, 254
Life Prospectus for India, quoted, 77
Life, expectation of, 53, 77; Hindu women non-insurable, 77
Light, Lahore, Muhammadan support of *Mother India*, 212
Literacy: women in British India, 50-51; and orthodoxy, 84; in Baroda, 221
Living India. *See* Zimand, Savel
London, infant mortality rate in, 198
Londres, Albert, author of *The Road to Buenos Ayres*, 161
Longley, Rev. W. J., editor of *The Baptist Missionary Review* (q.v.), 125
Low, Sir Sidney, *Indian States and Ruling Princes*, 221
Lytton, The Earl of, 'India Seen and India Served,' 197

McClelland, D. F., signs letter of protest, 121, 135
Macnicol, Rev. Dr., signed National Christian Council statement, 138-139
MacPhail, Dr., on early marriage, 55
Maddock, Colonel, operated on Gandhi, 33-34
Madras, Bishop of. *See* Whitehead, Rt. Rev. Henry
Madras, City: maternity hospital statistics, 49; Western influence in, 50; infant mortality in, 198; meeting in, 119, 272
Madras, presidency: Elihu Yale, Governor of, 50; oldest British settlement, 50; Legislative Council Debates quoted, 54, 71, 86-87, 151-155, 157-158, 161-162; Advocate-General on child marriage and widows, 100; Devadasi Association Manifesto, 156, 160; Untouchables' memorandum to Indian Statutory Commission, 164; condition of Untouchables, 166-168
Madras Law College Magazine, on legislation against prostitution, 157
Madras Mail, The, D. P. Krishnamacharya on religion and early marriage, 66; Dr. (Mrs.) Muthulakshmi Reddi on child marriage, 132; quotes M. B. Mullick on Untouchables, 165-166; quotes Rev. J. C. Chatterji on schools for Untouchables, 169; Mr. Sicar's letter on Lord Sinha, 181
Mahadev Desai, Gandhi's 'Boswell,' 36
Mahasabha, 117
Mahatma, Gandhi's right to title withdrawn, 202
Mainpuri, The Sessions Judge at, sentences Ramsarup's murderers, 178
Malabar coast, age of puberty, 69
Malaviya, Pandit Madan Mohan: on child marriage, 82, 89; purification of Untouchables, 177
Mallik, Surenda Nath, on child marriage, 64-65
Manchester Guardian, The: on effect of *Mother India*, 9; Tagore's letter on *Mother India*, 190-191; on refusal of appropriation for Age of Consent Committee, 222

Mandal, B. C., on Untouchables, 177
Mandi, reforms in, 221
Mangal Singh, Sardar, on age of puberty, 70
Manjiah, J., on child marriage, 84
Mankar, Jayanthai, advised by Gandhi against Western humanitarianism, 201-202
Marichi, cited on marriage, 72
Marriage, as betrothal, 48, 61, 62, 79, 116, 117; age of, 57-61, 65, 79; registration of, 66, 210-211; citation from Marichi, 72; age of consent (1892 and 1925), 85, 111, (and 1860) 111. *See also* Child marriage
Marriage, consummation of: before or at puberty, 59, 63, 65, 66, 71, 79, 81, 91, 134; after puberty, 62, 71, 116-117; in secret, 118. *See also* Age of consent
Marwari Association, The, Calcutta: on age of puberty, 70-71; on child marriage, 99
Maternity and Infant Welfare Organisation, Simla, 199
Maternity statistics, 49-56
Mathews, Basil: on Miss Mayo's sincerity, 207-208; on responsibility for reform, 208
Maturity of females, 66-73. *See also* Puberty, age at
Mayo, Katherine: visits Gandhi, 26-29, 36; accused of misquoting Gandhi, Tagore, Lord Sinha, Miss Bose, Roy's luncheon (q.v.); declared to be paid propagandist, 136, 224, 225-226; as yellow journalist, 164; alleged Britisher, 224; alleged subsidised, 225-226; no extraordinary assistance given by Government, 226-228, 233-249; biography of, 253-262
Medical institutions, number of, 51
Meetings: denouncing *Mother India*, epigraph, 9, 21; in favour of the Hindu Child Marriage Bill, 119, 267-269; protesting against the Hindu Child Marriage Bill, 119-120, 270-273; against Untouchables, 171; against Gandhi, 201-202
Michigan, University of, 39
Midwives, native, 52, 197
Millet, 126-127
Miss Mayo's Grandhakhandanamu, edited by Pandit Puranam Suryanarayana Thirthulu, a reply to *Mother India*, 23
Miss Mayo's Mother India, A Rejoinder, by K. Natarajan (q.v.), 22, 136, 185-187
Missionaries: and *Mother India*, 121-150; denouncing, 121, 135, 138; supporting, 139-140, 147-150; reticent to express opinion, 139; and conversion, 145-146
Mitra Mandal, The, on age of puberty, 69
Modern Review, The, Calcutta: 'The Shame of India,' 208; Native States reforms, 221
Moidoo Sahib, Khan Sahib T.M., on age of puberty on Malabar coast, 69
Montagu-Chelmsford Reform Act, 172
Moore, Arthur, on education of Untouchables, 173-174
Moscow, suggested origin of *Mother India*, 225
Mother India, first published, 15; proposed ban on, 18, 242; criticised without being read, 17-21; quotations analysed, 75-76; as propaganda, 136, 138, 191, 205-206, 260; choice of title, 213; alleged differences between American and English editions, 212-213, 236-237; alleged Government subsidies

and help, 226-227, 233-249; has stimulated action among Hindus, Introduction, 9, 231-232; no complimentary copies to Government officials, 233, 240, 246. *For* 'Replies' to, *see* Bibliography, 275
Mother India Aur Uska Jawab, a reply to *Mother India*, by Srimati Uma Nehru, 23
Mother India Ka Jawab, a reply to *Mother India*, by Mrs. C. Lakhanpal, 23
Motherhood, age of, 49-65, 131-134
Moti Lal Kaestha, on age of puberty, 69
Mounted Justice, *New York World* on, 257-258
Muddiman, Sir Alexander, 115
Muhammadans: and child marriage, 51, 114; and thuggee, 105; no enforced widowhood, 114; and Hindu Child Marriage Bill, 114; support *Mother India*, 211-212; and alleged deletions in American edition of *Mother India*, 212-213, 236-237 *et seq.*
Mukerji, Dhan Gopal: author of *A Son of Mother India Answers*, 22; publishes first reply to *Mother India* in America, 22; left India at eighteen, 22; married an American, 22; went to an American college, 22; offers to rewrite *Mother India*, 23; on early motherhood, 57-58; misrepresents *Mother India*, 57; prints only a part of sentence in the census, 60-61; on maturity, 70; on the untenable thesis of *Mother India*, 75; on the Indian Penal Code, 85; on Miss Mayo's sincerity, 206-207; on Americans and pornography, 226
Mullick, M. B., on Untouchables, 165-166
Murders: of William Francis Doherty, 40-43, 263-264; of Ramsarup, 178-179; of Samuel Howell, 254-256
Muslims. *See* Muhammadans
Muthulakshmi Reddi, Dr. (Mrs.): on early motherhood, 53-56; on age of puberty, 71; on child marriage, 132-134; on devadasis, 151-154, 157-158
Mysore Legislative Council, raises the age of consent, 221

Naidu, Mrs. Sarojini: Gandhi approves her visiting America, 38; sent to Mrs. Doherty by Gandhi, 38, 42-45; 'Gandhi ordered me to come,' 38, 46; lands in New York, 46; on child marriage as betrothal, 48; on widow remarriage, 48; on Purdah, 48; on devadasis, 188-189
Namasudras, 165. *See* Untouchables
Narasimhacharlu, Rai Bahadur T. M., on child marriage, 98
Natarajan, K., author of *Miss Mayo's Mother India, A Rejoinder*, and editor of *Indian Social Reformer*: on *Mother India*, 22, 136, 185-187, 189-190, 231-232; on Abbé Dubois, 185-188; at Indian National Social Conference, 188-190; on alleged misquotation of Tagore, 192; on Miss Mayo as propagandist, 205
Nateson, The Hon. G. A., on Miss Mayo and free railway passes, 148
Nation, New York, letter from Tagore on *Mother India*, 191-192, 194-195
National Christian Council of India, Burma, and Ceylon,

138-150, 198; widely quoted, 23; statement denouncing *Mother India*, 134, 138-139; statement appears in *Bombay Daily Mail*, *Indian National Herald*, *Amrita Bazar Patrika*, *Indian Social Reformer*, 138
Native States, and Swarajists, 182; number, area, and population, 220-221; reforms in, 221
Navalrai, Mr. Lalchand, on Government and *Mother India*, 247
Nayar, Diwan Bahadur M. Krishnan, supports abolishing of devadasis, 155
Nazimova, Madame Alla, in playlet, *India*, 183-185
Nehru, Mrs. Brijlal, on child marriage, 64
Nehru, Srimati Uma, author of *Mother India Aur Uska Jawab*, 23
Negro problem, in United States of America, 231
Neogy, Mr. K. C., on differences in editions of *Mother India*, 236-237
New Empire, Calcutta, on playlet *India*, 183
New India: on letter of protest to *The Times*, 19; J. Krishnamurti on Hindu customs, 93; on appointment of Age of Consent Committee, 222. *See also* Besant, Dr. (Mrs.) Annie
New Jersey, 253
New Oxford Dictionary, on age of puberty, 68
New Republic, The, 260
New Statesman, The, review of *Mother India*, 15-17, 190
New York City, discussion on *Mother India*, 163; infant mortality rate in, 198
New York Evening Post: articles by Katherine Prence (1896), 253; on *The Standard Bearers*, 257; on *Isles of Fear*, 259-260
New York Legislature, 257
New York State Police Bill, 257
New York State Troopers, organisation of, due to Miss Mayo, 257
New York Times, The, prints Gandhi's review of *Mother India*, 23; on Age of Consent Committee, 73
New York World: J. Krishnamurti in, 93; on *Mounted Justice*, 258
New Zealand, infant mortality in, 198
North American Review, on Miss Mayo and propaganda, 258
North-West Frontier Province, 51
Northcliffe, Lord, statement concerning the murder of William Francis Doherty, 42, 263-266
Norton, Esther, interviews Mrs. Naidu, 38

Officials, reticent regarding India, 16
Olcott, Mason, signs letter of protest to *Mother India*, 121, 135
Opinions on the Hindu Child Marriage Bill, 71, 87, 96-104
Orthodox Hindus: on child marriage, 83, 84, 134; literacy of, 84
Outcastes. *See* Untouchables
Over-Seas Daily Mail, The, Lord Northcliffe's statement, 263-266
Oxford History of India, The, by Vincent A. Smith, 108

Pandita Ramabai Sarasvati, by Clementina Butler, 95
Pariahs, 173. *See also* Untouchables
Parliamentary Debates: House

of Commons, 226-227; House of Lords, 227
Parsis: do not practise child marriage, 50; literacy of females, 50; social customs, 50; insurance of females, 77
Patna, school for the blind, 217
Penal Code. *See* Indian Penal Code
Penal legislation: failure of, 105-120; opposition to, 116
Pennsylvania State Police, books on, 256-258
Phadke, Dr. N. S.: on cohabitation, 62-63; on effect of child marriage, 63; cites Marichi on age of puberty, 72; on child marriage, 90
Philadelphia North American, on *The Standard Bearers*, 257
Philip, P. C., signed National Christian Council statement, 121, 135
Philippine Islands, Katherine Mayo and, 259-261
Phœnix Assurance Company, Ltd., Calcutta, 77
Physical status of Hindus, 62, 63, 74, 90, 188; Sir H. S. Gour on, 77; Dr. Clark on, 126, 129-130. *See also* Child marriage
Pickett, J. Waskom, editor of *Indian Witness* (q.v.), 141-142
Pioneer, The, 53, 88; memorial to the Indian Statutory Commission by the 'Untouchables of Bombay Presidency,' 164, 170; Deputation of Untouchables in Punjab to Indian Statutory Commission, 169
Pioneer Mail, The: letter on caste tyrannies, 211; letter from Mrs. Ida M. Willmore, 215-216
Plague, India as source of, 200
Plain Dealer, Wabash, quotes Rev. R. F. Porter on Miss Mayo, 224
Playgrounds, 130
Pooley, A. M., perceives motives of hatred and malice against British in *Mother India*, 225
Poona, infant mortality, in, 198; headquarters for Indian social reform societies, 198; National Christian Council at, 198
Poona Seva Sedan Society, 198
Population statistics, 50, 220
Porter, Rev. Reuben F., asserts Miss Mayo is English, 225
Post Office, Untouchables forbidden to enter, 165-166
Post Standard, Syracuse, N.Y., quotes Bishop Fred B. Fisher on *Mother India*, 206
Prence, Katherine: *nom de plume* used by Katherine Mayo, 253; articles in *N. Y. Evening Post* (1896), 253
Prince of Wales. *See* Wales, Prince of
Princes of India. *See* Native States
Prisoners, authority to operate on, 33-35
Privy Council, decides against appeal to permit suttee, 106
Propaganda, *Mother India* as, 136, 138, 191, 205-206, 260; *Mounted Justice* as, 258
Prostitutes, 151-162, 209; Bishop Whitehead on, 149-150, 160
Protest meetings: against *Mother India*, epigraph, 9, 21; against Hindu Child Marriage Bill, 119-120, 270-272; against Untouchables, 171; against Gandhi, 201-202
Provincial Councils, 223. *See also* Madras Legislative Council; Punjab Legislative Council; United Provinces Legislature
Puberty: *Mother India* on, 49; age at, 66-73; age among Occidentals, 68; age at, in Bombay, 68-69; in Malabar, 69; Kan-

gra (Punjab), 69; in Lahore, 70; in Calcutta, 70-71; Poona, 71; in Madras, 71; according to Hindu scriptures, 72; mean age in India, 72; attainment of, 104
Publicity Department of the Government of India, 233 *et seq.*
Punjab : principally Muhammadan, 51; age of puberty in, 69-70; favours abolition of child marriage, 101-102; infanticide statistics, 108; age of motherhood in, 131-132; Untouchable deputation to Indian Statutory Commission, 164, 168-169; village uplift in, 209-211
Punjab Addharm Mandel, Memorial to Statutory Commission, 164, 168-169
Punjab Legislative Council Debates, 249
Purdah system, Mrs. S. Naidu defends, 48; missionaries and, 141
Purshotamdas Thakurdas, Sir, on prevalence of child marriage, 82-83

Racial degeneration, 90, 91. *See also* Child marriage; Physical status of Hindu
Racial suicide, child marriage and 81
Rai, Lala Lajpat. *See* Lajpat Rai, Lala
Raizada Hans Raj, on *Mother India*, 249
Rajaram College, Kolhapur, 62
Rajok, reforms in, 221
Rajputs, exceptions to rule of child marriage, 90
Ram, Bhagat, letter to *Indian Witness*, 142-143
Ramabai, Pandita, 95
Ramesam, Justice : on age of puberty, 71; on child marriage, 98-99
Ramji, Sir Manmohandas, chairman of protest meeting against Untouchables, 171
Ramsarup, murdered for helping Untouchables, 178-179
Ranga Iyer, Mr. C. S. : author of *Father India*, 22; on prostitutes, 152-153; Miss Mayo as propagandist, 206
Rangachariar, Rao Bahadur T., on devadasis, 157
Rangaswamy Iyengar, A. *See* Iyengar, A. Rangaswamy
Rangini Devi, Sreemati, letter on *India*, 184
Rao, Justice Venkatasubba, 97
Rape : evidence of age in, 67; of wife by husband, 86-87, 91, 111. *See also* Age of consent
Ratcliffe, S. K., on *Isles of Fear*, 260
Rathbone, Eleanor F. : biography of, 59-60; on marriage statistics, 59; on *Mother India*, 197
Reddi, Dr. (Mrs.) Muthulakshmi. *See* Muthulakshmi Reddi, Dr. (Mrs.)
Reforms : Government of India, 105-120, 222; Native States, 221
Regulation XVII, on suttee, 105-106
Religious prostitutes. *See* Devadasis
Replies to *Mother India*. *See* Bibliography, 275
Report of the Royal Commission on Agriculture in India, on fodder-crops and feeding of cattle, 127-129
Review of the Churches, The, 197, 207-208
Ridgeway, Pennsylvania, Katherine Mayo born at, 224, 253
Road to Buenos Ayres, The, by Albert Londres, 161

INDEX

Robinson, Bishop J. W., dissents from National Christian Council's statement denouncing *Mother India*, 139
Roman civil law, on age at puberty, 68
Roosevelt, President Theodore: writes introduction to *Justice to All*, 256; on Katherine Mayo, 256
Roy, Himadri Bhusan, letter to *The Statesman*, Calcutta, 21
Roy, Mr. K. C., luncheon to Miss Mayo, 76, 182-183
Roy, Mrs. K. C., 183
Roy, Raja Ram Mohan, on suttee, 106
Royal Commission on Agriculture, constitution of, 127; *Report*, fodder-crops and feeding of cattle, 127-129
Ruthnaswamy, M., on *Mother India*, 242

Sambava Maha Jana Sangham, appeal to Sir John Simon, 164-166
San Francisco Chronicle, Mrs. Naidu on betrothal, 48
Sanatan Dharm Mahamandal, President of, on Hindu Child Marriage Bill, 100-101
Sanger, Margaret, writes foreword to *Sex Problem in India* (q.v.), 62
Sanskrit College at Benares, Principal of, on Sarda Child Marriage Bill, 96-97
Sarabhai Nemchand Haji. *See* Haji, Sarabhai Nemchand, 240
Saran, Munshi Iswar. *See* Iswar Saran, Munshi, 81, 238
Sarda, Rai Sahib Harbilas: on *Mother India*, 78; on child marriage, 79-80, 112, 230; on Swaraj, 80; on age of consent, 86; on Government attitude towards his bill, 114-115; describes girl wife's suicide, 218-219
Sarda Child Marriage Bill. *See* Hindu Child Marriage Bill
Sarojini Devi. *See* Naidu, Mrs. Sarojini
Sastri, C. V. Visvanatha, on marriage and consummation, 117-118
Sastry, N. Yagnesvara, 107
Sati. *See* Suttee
Saturday Review of Literature, on *Isles of Fear*, 260-261
Schools, use of by Untouchables, 165, 169-175
Scribner's Magazine, articles by Katherine Mayo, 253
Scudder, Dr. Ida, on early motherhood, 54-55
Secretary of State for India, 64, 227, 234-237
Servants of India Society, 198
Setalvad, Sir Chimanlal, sends letter to *The Times*, 251
Seva Sedan, Superintendent of, on age of puberty and consummated marriage, 71
Sex Problems in India, by Dr. N. S. Phadke, 62, 63, 72, 90
Shah, Mrs. Jelal, on child marriage, 92
'Shame of India, The,' by Har Dayal, 208
Sharp, Clifford, editor, *The New Statesman* (q.v.), 15
Shave, Mrs. M. C., on age at puberty, 70
Sheriff-constable system in New York, breakdown of, 255
Shetty, A. B., quoted on devadasis, 155
'Shilling shocker,' *Mother India* as, 226
Sicar, Mr., letter regarding Lord Sinha and *Mother India*, 181-182
Sikh Jats, age of puberty among, 70

INDEX

Simla, infant mortality in, 199; Infant Welfare Organisation of, 199

Simon, Sir John, Chairman of Indian Statutory Commission, 164-171

Simon Commission. *See* Indian Statutory Commission, 164-171

Singh, Gaya Prasad, on Miss Mayo in Lahore, 238, 239, 248

Singh, Rai Bahadur B. Vikramjit, on child marriage, 100

Singh, Ram Narayan, on *Mother India*, 243

Singh, Sandar, murdered Brahman who helped Untouchables, 178-179

Singh, Sardar Mangal, on age of puberty, 70

Sinha, Kumar Ganganand, on effect of child marriage, 80-81

Sinha, Lord: Miss Mayo accused of misquoting, 76, 181-182; interviewed in *Indian Daily Mail*, 182; and outcastes, 180

Slaves of the Gods: letter from Bishop Whitehead to Miss Mayo, 149-150; on title of *Mother India*, 213; Miss Mayo's seventh book, 262; appeal 'to women of Hindu India,' 262

Sister India, a reply to *Mother India*, by 'World Citizen' (S. G. Warty), 22, 180, 205

Sleeman, Sir William, eliminates thuggee, 108

Slums, in England, 231

Smith, Rev. James: letter to *The Times of India* supporting *Mother India*, 139-140; and National Christian Council, 139-140

Smith, Rennie, on government assistance to Miss Mayo, 226

Smith, Vincent A., on thuggee, 108

Social reform in India, *Mother India* as a power for, Introduction, 231-232

Son of Mother India Answers, A. *See* Dhan Gopal Mukerji

Spiritual Regeneration Movement, 84

Sports, 126, 129-131

Standard Bearers, The: N. Y. Evening Post on, 257; *Philadelphia North American* on, 257

Standard Dictionary, on age at puberty, 68

Statesman, The, Calcutta: letter from Himadri Bhusan Roy, 21; editorial, 214; reforms in Native States, 221

Statistical Abstract for British India, infant mortality, 198

Statutory Commission, 164-171

Stri-Dharma, on Mrs. Naidu's visit to America, 46, 48

Suhrawardy, Dr. A., on *Mother India*, 242-243

Suicide, of girl wife, 219

Sumati Bai, G., author of *Woman Awakened*. *See* Bai, G. Sumati

Sun, The, New York, interview with Mrs. Naidu, 38

Suttee, 105-107, 120; Regulation XVII prohibited, 105; Lord William Bentinck and, 105-107; Calcutta citizens appeal against prohibition of, 106; Raja Rammohan Roy and, 106; cases still occur, 106; number of cases recorded in 1818, 107; stopped by British not Hindus, 107

Suttee, by Edward Thompson, 106-107

Swaraj, definition of, 17; *The New Statesman* on, 17; Rai Sahib Harbilas Sarda on, 80; Untouchables on, 168; Native States and, 182

Tagore, Rabindranath : criticism of *Mother India* widely quoted, 23 ; alleged misquotation of, 76, 180, 190-195 ; letter on *Mother India* to *Manchester Guardian*, 190-191 ; to *The Nation* (New York), 191, 192, 194-195 ; on *Mother India*, 190-195 ; 'Indian Ideal of Marriage,' 192-193 ; on Aryuvedic medicine, 194-196
Talyarkhan, Mrs. F. S., on evils of child marriage, 92
Tarabai, Dr., on age of puberty, 70
Temple, Hindu, opened to Untouchables, 177
Temple prostitutes. *See* Devadasis
Thakurdas, Sir Purshotamdas, on where child marriage is most prevalent, 82-83
That Damn Y: Rev. Stanley Jones on, 122-123 ; reason for book's being written, 122-123 ; *Association Men* on, 123, 258-259
Thompson, Edward, *Suttee*, 106-107
Thompson, W. H., on Bengal marriage statistics, 59
Thuggee, 105-108 ; practically annihilated by British, 107-108, 120 ; recognised by Hindu and Muhammadan rulers, 107 ; a part of Kali worship, 107-108
Times, The (London) : reports protest meeting against Untouchables, 171 ; reports murder of Brahman for helping Untouchables, 178-179 ; on Age of Consent Committee, 223 ; letter by Jonathan Cape on *Mother India*, 228 ; editorial, "The Legend of *Mother* India,' 250-252
Times, The (London)—Protest letter to, on *Mother India*, 19-20 ; Surenda Nath Mallik signed, 64 ; Sir Chimanlal Setalvad signed, 251
Times of India, The: on the Prince of Wales' ovation in Bombay, 30 ; Dr. Balfour on expectation of life, 53 ; Mrs. Bhat on consummation of marriage, 71 ; on kidnapping of minor girls, 102 ; letter from Rev. James Smith, 139-140 ; letter on cruel treatment of girl, 215
Times of Malaya, The: reports demand to ban *Mother India*, 18 ; Dr. E. Stanley Jones on Miss Mayo, 122
Times of Manila, The, on *Isles of Fear*, 261
Tribune, Des Moines, quotes Mukerji on *Mother India*, 226
Tuberculosis, in Calcutta, 216
Tuberculosis in India, by Arthur Lankester, 80, 197
Twain, Mark, use of ridicule, 208

Ullah, Qudrat, on caste tyrannies, 211
Unhappy India, a reply to *Mother India*. *See* Lala Lajpat Rai
United Provinces : infanticide statistics, 108 ; Untouchable deputation to Indian Statutory Commission, 168 ; Untouchables in, 169
United States of America : lecture tours to counteract *Mother India*, 38, 48, 192 ; State Department of, 184 ; infant mortality rate in, 198 ; negro problem in, 231
Untouchability, 209 ; Gandhi's attitude, 25 ; J. Krishnamurti on, 93. *See also* Untouchables
Untouchables, 163-179 ; child marriage among, 82 ; and Christianity, 143 ; existence of,

denied in New York, 163; in Bengal, 165-166; in Bombay, 170-171; in Madras, 166-168; in United Provinces, 168-169; education for, 165, 169, 170-175; use of wells, 165, 167, 169; conditions of, 165-169; Indian Statutory Commission and, 164-165; Sir Manmohandas Ramji and, 171; Bombay Stock Exchange and, 171; Mr. Arthur Moore and, 173; Mr. N. M. Joshi and, 174-175; number of children of school age, 175; Hindus would rid their country of, 176; Arya Samaj and, 176; Brahmo Samaj and, 176-177; Wardha temple opened to, 177; purification of, 177; All-India Depressed Class Conference, 177; Brahman murdered for sympathy with, 178-179

Van Tyne, Professor Claude, describes Bombay riots (1921), 39-40
Van Doren, Alice B., signs letter of protest against *Mother India*, 121, 135
Venkatasubba Rao, Justice, on child marriage, 97
Victoria School for Girls, Lahore, 136
Vidhva Vivaha Sahayak Sabha, The, work for widows, 94
Village Uplift in India, by F. L. Brayne, 209-211
Villages, number of, 85; fodder in, 126-129; wrestling matches in, 130; sports in, 130-131; Untouchables in, 165-169; tanks in, 165; uplift of, 209-211
Villard, Oswald Garrison, on his indebtedness to Katherine Mayo, 253; on her judgment, 254
Wales, Prince of, popular ovation in Bombay, 26-30, 39, 43
Walker, Major, 108
Wardha, Hindu temple opened to Untouchables, 177
Webster's Dictionary, on age of puberty, 68
Wells, use of by Untouchables, 165, 167, 169
Western medicine vs. Ayurvedic medicine, 26, 31-34, 195-196
White, Horace, editor of *Chicago Tribune*, and *N. Y. Evening Post*, 254; on Katherine Mayo, 254
Whitehead, Rt. Rev. Henry, letter to Miss Mayo, 148-150; on prostitutes, 149-150, 160
Widow-remarriage, 120; Mrs. Naidu on, 48; restriction on, 94; Vidhva Vivaha Sahayak Sabha and, 94; Census on, 94; The Widow Remarriage Act of 1856, 94, 109-110; the Hon. Mr. J. P. Grant on, 110-111; Hindu scriptures on, 110
Widowhood, 94-104, 105, 106-107, 109-111; Gandhi on, 25; enforced, 141, 209, 214
Widows: statistics, 60, 94, 109-110; reason for large number of, 94; Pandita Ramabai and, 95; child widowhood, 94, 100; misery of, 95; widow-burning, 105-107, 120; Hindu rules for, 110; licentious life of, 111
Wilkinson, Miss Ellen C., alleged Government responsibility for *Mother India*, 227
Willmore, Ida Mary, letter to *Pioneer Mail*, 215-217
Wives, sent by force to husbands, 215-219
Woman Awakened, by G. Sumati Bai, 66, 72, 91
Women: position of, 16; literacy of, 50; treatment of, 93; traffic in, 102, 160; among backward

classes, 175 ; education of, 175 ; status of, 210-211, 214
'Women of Hindu India, Appeal to the,' by Miss Mayo in *Slaves of the Gods*, 262
Women's Christian Medical College at Ludhiana, 148
Woodroffe, Sir John, on suttee, 107
Woolf, Edgar Allen, author of playlet *India*, 183
World, The. See *New York World*
World Almanac, The, 198
World Citizen (S. G. Warty). *See Sister India*

Yale, Elihu, 50
'Yellow Journalist,' Miss Mayo as, 164
Young India: editor, M. K. Gandhi, 24 ; 'The Drain Inspector's Report,' 23-37 ; Gandhi's reason for sending Mrs. Naidu to America, 38 ; 'The Facts About India, A Reply to Miss Mayo,' 70, 260 ; Gandhi on Governments, 105 ; on killing of animals, 202-204 ; C. F. Andrews and Gandhi on *Mother India*, 206
Young Men of India, Burma and Ceylon, 'Is India Dying ?' 126-132 ; 'The Basis of Inter-religious Fellowship," 145-146
Young Men's Christian Association, The : Dr. Stanley Jones and Miss Mayo's war book on, 122-123, 258-259 ; and Miss Mayo in France, 122-123 ; record of work with American Expeditionary Force, 122-123, 258-259 ; secretary states Miss Mayo paid propagandist, 135-136 ; secretary alleges *Mother India* misquotes, 136 ; work in France, 258. *See also That Damn Y*

Zimand, Savel : author of *Living India*, 60 ; inaccurate census statistics, 60 ; quotes only a part of a sentence, 60-61 ; misquotes Mr. M. R. Jayakar, 113